CONFLI... ...NTION

Conflict: Resolution and Provention

John Burton
Center for Conflict Analysis and Resolution
George Mason University, Virginia, USA

First published 1990 by
MACMILLAN PRESS LTD
Houndmills, Basingstoke, Hampshire RG21 6XS
and London
Companies and representatives
throughout the world

ISBN 0–333–53192–2 hardcover
ISBN 0–333–53193–0 paperback

A catalogue record for this book is available
from the British Library.

Printed in Great Britain by
Antony Rowe Ltd, Chippenham and Eastbourne

Published in the United States of America 1990 by
ST. MARTIN'S PRESS, INC.,
Scholarly and Reference Division
175 Fifth Avenue, New York, N. Y. 10010

ISBN 0–312–03748–1

The Conflict Series

1. CONFLICT: RESOLUTION AND PROVENTION,* *by John Burton*

2. CONFLICT: HUMAN NEEDS THEORY, *edited by John Burton*

3. CONFLICT: READINGS IN MANAGEMENT AND RESOLUTION, *edited by John Burton and Frank Dukes*

4. CONFLICT: PRACTICES IN MANAGEMENT, SETTLEMENT AND RESOLUTION, *by John Burton and Frank Dukes*

*Provention
The term *prevention* has the connotation of containment. The term *provention* has been introduced to signify taking steps to remove sources of conflict, and more positively to promote conditions in which collaborative and valued relationships control behaviors.

Foreword to the Series

Samuel W. Lewis
President, United States Institute of Peace

We seem to know much more about how wars and other violent international conflicts get started than we do about how to end them. Nor do we understand very well how to transform settlements that terminate immediate hostilities into enduring peaceful relationships through which nations can continue to work out their differences without violence. The lack of attention to these questions, at least with regard to relations among sovereign governments, is due in some degree to the way international relations as an academic subject has traditionally been studied. By and large, more academic theory and analysis has been devoted to patterns and causes in international behavior with an eye to perfecting explanatory theory than to effective, usable remedies to international conflicts. We have assumed the remedies would become plain once the correct theory was found.

That imbalance is now being corrected. Interest is now growing in the theory and practice of "conflict resolution," a new field concerned specifically with the nature of conflict as a generic human problem and with techniques or initiatives that might be applied productively in addressing conflicts. This new emphasis is reflected in the emergence of alternative dispute resolution methods in the law profession, of peace studies or conflict resolution programs in many of the nation's colleges and universities, of research journals devoted specifically to conflict and its resolution, and of community mediation or problem-solving strategies at the local level and "second-track diplomacy" at the international level.

Providing much of the conceptual foundation for an explicit focus on conflict itself has been a small but growing group of interdisciplinary scholars engaged in a search for formulas and processes that seem to work in ending conflicts among nations and groups. They are seeking to identify those institutional and societal structures that have the best chance of ensuring a lasting and just peace among conflicting interests. Unfortunately, the work of these scholars has not reached the widest circles of policymakers, professionals, students, and researchers who could benefit from the stimulating explorations of the conflict resolution school of thought.

The United States Institute of Peace wishes to commend the four book Conflict Series: an effort by one of the acknowledged founding fathers of the conflict resolution field to summarize the main insights of the field to date for a wider readership. In these books, John Burton, with the assistance of other major contributors, delineates the distinctive scope of the conflict resolution field, defines its key concepts, explains how the field emerged out of existing approaches to conflict and peace and how it differs from them, summarizes the field's leading substantive insights about conflict and its resolution, collects some of the best readings produced by the field, and probes where the field needs to go in the future to strengthen its theory and applicability to real problems. The series also surveys extant practical techniques for conflict management such as mediation, adjudication, ombudsmen, interactive mangement, and problem-solving workshops and explores their utility for different types of conflict situations. Of course, the views expressed in these volumes are those of the authors alone and do not necessarily reflect views of the Institute of Peace.

Impressively, John Burton and Frank Dukes completed this broad examination of the conflict resolution field during Burton's year as a Distinguished Fellow of the United States Institute of Peace in 1988–89 while he was also a Distinguished Visiting Professor at the Center for Conflict Resolution at George Mason University in Virginia. No one in the world is better qualified to present the conflict resolution field's distinctive perspectives and unique contributions than is Burton, whom many in the field regard as its first leading explorer and one of its most ardent spokesmen before students, scholars, and governments since its beginnings in the late 1950s. In preparing this series, Burton has drawn on the wealth of his extensive academic training in economics and international relations and his 25 years of research and teaching at universities in three countries, as reflected in his previous ten books and numerous articles. He also has applied the lessons of his practical experience as a diplomat for the Australian government and as a third party facilitator in efforts to end such conflicts as Lebanon, Cyprus, Northern Ireland, and Sri Lanka.

The United States Institute of Peace is a non-partisan, independent institution created and funded by the United States Congress to strengthen the nation's capacity to understand and deal more effectively with international conflict through peaceful means. It serves this purpose by supporting research and education projects that will expand and disseminate available knowledge about the nature of international conflict and the full range of ways it can be resolved within a framework that maximizes freedom and justice. Within this challenging mandate, one of our tasks is to identify serious, innovative, but less well known approaches that may bear futher examination and to bring the insights from these approaches to wider circles so that fruitful dialogue among different perspectives is fostered.

John Burton's work complements another Institute project that is mapping all the major "roads to peace" – e.g., international law, diplomacy and negotiations, transnationalism, deterrence theory, nonviolence traditions, and international organizations – that have been emphasized in the scholarly literature and world of practice as important methods and tools for achieving international peace. The conflict resolution method and outlook is one of the approaches the Institute wishes to see more widely understood so their respective strengths and limitations can be sorted out and constructive syntheses can be developed. In short, we seek to stimulate much faster dissemination of ideas and cross-fertilization than normally would occur across the barriers of different academic disciplines, professions, governmental spheres, and private organizations that are concerned in various ways with international conflict and its resolution, although they may not necessarily describe their concerns in exactly these terms.

By supporting John Burton's work, the United States Institute of Peace hopes that the perspectives, insights, and new directions for analysis of this relatively new field of conflict resolution will be brought before, and enrich the work of, a wider readership of international relations and conflict resolution students; practitioners in fields such as law, government, labor and industrial management, and social work; policymakers at all levels; as well as scholars concerned with conflict issues.

Washington, D.C.

Preface to the Series

It is not easy for those who are seeking new approaches to move from deterrence theories and practices of conflict *settlement* and *management* to conflict *resolution* theory and practice. The jump to prevention and the predictive capabilities that prevention requires, is even more challenging. These are different fields with different assumptions. While they exist concurrently they are in different conceptual worlds. Some practitioners and theorists seek more effective institutional and management constraints, power-negotiating techniques and peace through technologies of mutual threat. There are consensus seekers who employ more sophisticated socialization processes largely within existing systems. Problem-solving advocates pursue more analysis of human behaviors and seek to deduce processes of conflict resolution and provention. There cannot be communication between different approaches, or with policy makers and the public generally, until there is a precisely defined language, appropriate concepts that enable a clear differentiation of the various approaches, and an adequate and agreed theory of human behaviors at all social levels. This is the purpose of these four books concerned with the study of Conflict.

The four books in this Conflict Series are:

1. *Conflict: Resolution and Provention.* This book seeks to provide an historical and theoretical perspective, and a framework for consideration of theory and practice in conflict resolution and provention. It is in five parts: Part I defines the approach; Part II deals with the political context of conflict provention; Part III is concerned with the theory of decision making, and with conflict-resolution processes; Part IV is concerned with the longer-term policy implications of provention; and Part V draws together some conclusions.

2. *Conflict: Human Needs Theory.* An adequate theory of behavior is required to provide a basis for the analysis and resolution of conflict, and particularly for prediction of conflict and a guide to conflict provention. "Needs theory" is put forward as this foundation. The chapters contributed in this book were written as a result of an international conference convened in July 1988 for that purpose.

3. *Conflict: Readings in Management and Resolution.* A new subject has origins in many fields, and this is an attempt to bring

together some earlier contributions from a broad spectrum of disciplines. A newly developing subject also has gaps requiring attention, and this book includes contributions requested to fill some of these gaps. It also contains an extensive annotated bibliography.

4. *Conflict: Practices in Management, Settlement and Resolution.* It is useful to survey practices generally, even those that proceed from contradictory theories. This book is a general survey of management, settlement and conflict resolution practices.

Conflict, its resolution and provention, comprises an *a-disciplinary* study, that is, a synthesis that goes beyond separate disciplines, beyond interaction between separate disciplines, and beyond any synthesis of approaches from several disciplines. An a-disciplinary approach accepts no boundaries of knowledge. Consequently, it has as yet no shelf in any discipline-based library. These four books seek to make a start.

JOHN BURTON

Acknowledgements

The preparation of four books on the study of conflict – this one on its resolution and provention, a second on human needs theory, a third providing readings, and a fourth on practices in conflict management and resolution – was made possible through the support of the United States Institute of Peace at Washington, D.C., and the George Mason University Center for Conflict Analysis and Resolution at Fairfax, Virginia.

The United States Institute of Peace made it possible for me, as the author of this overview volume and an editor of the Series, to spend a year as a Distinguished Jennings Randolph Fellow to interact with other Fellows at the Institute, and to complete the project relieved of other duties.

I wish to acknowledge the continuing support received from Faculty Members of the George Mason University Center for Conflict Analysis and Resolution, Professors James Laue, Christopher Mitchell, Richard Rubenstein, Dennis Sandole and Joseph Scimecca and, in addition, from the many others who from time to time took part in conferences and discussions. Through Center Faculty members it was possible to arrange for graduate students to read a draft and to make comments in class, and I wish to express my deep appreciation also to these students.

Several graduate students of the Center were involved in the research associated with these books, and they are identified in the acknowledgements in the relevant book. I wish, however, to acknowledge the continuing assistance given to me by Frank Dukes, during this time completing his Doctorate in Conflict Resolution at the Center. He also co-edited with me the third, and co-authored the fourth book in this Series.

The Center has received major support from The William and Flora Hewlett Foundation of Menlo Park, California, for the development of the Center as a theory center in the field of conflict resolution. Much of the basic research for this study was carried out with the support of their grant.

The German Marshall Fund of the United States made possible two conferences convened to promote this study. The first one, in January 1988, attended by scholars from the United States and the United Kingdom, sought to define the field and approach. The second, in July 1988, brought together scholars from nine countries to integrate theory and practice in conflict resolution, and it is they who have contributed to Volume 2 of this Series.

My special thanks are due to Betty Nathan whose editing of many drafts led, not merely to an improved exposition, but to important additions and modifications of the contents. The term "provention" is hers, introduced for reasons that will become clear.

While there has been this widespread consultation, I as the author of this book, and an editor of the Series, must take final responsibility for the approach and details of exposition.

JOHN BURTON

CONFLICT: RESOLUTION AND PROVENTION

Contents

List of Figures   xxiv

Introduction   1
The nature of the study   1
Definitions and scope   2
The human dimension   4
A problem-solving approach to conflict resolution and
  provention   5
Conflict resolution as a political philosophy   5
The role of a third party   6
A summary   7

PART I   THE APPROACH

Introduction to Part I   12

1 The Problem Area   13
An altering perspective   13
Deep-rooted conflict   15
Escalating conflict   16
The cost of treating symptoms   17
Provention and social problems   18
The methodological approach   19
The advantages of facing complexities   20
The question of values   21
Third-party facilitation and public policy   22
The individual and the common good   23

2 The Human Dimension   25
Specialists versus theorists   25
Conflict theory and practice   27
Abnormalities   29
The issue of fault   30
A generic human component and deep-rooted conflict   32
The significance of a human needs approach   33

3 Human Needs Theory   36
Needs   36
Values   37

Interests   38
The trading of interests, values and needs   39
Goals, tactics and ideologies   41
Ideologies and systems   43
Confusion over tactics and goals   43
Ideologies – ideal types and the pragmatic   44
Communication in conflict resolution   46
The common good   46
Decision making   47

4 **The Environment of Conflict**   **49**
The determinants of conflict   49
The escalation of conflict and violence   50
Exponential change   52
System change as a requirement of conflict resolution
   and provention   54
Dependency relationships   55
Appendix: Quality of Life and Entropy   58
Defining quality of life   58
The problem of entropy   59
A criticism of economics   62
Public policy implications   62
The economic perspective   63
An adequate theoretical framework   64

5 **The Influence of Tradition**   **66**
Problems of change   66
Political thought and law   67
A false dichotomy   68
Authority and repression   69
The legacy of tradition   70
Man, the state and war   72
The importance of models and language   74
Language   75
The misinterpretation of data   77
Choices, interests, values and needs   78
Belief or interest?   80

6 **Sources and Trends in Thought**   **83**
A recent interest   83
The experience of social workers   84

Industrial relations   85
High level conflict   85
Trivializing problems   86
Implications of power theories   87
The "ripening" thesis   88
Trends in thinking about a human dimension   90
The recent literature   92
Human needs and control theory   94
An assessment of control theory   97
The contemporary literature   98
The international literature   100

PART II THE POLITICAL CONTEXT

Introduction to Part II   106

7 Navigation Points   109
  Interest policies versus conflict resolution   109
  The subjective and controversial nature of politics   110
  An uncomfortable doctrine   112
  Empirical evidence of a human dimension   114
  Some recent whistle blowing   115
  The need for autonomy   116
  From subjectivity in politics to objective guidelines 117
  Politics not inherently controversial   117
  The challenge   118
  A question of process   119
  The two-track approach   120
  The separation of symptom treatment and problem-solving 121
  Theory and practice   122

8 The Legitimization of Authorities   123
  The conceptualization of legitimization   123
  The case for legality   124
  Conflict as non-legitimized relationships   125
  Reciprocity and legitimization   127
  The phenomenon of change   128
  A shift in thought   129
  The dilemmas of leadership   130

System legitimization 132
The measurement of legitimization 132
The realities of the political climate 133
The search for process 134

9 Multi-ethnic Societies **137**
Ethnicity and other identity problems 137
An issue of identity 138
The legitimization problem 139
Integration through separation 140
Zonal systems 141
The problem of mixed societies 144
Ethnic conflict and legitimization 145

10 The Individual and Society **147**
The source of conflict: institutions or persons? 147
The historical context 148
A problem-solving approach to the individual and society 149
The policy dilemma 150
Intellectual confusion 152
The social good and valued relationships 153
The demise of relationships 154
What are future goals? 156
The common good as compensation 157

11 Constructive Intervention **158**
The quality of intervention 159
A neglected subject 161
Needs theory and intervention 162
The relevance of quality intervention 163
International interventions 164
The problems of public policy making 166
Problem-solving processes 167
Principles of intervention 168
Conflict resolution and provention as providing an
 alternative system? 169

PART III CONFLICT RESOLUTION

Introduction to Part III **172**

12 Decision Making **173**
Conflict resolution as decision making 173

Contents

Reactive and interactive decision making 174
The power input–output model of decision making 175
Making puzzles out of problems 178
Legitimacy 180
Decision making and ideologies 180
Decision making and conflict resolution 181
Interactive models of decision making 183
The emergence of problem-solving 187

13 Trends in Conflict Management and Resolution 188
The emergence of the third party 188
Changing models: direct power confrontation 188
Summary view 192
An historical process 193
The behavioral component 194
Lessons from the past 195
The main variables 196
The questioning of assumptions and perceptions 197
A unified theory 199
Hypotheses 199
Process 200
Some additions to the model 200
The human dimension 201
The task ahead 201

14 Conflict Resolution as Problem-solving 202
The characteristics of problem-solving 202
The problem-solving process 204
The sponsoring role of the third party 205
Conflict resolution as an analytical and learning process 206
The problem of scope and the question of relevance 207
The filter 208
Concepts and models 209
Summary 210

15 Culture 211
The concept of culture 212
Culture and the human dimension 212
The process issue 213
Culture and attitudes 215

16 Acceptability of Conflict Resolution 217
The complexities of conflict resolution 217

Resolution processes   218
The power of ideas   220
The need for a paradigm shift   223
Creative thinking   225
Creativity and manipulation   227

PART IV   PROVENTION

Introduction to Part IV   **230**

17   From Resolution to Provention   **233**
Problems of prediction: probabilistic prediction   233
Games without end   234
Analytical prediction   235
Provention implies change   236
Vested interests versus uncertainties   237
Conflict resolution as a means of change   238

18   Second-order Change   **239**
Reframing   239
Is provention by change what is sought?   240
The situations requiring second-order change   241
The practitioner's perspective   243
Within-system disputes and conflicts   244
Conflict and system fault   247
The type of change required   248
Accumulated adjustments   249
The need for viable options   250
The reliability of processes   251

19   The Intellectual Challenge   **252**
Reliability and credibility   252
The recent nature of thinking about provention   253
Altered concepts   253
Thought processes   255
Remedial and provention approaches: two different fields   257

PART V   CONCLUSION

Introduction to Part V   **260**

20   Conflict Resolution as a Political System   **261**
Political movements in perspective   261
A universal phenomenon   264

System and process 265
Rights and needs 265
The future 266
Problem-solving processes within systems 267

21 A Summary Assessment **269**
Resignation 269
Resolution and provention as a challenge to resignation 270
The creative role of professionals 271
The availability of conflict resolution 272
Provention as the major policy focus 274
A problem of education 276
The need for thinking skills 276

A Short Bibliography 279

References 281

Index 287

List of Figures

4.1	An exponential change curve	53
12.1	Power inputs and allocations	175
12.2	Reactive decision making model	176
12.3	Cybernetic models	177
12.4	More complex stimulus–response models	178
12.5	Interactive models	183
12.6	Reactive power models	184
12.7	Transition models: interactive power models	185
12.8	Interactive problem-solving models	186
13.1	Coercive and problem-solving approaches	197
13.2	The problem-solving diagram	198

Introduction

The study of conflict, its resolution and provention, has two main concerns. The first is the *explanation* of conflict and violence within societies and the world society. It is only on the basis of an adequate explanation of a problem that we can evolve a constructive approach to solving it. The second concern is, given an explanation of the problem of conflict, to find the nature of a constructive approach to it: the principles of processes and policies that we derive from the explanation.

There are five features that define the scope and areas of concern of this study:

First, a clear distinction is made between, on the one hand, disputes which are a feature of normal and frequently collaborative and creative relationships, endemic in all social relationships, and an integral part of competitive systems; and, on the other, conflicts which are deeply-rooted in human needs, and which frequently require major environmental and policy restructuring for their resolution. While recognizing that the two are sometimes linked, disputes being sometimes symptoms of underlying conflicts, the latter is our special concern in this study.

Second, while limiting our definition of conflict in this way, we nevertheless include some behaviors, such as instances of street gang conflict, even occurrences of family and community conflict, that legally might be classified as ordinary crime. In some environmental conditions the distinction between crime, and situations of deep-rooted conflict between persons and groups or with authorities, is a fine one.

Third, the study is concerned with conflict as a universal phenomenon affecting all cultures, at all stages of political, social and economic development, and at all societal levels from the interpersonal to the international. It seeks a generic explanation of conflict from which to deduce the principles of its treatment.

Fourth, the study seeks to point to means of the *resolution* of conflict as distinct from its containment, suppression or enforced *settlement*. The study is thus concerned with the analysis and solving of the problems, whether human, institutional, or both, that give rise

1

to conflicts, and the discovery of the options that meet the needs of those involved.

Fifth, the study seeks explanations of conflict that make possible prediction, and, thereby, not merely prevention, but "provention" also. "Provention" implies the promotion of an environment conducive to harmonious relationships. The study thus enters the fields of political philosophy and policy making.

DEFINITIONS AND SCOPE

It will help to describe the nature of the study further if we give some preliminary definitions to terms used, and some indication of scope. (In Chapter 5 we return to the use of language to show the way in which traditional concepts have inhibited thinking on this subject. Throughout the study there is a great deal of emphasis on the need for clarity of terms and concepts because it is necessary to give special meanings to many terms in general use.)

A first distinction to be made is between *disputes* and *conflicts*. By *disputes* we mean those situations in which the issues are negotiable, in which there can be compromise, and which, therefore, do not involve consideration of altered institutions and structures.

By contrast, the behavior which is the main concern of this Conflict Series is the kind of behavior on the part of persons, groups or nations that goes beyond the normal disagreements and confrontations that characterize much of the usual social, economic and competitive life of societies. Overtly it is behavior that is, or has the potential of being, destructive of persons, properties and systems. The issues that lead to conflicts are not the ordinary ideas, choices, preferences and interests which are argued and negotiated as part of normal social living. They are those whose sources are deeply rooted in human behaviors.

This helps us to define *conflict*. Where such issues are involved, conflicts are likely to be intractable and to lead to behaviors that seriously prejudice the physical and psychological security, and the future development, of the individuals, groups, societies or nations concerned. Where and how we draw a line between disputes that are the normal and constructive features of social life, and conflicts that involve deep-rooted human needs, will become clearer in the analysis which follows.

By the *resolution* of conflict we mean the transformation of relationships in a particular case by the solution of the problems which led to the conflictual behavior in the first place. (Such a transformation does not necessarily eliminate future problems in relationships, or remove residual antagonisms: these are some of the complexities with which we deal in this Series.) We thus make a distinction between *resolution*, that is, treatment of the problems that are the sources of conflict, and the suppression of *settlement* of conflict by coercive means, or by bargaining and negotiation in which relative power determines the outcome.

Problem-solving Conflict Resolution has, therefore, a special meaning. Its practice is analytical, and designed to assist parties to conflicts to understand and accurately to cost the consequences of their behaviors. Its philosophy is one of a reconstructed sense of political realism, a realism that takes fully into account the inexorable nature of human behaviors. For this reason it is conceptually and in practice removed from traditional forms of dispute and conflict *settlement* or *management*. It does not include deterrence strategies as applied to domestic or international situations, or repression and containment of conflict. It is not concerned with the management of conflicts by arbitration, or with mediation processes based on compromises. It is not concerned with peace-oriented reactions to deterrence strategies and the advocacy, for example, of peace through arms reductions. It is not concerned with just arriving at a consensus among disputants, for if there were an ill-informed consensus there would be no guarantee of a solution to a problem. Each of these approaches may have its own applications and justifications, but problem-solving conflict resolution is fundamentally different from them.

Conflict Provention means deducing from an adequate explanation of the phenomenon of conflict, including its human dimensions, not merely the conditions that create an environment of conflict, and the structural changes required to remove it, but more importantly, the promotion of conditions that create cooperative relationships. The term "provention" is invented because "prevention" has a negative connotation. The absence of a suitable word reflects the fact that prevention of an undesirable event by removing its causes, and by creating conditions that do not give rise to its causes, has not been a focus of attention of societies or of scholars.

THE HUMAN DIMENSION

We give a special meaning to *deep-rooted human needs*. Some preliminary definition or explanation is appropriate as this is a core concept in this analysis.

It has been a largely unquestioned assumption in traditional thought that conflict is to a large degree the consequence of inherent behaviors that are malign (see Chapter 5). Authorities, not wishing to reflect adversely on their institutions or policies, have tended to hold personal malevolence responsible for conflict among their subjects, between themselves and their subjects, and with other authorities. This theory of behavior logically required the punishment or constraint of persons and groups involved both as a means of dealing with the present situation, and as a means of deterring others from such behaviors in the future.

These traditional methods of conflict management are, however, failing in modern societies to a degree that is becoming increasingly unacceptable. There are, furthermore, both empirical and theoretical reasons to believe that there will be a continuing escalation of levels of protracted conflicts in most societies, and also internationally (see Chapter 4). In many cases the incidence of conflict is already outside the bounds of authoritative containment.

This reality forces a reconsideration of the basic hypothesis on which coercive policies were, and are, based. Is it a valid assumption that behaviors, even if they are correctly interpreted as basically evil or anti-social, can be contained by coercive means?

We argue in this study that there has been a fundamental error in the traditional assessment of the human dimension involved in conflict and its management. It is a mistake not only in theory, but also pragmatically when coercive and authoritative processes of control are used in an attempt to preserve existing interests and institutions (Chapters 1 and 2).

It is insights into the wellsprings of human behavior, gradually developed over some decades (see Chapter 6), that has made possible the present study of conflict, its resolution and provention, and that justifies the assertion that a problem-solving approach to conflict resolution is, in practice, politically more realistic than the suppressive policies of the traditional "power political realists". If it is a valid perspective that there are some behaviors that cannot be altered by socialization processes or deterred by coercion, it follows that there are effective limits to the use of coercion by authorities over citizens, and by more powerful persons and groups over others with whom they are in dispute.

A PROBLEM-SOLVING APPROACH TO CONFLICT RESOLUTION AND PROVENTION

As indicated, the approach we are adopting to conflict, its resolution and provention, is a problem-solving one. Problem-solving has two special connotations:

First, problem-solving implies a concern with the causes that lead to conflict – for example, the underlying and causal sources of gang warfare and of terrorism, or the institutional and human origins of ethnic conflict – rather than with the overt violence and disruptions that are the manifestations or symptoms of such problems. It may be necessary as an expedient to contain some behaviors, but unless underlying causes of conflicts are treated there can be no *resolution* of a particular conflict, let alone prevention of such conflicts in the future. In the absence of the treatment of causes there can be, at best, only containment. We are as much concerned with the analysis of social problems that give rise to conflict, that is *the environment of conflict*, as with the features of particular conflicts and processes of resolution (Chapter 4).

Second, conflict resolution through problem-solving implies that, in order to reveal the nature of conflict and the sources of particular conflicts, the approach must be analytical. It must include not only clarifications of terms and concepts, but also a questioning of assumptions. Throughout this overview references are made to the nature of analytical reasoning, for it is this which makes possible problem-solving and, therefore, conflict resolution and provention (see Chapter 14 for a further discussion on problem-solving).

CONFLICT RESOLUTION AS A POLITICAL PHILOSOPHY

Dealing with a particular conflict situation, a street confrontation or an ethnic conflict, does nothing to prevent the occurrence of another case of the same kind. The particular case can, however, throw light on the broader causal problems, thus leading to some predictive capacity, and to policies of prevention of future conflicts.

Problem-solving conflict resolution is thus more than a resolution process with respect to a particular conflict. It provides an alternative to coercion or authoritative approaches to policies generally. There is, therefore, an important link between resolution and provention, the one throwing light upon the other. Problem-solving conflict resolution brings to attention a major decision making dilemma: to aim for *needs satisfaction*, or to employ the simpler expediency of *needs suppression* by power.

This dilemma is being highlighted by events: needs suppression by coercive means is failing at both domestic and international levels. There is now no viable option but problem-solving conflict resolution that is designed to discover means by which human aspirations can more fully be satisfied within the context of the social good. In theory at least, problem-solving conflict resolution is thus a political philosophy, perhaps the foundation of a political system that in time will be a supplement to, if not an alternative to, traditional political relationships.

There are inherent practical and political resistances to new thinking, and to processes that are a departure from the traditional, unless they can be shown to be viable options that do in practice solve the problems that are being experienced. It may be that the complexities of problem-solving in respect to situations of conflict in both modern societies and the international system are now beyond human capabilities. It may be that the simpler coercive approach of conflict suppression is becoming even more expedient as societies are increasingly threatened by their own system failings. This study seeks to examine these and related issues, and to determine whether there is an alternative, or a supplement to, the prevailing power consensus in the study of conflict, its resolution and provention.

THE ROLE OF A THIRD PARTY

Treating problem-solving conflict resolution and provention as a political philosophy does not negate the importance of facilitated processes of conflict resolution in particular cases. On the contrary, the philosophy provides the foundation of such processes. Such processes provide, in turn, the means of validation of the theoretical and philosophical approach.

A problem-solving decision making process is by nature far more complex than a coercive process. Parties involved in a conflict – authorities and dissidents, rival communities, nations and states – are not likely to have sufficient knowledge either of the sources of their conflictual relationships, or of the options available to resolve them. In the absence of adequate knowledge there can be no accurate costing of policies, or of the consequence of behaviors. A problem-solving approach to conflict resolution as applied to particular situations requires, therefore, a most knowledgeable and skilled "third party". (The term "third party" has come into use because in an analytical framework it is usually necessary to break a conflict down into parties and issues, treating each interaction separately. There are, therefore, two interacting protagonists, and the third party facilitator; see Part III on Conflict Resolution.) It is probably only in the presence of such a third party that the necessary insights are likely to emerge, and the required longer-term costing of policies, and non-bargaining and analytical discussions, are likely to take place. The wider political philosophical area implied in provention is an essential part of the intellectual background of such a "third party".

A SUMMARY

This extensive field of study has, for purposes of exposition in this book, been separated into five Parts:

– The Approach
– The Political Context
– Resolution
– Provention
– Conclusion

Part I, *The Approach* commences with an introductory chapter defining *The Problem Area*. It seeks to clarify the scope of the study. Then we describe the approach by dealing at the outset with *The Human Dimension* (Chapter 2), followed by some explanation of *Human Needs Theory* (Chapter 3). In Chapter 4 we indicate the way in which an *Environment of Conflict* is emerging and can be expected to escalate. Then we turn to the *Influence of Tradition* and the way in which decision making has over the years helped to create an environment of conflict (Chapter 5). We finally pull together the chapters of Part I by reviewing trends in thinking that have led over some decades to this approach (Chapter 6).

In Part II, *The Political Context*, we examine that background knowledge which enables a third party facilitator to provide the analytical input required by parties in their endeavors to see clearly what is before them, and to help to resolve their perceptual and real problems without compromise of their fundamental goals and values. This touches, also, on the knowledge required by decision makers to provent conflict. We argue that contemporary knowledge of behavior leads to some *Navigation Points* – that is, objective criteria – by which meaningful definitions can be given to concepts and terms, and by which assessments can be made of policies, thus reducing the role of ideologies (Chapter 7). This enables us to discuss *The Legitimization of Authorities*, which is clearly an important consideration in analyzing relations between authorities and those over whom they exercise authority at all social levels (Chapter 8). *Multi-ethnic Societies* present a special problem of legitimization (Chapter 9). We are then led to discuss the more general question of *The Individual and Society*, raising the issue of the common good (Chapter 10). Finally, in Part II, we give consideration to the role of authorities, and distinguish between *Constructive Intervention* and restrictive policies (Chapter 11).

Part III, *Resolution*, deals in detail with processes of *Decision Making* (Chapter 12), and with *Trends in Conflict Management and Resolution*, and how both have emerged out of decision making theory and experience (Chapter 13). This evaluation reflects a growing awareness of the practical need to take human responses into account in decision making, leading to *Conflict Resolution as Problem Solving*, a process that seeks to discover options that satisfy the human needs of all parties within the context of the interests of societies (Chapter 14). There follow some comments on *Culture* and its consequences for conflict resolution (Chapter 15). Finally we examine the conditions that make such processes acceptable to protagonists (Chapter 16).

In Part IV, *Provention*, we develop the concept of provention (Chapter 17), and then explore the inherent difficulties in making *Second-order Change* in social systems (Chapter 18), and *The Intellectual Challenge* it presents (Chapter 19).

In Part V, *Conclusion*, we examine *Conflict Resolution as a Political System* (Chapter 20), then we make a *Summary Conclusion*, finally suggesting that conflict provention is ultimately a question of education and an altered consensus (Chapter 21).

Throughout, references are made to articles and contributions that are in the other three books in the series. In addition to the usual list of references made in the text, there is attached to this overview a small selected Bibliography of recent books which are relevant, and should be available readily in most libraries.

I
The Approach

Chapter 1   The Problem Area   13
Chapter 2   The Human Dimension   25
Chapter 3   Human Needs Theory   36
Chapter 4   The Environment of Conflict   49
Chapter 5   The Influence of Tradition   66
Chapter 6   Sources and Trends in Thought   83

Introduction to Part I

The general area of concern is the discovery of means of resolution, or better still, the elimination of conditions that give rise to deep-rooted conflict. Chapter 1 is a general one describing the problem area.

Any human problem must commence with some indication of the assumptions about behavior that are at the basis of the analysis of the problem. Chapter 2 deals with this human dimension, and Chapter 3 develops it further indicating its practical significance. Chapter 4 deals with the environment that gives rise to conflict, and offers expectations that increases in levels of conflict at all societal levels must be anticipated. One reason is the burden of past policies (Chapter 5).

In order not to distract from the exposition we have not made many references to the relevant literature in these chapters describing the problem area and the approach, but it is important to place this evolving subject in its wider context of scholarly thought. This we do in Chapter 6.

1 The Problem Area

A prevailing view is that all potential conflictual behaviors can be deterred, but that failing this, all conflicts can be contained provided sufficient coercion is employed.

We are, however, becoming increasingly aware of the many complex conflicts, within societies and internationally, that are not contained when treated by the enforcement of legal norms or by coercive power means. These include not only cases of communal conflict, such as ethnic disputes, but also a variety of other conflicts within and between societies, ranging from family violence and drug-related disputes and the conflicts that underlie them, to the conflicts that result from foreign interventions and threats to independence. It would appear that in all these cases there are frustrations and concerns under the surface that are not negotiable and cannot be repressed, adjudicated by courts or negotiated.

A failure to recognize that there are two quite different types of conflicts – those that are subject to the application of social and legal norms and coercive processes, and those that are not – has been at the heart of legal, political, academic and social disagreements over the handling of conflict within and between societies.

This observation is not made as a criticism of systems, leaderships or thinkers. All are a product of the past. There is a continuum from primitive forms of feudalism to modern societies. The relevant historical space is only a few hundred years. It is not surprising that there are still significant elements of authoritarianism and power politics in modern societies. (What is surprising is that we do not generally recognize this short time period and legacy of the past in our daily lives and thinking, and do not acknowledge that we are still in a quite primitive stage in social development, requiring an analysis of problems rather than just the defense of the present.) Our task is, in a non-judgemental way, to pinpoint sources of conflict, to direct attention to them, and to find means of resolving and proventing them.

AN ALTERING PERSPECTIVE

Societies, and Western industrial societies in particular, have moved

13

to a stage of ambiguity and confusion in social controls that can only be described as a mess. Governments seem to be at a loss in foreign and strategic policies in this nuclear age. There is a growing number of ethnic and tribal conflicts that remain unresolved in addition to problems with military governments. At home jails and correction centers are overcrowded and, moreover, seem not to achieve their purposes. (Two thirds of those sent to jail return within three years, US Justice Department Report, April 1989.) Deterrent and coercive approaches do not lead to the discovery or removal of causes of conflict in the particular case, and do nothing to stop others occurring.

Theoretical evidence, as we shall see in Chapters 2 and 3, suggests the behavioral reasons why authorities are failing to maintain an orderly society, sometimes despite the most repressive of measures. It appears that in the longer term the pursuit of certain inherent human drives may be more powerful than are institutional constraints. There are reasons for predicting that no form of coercion or control is likely to suppress conflict and its violence in the family, the street, the community, or within the national or international society, while there exists an environment promoting conflict. Later we will seek to define what constitutes such an environment (see Chapter 4).

Furthermore, some sources of conflict lie in frustrations resulting from constraints on behaviors. Containment of conflict can provoke it in the future. There are situations in which civil strife has been restrained by military regimes, as in some countries in South America, only to lead to further strife that finally defeats the regimes. There have been situations, such as in Vietnam, in which the exercise of vastly superior military and economic powers has provoked responses that out-matched it.

Short-term political expediency can, obviously, have long-term consequences of proportions that reach beyond the bounds of adjustment of which societies seem capable. Ecological, social and political adjustments that changing circumstances require have been resisted. We thus have a potentially disastrously increasing gap between escalating increases in conditions creating conflict, and steps taken to deal with them. This is a political reality that problem-solving conflict resolution and provention must confront.

The burden of past institutions and attitudes, the human behavioral dimension of which we still understand little, the growing gap between required change and achieved change, combine to present a social problem of immense complexity and dimension. To tackle it, we must start with clear concepts and an agreed language with which to make an analysis; but here, too, we have a burden from the past (Chapter 5).

DEEP-ROOTED CONFLICT

Deep-rooted conflict includes cases of conflict with authorities, between authorities, and among persons and groups within societies. It involves cases that arise out of demands on individuals to make certain adjustments in behavior that are unacceptable, and probably beyond human tolerance and capabilities. Symptoms of deep-rooted conflict – and these are merely symptoms – include hostage taking, illegal strikes, public protest movements, ethnic violence, terrorism, gang warfare, and many other forms of intractable opposition to authorities at one social level or another.

In such cases, it is not possible to contain conflict within existing frameworks, except over severely limited periods of time. Such cases, therefore, require alterations in norms, institutions and policies to bring adjustment within the range of human acceptability and capability. In other words, these are cases in which there has to be an analysis of the total situation and an appropriate remedy, rather than merely the containment of dissident behaviors. (Let us note that while deep-rooted conflict is apt to result in violence, we should not equate deep-rooted conflict and violence. Violence can also result from disputes that are over negotiable interests, and from psychological problems.)

It should not be assumed, however, that this study does not touch on the disputes and conflicts of everyday life with which lawyers, social workers, industrial arbitrators, administrators and managers are engaged. There is a close relationship between what have been regarded and treated as ordinary, negotiable, interest disputes, and deep-rooted conflicts likely to result in high tensions, and violence between peoples and communities. In many more cases than is realized, courts, lawyers, mediators and public officials have been treating disputes in a dysfunctionally superficial way. There are cases that traditionally go to courts, to arbitration or to power bargaining negotiation that require far more analytical treatment if there are not to be adverse and costly social and political consequences in the longer term. Settlement of landlord and tenant disputes can set patterns that in the longer term can lead to major social problems in housing, leading in turn to problems in social relationships.

Unemployment relief, not accompanied by other requirements of social living, can help in providing food, but can also lead to lack of stimulus and to alienation. "Closure" in a particular case is not necessarily a measure of effective resolution. Even normal disputes may become deep-rooted and sometimes violent. This can happen because of inappropriate processes of third party intervention: deep-rooted conflict can in some circumstances be generated by processes of interaction and intervention in dealing with quite ordinary and potentially functional disputes.

(These are among the reasons why we make few references in this study to an extensive literature that deals with bargaining and negotiation over interests: see, for example, Fisher and Ury, 1978 and Goldberg, Green and Sander, 1985; we are treating bargaining and negotiation as a separate field, our interest being problem-solving in cases in which there are needs to be satisfied without compromise, making bargaining and negotiation irrelevant.)

ESCALATING CONFLICT

We will be asserting in Chapter 4 the probability of a universal escalation of conflict. Deep-rooted conflict is in modern times a problem at all social levels and in all cultures on a scale not previously experienced. This assertion does not rely on statistical support alone. Numbers of murders, ethnic conflicts, terrorist activities, and other symptoms of social problems can be interpreted to show quite different explanations and projections. In considering provention in particular, statistics may not provide a predictive base. Early statistics of persons with the AIDS virus did not alert societies to the extent of the problem. It was only when the nature of the virus was known, the ways in which it could unknowingly be communicated, that there was a realistic appreciation of the extent of the problem, and reliable predictions as to future casualties. The drug epidemic was not predicted. So it is with conflict generally. It is not statistics of past incidents, not even statistical projections, that give us a true picture. Reliable prediction is based on an understanding of the problem of conflict, its origins and its implications.

THE COST OF TREATING SYMPTOMS

Problems that relate to social stability and human survival are not solved in the absence of an explanatory and a proventive approach to them. At best, the problems which give rise to conflicts, and the conflicts themselves, are then treated merely as part of the totality of environmental conditions to which humanity must adjust, or finally succumb. Indeed, this describes our contemporary approach to the bulk of unwelcome conditions that adversely affect our quality of life. In the last few decades we have developed a major and costly industry in security checks, but have spent far less thought and resources on the reasons for robbery and terrorism. We spend more and more on jails, but very little on the sources of deviant behaviors. At great cost we try to make air travel secure, but give little attention to the sources of sabotage. We try to curb drug trafficking and consumption, with little attention being paid to the reasons for drug production and consumption. We use police measures to deal with gang violence, with little consideration of the alienation and identity reasons for gang formation. Greater powers seek to impose their institutions and values on peoples of other nations in the name of democracy and freedom, but there is little analysis and understanding of the oppressive circumstances that have led peoples and nations to their present condition, or of their present felt needs for taking steps toward their independent development.

Meanwhile, the costs of containing conflict and violence – that is, of treating symptoms by traditional coercive means – are more than societies can afford. The costs of building jails and interning people and then releasing them as less desirable citizens, the costs of ethnic conflict which destroys the economies of nations, the costs and uncertainties of thermonuclear deterrence, are costs never before experienced, and they have grown beyond the capacities of even the wealthiest of nations. Suppression and containment, perhaps possible when societies were smaller and less complex, are no longer practical options either technically or financially. We conclude that there is now no option but to pay attention to the problems which give rise to conflict, even though this may require altered institutions and policies.

PROVENTION AND SOCIAL PROBLEMS

The introduction of the notion of conflict *provention* – that is the removal of causal conditions, and the positive promotion of environments conducive to collaborative relationships – extends the scope of our concerns beyond the narrow area of conflict resolution. Conflict resolution implies specific parties and their specific issues that are to be resolved. A matrimonial conflict over child custody, or an ethnic conflict over constitutional provisions, requires accommodation of emotions and human needs, but could possibly be resolved without consideration of events that led to the conflict. Once we introduce the notion of prevention the total social environment and sources of conflict become relevant. Conflict provention addresses problems of social relationships, and all the conditions that affect them.

Provention is thus concerned with social problems generally, with altering the environments that lead to conflict, and with creating environments that mitigate conflict. This may, in practice, seem to be largely irrelevant in respect to conflicts, such as matrimonial and ethnic conflicts, that are widespread and now treated as a normal part of social relationships in most countries. There are, however, other conflict areas in which there can be no resolutions, and where there must be provention. Take, for example, drug-related conflicts, gang violence, terrorism and international conflicts. As phenomena these cannot readily be contained, and often such conflicts involving particular parties cannot be resolved. They require provention – that is, elimination by removal of their sources. There is probably much that could be done also in the provention of conflicts such as "normal" matrimonial and ethnic ones, if only we were to give some thought to tackling them from this broader perspective.

In short, once we move beyond resolution to provention, we can no longer confine conflicts to specific parties and issues, and are in the area of social problems generally out of which emerge specific conflicts. "Conflict" is redefined to include social problems generally, and any set of circumstances that are symptoms of, or sources of conflicts between specific parties.

To be practical we must, however, confine conflict *resolution* to conflicts between identified parties, thus separating resolution processes from means of provention. In this sense they are two different areas of concern. It needs to be realized, however, that resolution will frequently be possible only if the parties concerned appreciate that "fault" may be with the environment or sources over which they have no control, and not with the protagonists in the conflict. Conflicts between factions *within* the Protestant or Catholic communities in Northern Ireland, and *within* the black and white communities in South Africa, are conflicts that have their sources in the wider conflicts in which these communities are engaged. Family and social conflicts frequently have sources in conditions of education, work or housing. Parties to conflicts frequently have no option but to accommodate to environmental conditions for which they are not directly responsible. Knowledge of provention, that is knowledge of environmental sources of conflict, may thus be a part of conflict resolution in the particular case.

The separation of conflict between specific parties, and social problems that lead to anti-social behaviors is, analytically, an artificial one. The inclusion of policy aspects of provention in the study of conflict resolution is necessary to an understanding of the particular conflict, even though little may be done about provention in a relevant time frame.

THE METHODOLOGICAL APPROACH

Whether we are concerned with resolution or provention we have to explore widely and find means by which to isolate the fundamental sources of conflict in particular cases and generally. These means must be both theoretical and empirical. The theoretical prove to be the more rewarding, subject to testing at the empirical level. The reason is that empirical evidence is likely to be misleading, especially in human studies, because it is confined to superficial or observable phenomena. Our perceptions are, moreover, guided by our preconceptions and expectations (see Chapter 2).

The thinking of a late nineteenth century mathematical philosopher, C. S. Peirce (see Rescher, 1978), whose writings have only recently been analyzed, is most useful to students of problem-solving conflict resolution. He stressed the need, first, for hypothesis projection – that is, postulating in an imaginative way possible explanatory hypotheses. These are not guesswork or trial and error, but imaginative hypotheses based on available knowledge, intuitions and insights. This he called an "abductive" process. Second, he attached importance to the questioning and elimination of hypotheses, not just on empirical grounds, for testing is sometimes impossible, but on analytical, common-sense, intuitive grounds. This he termed "retroduction." He did not attach a great deal of value to trial and error and testing, for testing may suggest a fault, but it cannot provide a better theory.

Such an approach is especially appropriate for social problem-solving and conflict resolution because in many instances there cannot be testing, and even if there could, it would be fatal if the hypothesis proved to be false. The hypothesis that nuclear deterrence deters is not one that should be entertained as a trial and error proposition. It is in this sense that Peirce claimed that he was advocating a logical and self-correcting process, the self-correcting element not resting wholly or even mainly on testing. The emphasis on improving theory, and not on quantitative induction based on examination of cases, is one that meets the requirements of social problem-solving.

We will be giving a great deal of attention to methodological issues, the questioning of assumptions, and the way in which such methodology enters into the conflict resolution process when parties are interacting. Conflict resolution as a process is itself a means of tackling methodological problems of research and discovery. Parties interacting within a facilitated and analytical framework are questioning assumptions, preconceived notions and perceptions, and thus making discoveries, not only about their own situation, but also about human behavior generally.

THE ADVANTAGES OF FACING COMPLEXITIES

Conflict, its resolution and provention, is inevitably a study which knows no boundaries of thought. It involves the whole person, the nation or identity group of the person, the political system, and the physical environment. It is a study with a univeral application. It cuts across cultures. It cannot be broken up into "aspects" of behaviour. Conflict resolution is a study that transcends separate compartments of knowledge, known as disciplines, and seeks to take a holistic view of human conflictual behavior, without being politically unrealistic, or in any sense superficial.

Despite the obvious complexities of such a comprehensive approach, experience suggests that it may be more practical and cost effective than a specialist and reductionist approach that leads to the treatment of only some aspects of problems, and perhaps to the treatment only of symptoms. Conflicts can be tackled at source by an adequate understanding of them, and by appropriate processes. Complexity could, indeed, be the means to greater simplicity, and greater intellectual and practical achievement. In theory and in practice the behavior of the whole person, acting separately or as part of a wider identity group, is proving to be far more easily understood and predictable than the unreal constructs of the person, constructs such as "economic man," which were invented for reasons of "scientific" precision in theorizing.

THE QUESTION OF VALUES

Dealing with the totality of behavior in this way, conflict resolution and provention does not assume as given any goals or values, no matter how traditional and established, that are inconsistent with human development generally. This focus on human development in dealing with critical problems of conflict and survival does *not*, therefore, rest on any ideological notions of justice as such. It rests on the reality that conditions of social stability and harmony require the satisfaction of certain human needs. Events, surveys and experiences relating to alienation, gangs, terrorism and dissident behaviors generally demonstrate that conflict of the type which is of concern to us is the consequence of frustration of certain ontological human needs (Winfrey, 1988). As we shall see (Chapter 2), theory leads us to this conclusion, but so does the history of slavery, feudalism, imperialism, racism, sexism and all other forms of frustration of human development, and the conflicts associated with them. The reality is that the human dimension has to be taken into account if pressing social problems are to be solved in the common interest.

The only value orientation that is inherent in a study of conflict, its resolution and provention, is the goal of resolving and proventing conflict. Just as economics has the goal of the best use of scarce resources, so conflict resolution has its own self-defined goal. This goal, however, is the only value orientation. It is hard for anyone to prevent values entering into judgements; but, as we shall argue in Chapter 2, an adequate theoretical framework helps greatly to prevent this happening.

This value issue is stressed because conflict resolution and provention, being associated in the minds of most people with "peace" and pre-conditions of peace, such as "justice," is frequently dubbed ideological or value oriented in the sense of being unrealistically "liberal" or pacifist. In practice it is concerned with the political realities of behavior in a far more realistic fashion than are power theories and ideologies that ignore human dimensions, and for this reason become self-defeating.

The value issue is important, also, because of its implications for process. When parties are in conflict it may not be useful to try to convince one party that it "should" or "ought" to treat the other in some particular way dictated by value considerations. Conflict resolution is a costing process. The argument is that, given a problem-solving forum, each party, in its own interests, will seek to find means of satisfying, not only its own needs and interests, but also those of others in order to avoid costly and dysfunctional conflicts. In practice this is what happens (Burton, 1969 and Azar and Burton (eds), 1986).

It needs to be added, however, that the goal of universal human development is an unattainable one. Even the satisfaction of basic physical needs of food and shelter seems to be beyond the organizational capacities of societies and the world society. The satisfaction of human needs of autonomy and development is even more remote. As a consequence, conflict resolution can never attain its ultimate value or super goal. In addition to resource and opportunity scarcities there is the problem of individual deformities that are not environmentally related, the extent of which is still unknown. We have had the experience of elected leaders of great powers who were mentally unstable, of large numbers of persons who are unlikely to be able to cost accurately the consequences of their behaviors, and to deal with environmental conditions that promote misperceptions and confrontations. Conflict resolution must, therefore, also deduce those processes of decision making that can reliably provide for the probability of continued needs frustrations and non-rational behaviors. It must include considerations of frameworks or structures that serve as a backstop, such as constraints that seek simultaneously to overcome the causal problems. This link between problem-solving and constraints is a by-product of the study of conflict resolution that has not yet been explored widely in public policies, though it has received some attention in remedial education and therapy.

THIRD-PARTY FACILITATION AND PUBLIC POLICY

Conflict resolution has been associated in the minds of most knowledgeable people with process. Traditionally it has been held that, with good-will, parties to a dispute can settle their differences by negotiation and compromise. In difficult cases some skilled third-party intervention may be needed to help dialogue, and to move toward an informed consensus. Indeed, this thinking has led to a major industry in training negotiators, including corporate managers and diplomats. The aim has been, however, to improve bargaining positions – that is, to improve chances of "winning." These processes have little relevance in situations in which the issues are deep-rooted and not negotiable. "Winning" in these cases is only a prelude to protracted conflict, as many parents, industrial managers and governments in multi-ethnic societies come to learn.

As we will see in Part III, *Resolution*, a third party needs to have a wide knowledge of public policy issues, and to have the ability to place something on the table that attracts protagonists, and provides acceptable frameworks for discussion (see Chapter 16). It follows that the student of conflict resolution, as we define it, is not mainly concerned with process. Process is a small and ancillary part of the study of special interest even to the third party facilitator. A facilitator needs the wider knowledge that is required of the policy maker. The background knowledge required is the same in both cases. The goal of conflict resolution theory and practice is problem-solving, which means, ultimately, policy making. It is a philosophy, an education and a guide to public policy that seeks to look ahead more than is usually possible within an institutionalized political framework. While it is an essential part of facilitation training, it is also relevant for many influential and significant professions that involve decision making.

THE INDIVIDUAL AND THE COMMON GOOD

This approach raises fundamental issues of social control and the common good. Conflict resolution and provention have no ideological orientation: they are analytical. But they do start from the hypothesis that there are limits to the extent to which the human person, acting separately or within a wider ethnic or national community, can be socialized or manipulated. They assume that there are human development needs that must be satisfied and catered for by institutions, if these institutions are to be stable, and if societies are to be significantly free of conflict. Unless we can substantiate this assumption that there are limits to the capabilities of the individual to conform, the whole framework and justification of conflict resolution and provention is destroyed. But to the extent that it is substantiated, to the extent that it is found that deep-rooted conflicts cannot be contained or repressed by coercive means, traditional approaches to authoritative conflict management must give way.

Societies will, however, have no option but to continue to rest on coercive techniques in social control unless an option is perceived to be practical and available. There is a need for a clear picture of different approaches, their strengths and weaknesses and the types of cases which are best handled by each. It is also necessary to define those cases that require greater in-depth analysis than traditional techniques can provide. It would be absurd to employ the sophisticated techniques of analytical problem-solving conflict resolution, which may involve panels of facilitators, for cases which can be handled effectively by a single facilitator or by an arbitrator. We must, therefore, be descriptive of both processes and situations that are respectively relevant. Observations in this overview volume are supplemented in Volume 4 in this Conflict Series, *Conflict: Practices in Management, Settlement and Resolution.*

2 The Human Dimension

SPECIALISTS VERSUS THEORISTS

One of the major obstacles in dealing with basic problems such as deep-rooted conflict has been the absence of an adequate theoretical framework and, even more serious, the absence of a realization that such a framework is necessary for solving a problem. The responsibility for failed policies is frequently not with policy makers, but with those who have emerged out of "social sciences" as "specialist" and "expert" advisers. Sometimes they are policy makers, sometimes administrators, and sometimes consultants. They are specialists or experts in a particular field through experience or academic training that focuses on empirical data, but usually with little theoretical background that would enable them to select and to interpret data.

This is a severe criticism to make and will be resisted by the majority of trained persons associated with policy making, advising, and even some professions that involve interventions into human relationships. But the absence of a well-considered theoretical framework is at the core of problems associated with conflict provention.

A telling example is the area specialist in international affairs. Knowledge of regional conditions and local politics does not, by itself, qualify a policy maker, an administrator or an adviser. Vietnam and North Korea were policy failures for the US. Why? Interventions in many other countries in Central and Latin America, and in the Middle East, have been costly failures. Why? Regional "experts" have a wealth of knowledge about local conditions, but it does not follow that they have an understanding of the issues at stake. To have understood Vietnam and North Korea in a way that would have enabled an assessment of the wisdom of military interventions, a knowledge would have been required of independence movements, their past history, the effects of past interventions and occupations, such as the French and Japanese occupation of Indo-China, nationalisms and struggles for the preservation of cultures and of autonomy and identity. These are not studies that are confined to regions. They are studies that emerge out of deep analysis of human behaviors, behaviors that are common to all societal levels, though perhaps

25

exhibited in different forms. (It will be noted that in the "rules" governing facilitated conflict resolution printed in book IV in this Series, there is one which suggests that "specialists" on the countries or region concerned should *not* be on a third-party panel. It is the protagonists that must define the problem, the panel members confining themselves to the deeper behavioral issues that might be involved and which are deduced from a theoretical framework.)

So, too, with domestic problems of juvenile delinquency, drugs, street violence, corruptions and others. The "experts" tend to deal with symptoms, because it is these that are immediately and politically important. Treatment of symptoms tends to make situations worse. Members of the scholarly community who act as advisers at any societal level have a special responsibility to ensure that their advice is theoretically based, and that interpretations of data are not based on preconceived beliefs or on ideological perspectives. The fact that politicians in some administrative systems are able to seek out their own advisers is itself a criticism of scholarship.

Delving deeper, an examination of education systems from early years through to post-graduate studies, shows how there has been particular attention given to empirical data, knowledge of "facts," including "historical facts," that are selected and interpreted in the context of sets of traditional and consensus assumptions and beliefs that are usually not examined. Japanese "aggression" in the Second World War is history. What is not so widely known are the circumstances in which Western trading policies during the preceding Great Depression years gave Japan no option but to be "aggressive."

So, too, with domestic problems. It is a fact that there are proportionally more blacks in the US and Maoris in New Zealand in jail than whites. Why? What conclusions are to be drawn? There can be all manner of differences of opinion, reflecting different explanations, prejudices, values, fears and interests, given by different "expert" advisers. Only an adequate theoretical framework, one that has a universal application, and is not one that emerges from consideration of local empirical evidence only, can lead to reliable definitions and policies.

It is for this reason that, having described the problem area, we commence this analysis of conflict, its resolution and provention, with a consideration of theory. It is from theory that conflict resolution processes and provention policies must be deduced. Evidence drawn from past situations, or from present empirical data, must be subjected to the tests of theory. If there is fault to be found with an analysis –

such as the one we are making in this overview – it must be either in the theory on which it is based, or in the logical deductions made.

CONFLICT THEORY AND PRACTICE

So we turn to theory. In the study of conflict, its resolution and provention, in which there are so many subjective perceptions, and ideological and value stances, the main problem area is the finding of an adequate explanation of conflict from which to deduce remedies, and by which to avoid policies that could lead to dysfunctional outcomes immediately or at a later date.

Conflict resolution and provention designed to deal in this way with deep-rooted conflicts does not have its origins in any recent privatization of dispute settlement. Its origins precede the recent expansion of alternatives to judical processes. They are found in theories of behavior that were developed in response to empirical evidence of crucial failures in public policies as we shall see when reviewing the history of thought in this area (Chapter 6). A few decades ago, with greater insights into human behavior, it came to be understood that normative, coercive and containment processes may not be appropriate in certain cases.

Traditional means of settling disputes and conflicts follow from a framework that attaches importance to the preservation of institutions, to the socialization of the individual into certain behaviors, to the role of power in relationships, and to the application of elite norms. Courts, arbitration, bargaining, negotiation and the employment of force are the pragmatic consequences of such a power and institutionally-oriented framework. In the same way, the problem-solving means by which deep-rooted conflicts may be resolved or provented are deduced from an analytical approach to the topic. Conflict resolution and provention processes are not pragmatic responses to situations, but are deduced from a generic theory of conflict. The issue at stake is which or what theoretical framework is valid.

Essentially the conflict resolution process is concerned with two elements, definition and costing. On the basis of an accurate definition and understanding by the parties of a conflict situation (including the human dimension in all its aspects), and on the basis of an accurate costing of the consequences of actions and policies, agreed and lasting outcomes are sought that take into account the social good. The attempt is made in a specific case of conflict resolution to reveal the experienced deprivations, and to discover policy, structural, and institutional options that resolve the problem. The actual procedures and the principles followed are a matter for later attention in Part III, and also in *Conflict: Practices in Management, Settlement and Resolution*.

The study of conflict, and the practices of resolution and provention rely, therefore, on redefinitions of situations, derived from insights into the nature of behaviors, and of why conflicts occur. Teenage prostitution, for example, has become a major social problem in many cities in industrial societies. It has widespread consequences including organized interests, violence and murder. Prostitution is usually a criminal practice, and there are corresponding punishments. From a behavioral perspective the young people involved are the victims of conditions and of the behaviors of others, and it is not they or their clients who are the culprits. Young people come to the city seeking jobs. They can find none for which they are skilled. For some of them prostitution is a means of living. Previous sexual or physical abuse by parents or relations has, for many of them, prepared the way.

This redefinition, by pointing to sources of the problem, opens up the way for dealing with it by means that may be constructive problem solving. "Right" and "wrong" as defined by traditional norms, become limited in their meaning. While there may be a social "wrong" there may not be a situation in which blame can be attributed. In facilitated conflict resolution there is no need for a third party to take sides, regardless of the character of the dispute and the issues at stake. The dispute creates a problem. There is a need for a third party to help solve the problem without attributing blame.

How far can such an analysis be extended? To other teenagers who join competitive gangs and peddle drugs? To terrorists who seek to redress perceived discriminations and injustices that affect their cultural or national groups? To rebels within multi-ethnic communities who resist the rule of the majority? To members of nation-states who feel exploited by greater powers? To great powers who respond to the perceptions the one has of the motivations of the other?

Since the 1960s there has been an increasing scholarly concern with problem-solving, as opposed to problem suppression. From the point of view of public awareness and policy, however, this is a new field of study. The political consensus still favors repression rather than problem-solving on the grounds, not only that crime must be punished, but that there is something inherently wrong with the individual who commits a crime. This will remain the case until alternative explanations are articulated clearly, making possible a shift from fault and punishment to the institutionalization of problem-solving processes. Do we assume that conflicts are due to human aggressiveness, requiring and justifying authoritative political structures and processes of punishment and containment as the means by which to control conflict; or do we assume that there are inherent human needs which, if not satisfied, lead to conflictual behaviors? In the latter case, appropriate processes would be ones that revealed such inherent sources so that there could be introduced the environment that might be required to resolve or to provent conflict.

ABORMALITIES

It could be that the normal human being is not typically aggressive or conflictual even when human needs or desires may have been frustrated, and that those who engage in conflict are, indeed, aggressive and require containment. It could be argued that usually individuals, groups and nations accept social responsibilities and conform with social norms for the sake of the wider society.

This viewpoint accords with conventional wisdom that crime, violence, terrorism, wars and conflict generally are an individual or group fault. Majorities in most countries accept the need for sanctions and interventions of many kinds against other states, and within societies, the need for capital punishment, life imprisonment and detentions as punishments for crimes, and do not attach significance to environmental causal influences.

In his interesting history of crime and punishment, *The Roots of Evil* (1963), Hibbert traces shifting attitudes toward crime and criminals in Britain and the US from the year 602 to 1960. They range from the admonishment of Judge Jeffreys (1685), "Hangman, I charge you to pay particular attention to this lady. Scourge her soundly, man. Scourge her till her blood runs down," to that of Sir Samuel Romilly (1813) "I call upon you to remember that cruel punishments have an inevitable tendency to produce cruelty in the people. . . ." The *Gentleman's Magazine* recorded with approval in 1750 "Executed at Tyburn, July 6, Elizabeth Banks, for stripping a child; Catherine Conway, for forging a seaman's ticket; and Margaret

Harvey for robbing her master. They were all drunk." Even at the most liberal level of Cesare Beccaria (1764), "It is better to prevent crimes than to punish them," it was clear that there was no thought given to the possibility that crime may be the product of circumstances, and that the means of prevention could be provention.

THE ISSUE OF FAULT

In the 1980s punishments were popularly regarded in developed countries such as the US and Britain as being too lenient, especially when their duration was dictated by prison accommodation scarcities. As crimes increase in numbers there are more demands for stiffer sentences. This is especially the case when crime is committed by persons who suffer some mental abnormality. Indeed, a widespread view has been that crime in all its forms is due very largely to those who are mentally deformed or, alternatively, "evil." George Will, a noted Washington columnist, argued in 1989 that "A society that flinches from the fact of evil will flinch from the act of punishment. It should not wonder why it does not feel safe." The "human needs" approach would not have found a sympathetic audience in the past, and usually does not today. It certainly does not win support in respect to international relations problems.

In this analysis we are avoiding the issue of mental abnormalities as a source of conflicts. There can be no doubt that mental problems are frequently a causal factor. Incarcerations and treatments may then be required, and any analysis based on provention would have limited application. We are excluding such cases from our definition of deep-rooted conflict because we are concerned with conflicts between persons, groups and nations where violence is employed rationally and deliberately to achieve some goal. At the same time we are mindful that there are recorded cases of conflicts within and between nations that might not have occurred, or that might have been terminated earlier, if it were not for leadership paranoia.

The attribution of fault to the individual has certainly dominated thinking and policy throughout history. Just as there is an economic construct, "economic man," so there has been a political–social–psychological construct. Economic man suits the requirements of economic theory in a free-enterprise system. The political–social–psychological construct has been no less the product of the system into which it has had to fit.

This construct takes the form of a person who is probably aggressive by nature, or as an acquired consequence of the need to compete for scarce resources, or for some other reason depending on the micro-theory advanced, and who, therefore, needs to be socialized into conforming behaviors. Ernest Becker in his *The Structure of Evil* (1968) reviewed the thinking of most scholars who had expressed themselves on this issue during the previous 200 years. He noted the micro-theory differences, but believed that he discovered a "simple unifying principle." "The whole early training period of the child can be understood in one simple way: it is the period in which he learns to maintain his self-esteem in more-or-less constant fashion by adapting his reactions to the dictates and the possibilities of his human environment."

From an historical–institutional perspective this is an understandable construct for it, like "economic man," assumes and justifies existing institutions. It readily deals with evil, sin and maladjusted personalities, such as the deviant, the addict, the terrorist, the gang member and others, these being those persons who do not willingly submit to the "dictates" of society. Fault in any social setting thus lies with the individual for being evil or unsocialized. An alternative focus on environmental conditions which might provoke aggressive or anti-social behaviors, suggesting the need for change in structures, institutions and policies, would be seen as destabilizing.

The construct of the evil person and its implications, furthermore, justifies the conventional wisdom that authoritative power at all social levels, from the parent to the state, is the foundation of peace domestically and internationally, for only power can control inherently anti-social human behaviors. The legal view expressed in 1964 by Lord Lloyd in his *The Idea of Law* (1964) (quoted in full in Chapter 3) is thus validated: there are those who have a right to expect obedience, and those who have a moral obligation to obey.

There can be no doubt that there is in all human relationships a large degree of adjustment, leading to conformity and, in this sense, socialization. But the traditional view of behavior implies that this socialization process has no limits. This convenient construct presupposes that the person has no needs to be satisfied that are inherent or human. The individual is expected to adjust to all environments, all relationships, all deprivations of self. What is required is the willingness to learn, conform and accept the "dictates" of society and betters. The construct promotes the view that the individual exists to serve society, but that society does not necessarily have obligations to serve in the development of what is human in the individual.

A GENERIC HUMAN COMPONENT AND DEEP-ROOTED CONFLICT

In Chapter 2 we seek to argue the case for a human needs approach to conflict, and by implication, to crime and anti-social behaviors generally. We wish to argue that the traditional orientation that focuses on the primacy of authoritative institutions as the means of control implies an invalid assumption: that social conflict is due to human deformities rather than to structural or institutional deformities, and can be controlled, therefore, by deterrents, constraints and coercion.

In the last decade or so insights from different disciplines and from experience have begun to come together, and we are beginning to see what could be looked back upon in the future as a critical turning point in the history of thought, leading to a turning point in the history of institutions. We are catching the first whispers of a theory of human behavior that argues that the human being, whether or not by nature evil or anti-social or requiring socialization by parents and society, has certain needs that are basic, that are not malleable, that must be satisfied if there is to be individual development leading to conforming behavior.

The human being that is now being discovered is a far more complex and difficult product to accommodate socially than is the traditional and socially-convenient construct. If the human being were simply aggressive by nature but, nevertheless, malleable, social organization would be much easier than it is turning out to be. Coercion could possibly be effective if there were enough of it. Law and order could be enforced.

Human beings, however, appear to have certain inherent drives that are not within their ability to control, and which certainly cannot be suppressed by external socialization, threats and coercion. While this difficult but real human being is responsive to opportunities for development, and in this sense malleable, there is no malleability in acceptance of denial of needs such as recognition, autonomy, dignity and bonding – all of which could be regarded as a precondition of individual development. It follows that systems, no matter how coercive – including, by the way, the isolation of nations and personal incarcerations – that neglect human needs must generate protest behaviors and conflict.

Becker, and those whose thinking he surveyed, asserted that an inherent desire for self-esteem provides the opportunity for parents and societies to socialize the individual into required behaviors. Human needs theory argues, on the contrary, that there are certain ontological and genetic needs that *will* be pursued, and that socialization processes, if not compatible with such human needs, far from socializing, will lead to frustrations, and to disturbed and anti-social personal and group behaviors. Individuals cannot be socialized into behaviors that destroy their identity and other need goals and, therefore, must react against social environments that do this. Parents, teachers, societies, political philosophers or scholars in separate disciplines such as economics and politics, have probably never fully appreciated that there are human needs more compelling in directing behaviors than any possible external influences, and that these are easily frustrated by environments, sometimes seemingly caring family and social environments, that deny opportunities for development.

What these human drives are is still far from clear. They seem to relate to the individual's need for identity and recognition, and these relate to the need for security, and perhaps, ultimately, for development. In 1979 scholars from many countries met in Berlin seeking the basis of an interdisciplinary theory of development. Their papers were printed in 1980 under the title *Needs Theory* (Lederer, 1980). Some of these scholars and others met in 1988, and their papers are those included in *Conflict: Human Needs Theory*. There are many contributions to this book that suggest a major shift in thinking is taking place. Insights at this stage are like early insights at the beginning of atomic science: the long-term policy implications are not yet within our imagination, but their importance for education and policies generally cannot be in doubt.

THE SIGNIFICANCE OF A HUMAN NEEDS APPROACH

Once one denies the traditional assumption about the social malleability of human nature, and asserts the existence of some human needs that will be pursued, regardless of circumstance and consequences, some important insights emerge into the nature of conflict, its resolution and provention. Deterrence theory, the basis of domestic enforcement and international strategic policies, is undermined because deterrence cannot deter in conditions in which human needs are frustrated. Attention is directed to the political power of human behavior, both at the individual level and at the level of identity groups (Coate and Rosati, 1988). If conflicts cannot be settled by coercively controlling people or nations, there is no option but to seek their provention by dealing with their environmental origins.

Let us dwell a little on the significance of the discovery of this recently defined person. This explanation of behaviors on the basis of human needs relates closely to our experience. It seems to provide, for example, an explanation of why a small Catholic minority in Northern Ireland could not be controlled by a large British army, why a majority government in Cyprus led in the 1960s to multi-ethnic clashes and in due course to separate states, why there were ethnic conflict in Sri Lanka, the Soviet Union, and in sixty or so other nations in the 1980s. It helps us to understand why the white population in South Africa could not voluntarily accept one-man-one-vote as demanded by the black majority, and thereby place itself in the same minority position as were Catholics in Northern Ireland and Turks in Cyprus. A human needs approach demonstrates that our idea of unqualified majority government is turning out to be repressive and conflict making when applied to societies that are divided by ethnicity or some other identity need. Within a human needs framework it is understandable why Iran, having been subjected to greater power interventions over many generations, reacted in the late 1980s in ways which, in traditional thinking, could be described only by the use of the term "irrational." Our new explanation of human behaviors explains how Ghadafi of Libya reacted against generations of foreign invasions, which he learned about from his father and grandfather, and why he sought, as his biographies make clear, a real independence, acceptance and identity as an Arab state. If it is true that there are inherent human needs of identity, recognition and autonomy, we must expect leaders and people to react in extreme ways. Behaviors that are a response to frustration of such human needs will often seem aggressive and counterproductive, but they are understandable in this context.

Such a theory of behavior also explains why large industrial cities spawn street gangs comprised of young people who are alienated and unconsciously seeking some role, recognition, valued relationships and opportunities for development. In this framework those who belong to privileged majorities can have at least some appreciation of what it must be like to be a member of a minority group, especially one that receives less health and educational attention than other members of the society. A human needs theory opens up a new world, different interpretations of the past and different predictions of the future, and different policy possibilities.

It is for this reason women and persons who have had the experience of being a member of a minority community have a special role to play in the area of conflict and its *pro*vention. It is not that females are more peace-oriented or less forceful than males, but that they, along with minorities within societies, have been treated as an artificial construct, like "economic man," that has been socially convenient over the years. Because of their social experiences they have a better understanding of human needs theory, and the consequences of the denial of needs fulfillment.

3 Human Needs Theory

In the light of observations in Chapter 2 which stressed the importance of theory, and suggested the relevance to conflict of a theory that hypothesized certain ontological needs as an explanation of behaviors, let us examine human needs theory from an applied perspective.

It is reasonable to assume that human motivations include some that are required for the development of the human species, some that are culturally specific, and some that are of a transitory nature, even merely wishful-thinking desires. We need a common language that at least differentiates those motivations that are socially and politically significant. Three categories appear to be the main ones from a practical policy viewpoint: those that are universal in the human species, those that are cultural, and those that are transitory.

For our purposes we label these as "needs", "values" and interests." They are separate phenomena, and we should endeavour to define them as such. Even in the scholarly literature these terms do not have precise and agreed meanings. We can deduce that there is no general understanding of any differences between negotiable interests and non-negotiable interests – which we have termed "needs."

NEEDS

Needs, as we have used the term, reflect universal motivations. They are an integral part of the human being. Maslow and many others (and we survey the literature in Chapter 6) have argued that in addition to the more obvious biological needs of food and shelter, there are basic human needs that relate to growth and development. There cannot be learning and development by an infant until there is an identity separate from the mother. Then there must be consistency in response if language and behavior are to be learned. Human needs in individuals and identity groups who are engaged in ethnic and identity struggles are of this fundamental character.

From the perspective of conflict studies, the important observation is that these needs will be pursued by all means available. In ontological terms the individual is conditioned by biology, or by a primordial influence, to pursue them. It follows that unless satisfied

36

within the norms of society, they will lead to behavior that is outside the legal norms of the society. The issue whether behavior is determined genetically, environmentally, or both, is not a profitable one for us to engage in at this stage of knowledge. The fact that there are behaviors that cannot be controlled to fit the requirements of particular societies is our concern, rather than the evolutionary explanation of this phenomenon (*Conflict: Human Needs Theory* seeks to deal with these issues in depth).

VALUES

Values are those ideas, habits, customs and beliefs that are a characteristic of particular social communities. They are the linguistic, religious, class, ethnic or other features that lead to separate cultures and identity groups. Values, which are acquired, differ from needs in that the latter are universal and primordial, and perhaps genetic.

In conditions of oppression, discrimination, underprivilege and isolation, the defense of values is important to the needs of personal security and identity. In this sense they impinge on needs and can be confused with them. Preservation of values is a reason for defensive and aggressive behaviors. It is the pursuit of individual needs that is the reason for the formation of identity groups through which the individual operates in the pursuit of a wider ego, and of security and cultural identity. It is values that have divided Lebanon, Northern Ireland and many other multi-ethnic and multi-communal societies.

Over periods of time, after a generation or two of social and economic integration and shared education, values may alter. Given conducive environmental circumstances, persons of different cultures can be assimilated into one culture, which is likely to absorb some features of all. However, even in the best of circumstances this is a long process. It requires a sense of security, which in turn depends on an absence of discrimination, and on opportunities for development.

The more usual situation is one where separate customs, life-styles, dress, religion and language are bases for discrimination, and also a means of defensive identity against the consequences of such discrimination. Wars are fought to preserve cultural values and identity. Leaderships emerge to defend them – and also to use them for political purposes.

Values, however, have a connotation wider than ethnic or national identities. Cultures exist even within such groupings. There are class cultures and social identities associated with the many different groupings to which individuals belong. Values include the preferences and priorities associated with these.

INTERESTS

Interests refer to the occupational, social, political and economic aspirations of the individual, and of identity groups of individuals within a social system. Interests are held in common within groups in a society, but are less likely to be held in common nationally. Typically they are competitive, having a high win–lose component.

Interests are transitory, altering with circumstances. They are not in any way an inherent part of the individual as are needs, and as values might be. They typically relate to material goods or role occupancy. (Role itself may relate to needs when there are identity issues involved.) Interests influence policies and tactics in the pursuit of needs and values.

The assumption has been that this interest motivation – material gain – because it is the driving force of the economy, is the dominant one in social and political life. The term "interests" has, therefore, often been used in a generic sense, to cover all motivations, including needs and values (Pruitt and Rubin, 1986). However, our more restricted meaning of the term gives us an appropriate means of differentiation.

The relationships between interests and needs is an important one in practice. The absence of incentives, some of which can be defined as interests, and of a sense of role, can finally threaten identity and undermine the social cohesion and sense of sharing that are so necessary in a society planned to achieve equalities. There are signs in socialist societies that the need for some market incentives is necessary for initiative. While the pursuit of individual interests must be curbed somewhat in a sharing society, in a society that seeks to solve economic problems through individual initiative and productivity the pursuit of individual interests must not be inhibited. This presents serious problems. The outlook for societies that rest on the pursuit of interests is as dismal as the outlook for societies that restrict them. We have many examples in the developed and the developing world of societies that are in jeopardy just because interest groups are uncontrolled in their promotion of projects that endanger the environment and security, and in their exploitation of others. Such societies are characterized by gross inequalities and high levels of alienation. In both cases, therefore, societies are at risk. The promotion of an expanding stable society based exclusively on the social interest, or solely on personal interests, is difficult and perhaps impossible to achieve. These are polar examples of the problem. Such societies tend, in the one case, to lack drive, and in the other, to suffer from excess internal competitive and conflictual relationships.

Clearly, in the continuum from wholly planned and controlled societies to the other extreme of wholly free societies, there will be degrees of control so that individual interests and societal interests are balanced according to the importance attached to law and order, the environment, economic justice and other societal values. Differences in philosophies or political approaches leading to different social organization rest very much on these different balances decided upon to achieve the common (but not necessarily compatible) goals of increased individual welfare and improved social relationships.

All discussion of these issues, and the public policies implied, depend on clear definitions of interests, values and needs: policy disagreements stem to a large extent from lack of precision in the use of these terms.

THE TRADING OF INTERESTS, VALUES AND NEEDS

A feature of interests is that they are negotiable: it is possible to trade an individual interest for a social gain. Taxation is one means by which this is done. All functional laws, such as the rules of the road, involve this trading. In a free-enterprise system, negotiation is an important part of everyday life. It takes the place of many of the detailed decisions that govern trading and social relationships in a centrally planned society.

When we are considering the ways in which social systems differ – for example communism and capitalism – we are concerned mainly with the degree to which individual interests are curbed or given free expression in the promotion of the social good. As interests are negotiable, there can be many variations in types of system, and many changes in systems from time to time.

By contrast, it follows from the definitions given above, that needs and values are not for trading. Needs, in particular, are inherent drives for survival and development, including identity and recognition. It is not within the free decision making of the individual to trade them. Needs for identity that are frustrated or denied may give rise to behaviors that are inconsistent with the normal behavior, and even with the interests of the individual. This is the core of contemporary domestic and international problems. Ethnic conflicts are being treated in sixty or so countries, where boundaries have been drawn as a result of colonialism or conquest, as though the individual can be coerced to accept majority rule which denies ethnic or cultural identity. Majority rule and power sharing (which is still majority rule) are legitimized by the label "democracy." This is an ideological misinterpretation of the notion of democracy, and such "democracy" is a source of protracted conflicts in many multi-ethnic societies. (Because the concept is so important, especially in multi-ethnic communities, we discuss it further in Chapter 9.)

In the global society, great powers are still operating on the traditional assumption that other nations can be coerced into behaving in certain ways. This is the approach adopted by greater powers to "terrorism," to competing economic and political systems, and to small states which seek to establish alternative political systems. It is predictable that war is frequently the result, despite the relatively weak position of small states. It should come as no surprise that small states can "win" conflicts with greater powers. Great powers have not yet come to terms with their failures to control by military force, because they have as yet little understanding that there are human needs that are not for trading and cannot be suppressed.

The distinction between interests that are negotiable, on the one hand, and values and needs that are not, on the other, is a recent one. It is an insight gained primarily from facilitated conflict resolution processes. These seek to be analytical and to reveal the underlying sources of conflict, rather than merely to negotiate from fixed positions of relative power. They reveal, therefore, these differences in motivations (Burton, 1979 and 1984, and Azar and Burton (eds), 1986). It is a distinction that was not part of traditional thought, and is not welcome in contemporary times to those who are in a majority or powerful position. It is a distinction, however, that must be made if there is to be an understanding of conflicts, and the formulation of policies calculated to avoid or to resolve them.

The emergence of the three distinct concepts – needs, values and interests – reflects a transition in thought and practice from elite interests in the institutions of government, in property and in control, to the human needs of peoples who comprise societies. A continuing confusion between needs and values, on the one hand, and interests, on the other, is part of the transition. It is sustained by an unwillingness (based both on inertia and interests) to make the shifts in political, social and economic institutions that social evolution and the pursuit of needs require.

GOALS, TACTICS AND IDEOLOGIES

Still differentiating on the basis of needs theory the terms that are relevant to conflict and its resolution, we move now to clarify the notions of goals and tactics.

Fierce and sometimes violent opposition can result from different responses to conditions experienced in common even by persons and groups who have shared goals. The reason is that different tactics may be employed in the pursuit of common objectives. A "tactic" implies a choice of a satisfier, and this could be conflict making. Satisfiers may include resources that are in short supply, and this scarcity then becomes a source of conflict. For this reason it is important to separate goals and tactics in any analysis of conflict so that negotiable differences over choice of satisfiers can be separated from the issue of non-negotiable goals which, in any event, are likely to be held in common.

Inevitably there is a blurring of goals and tactics. The long-term goal may be national security; the tactic or satisfier may be the occupation of some strategic role or vantage points, which then becomes a pressing immediate "goal."

Sometimes belief systems govern tactics. When the nature of a problem is not understood, an approach is adopted that may not relate to the essence of the problem. The problem may be an increase in terrorism, and the goal to abolish it, but the tactic dictated by a prejudice or a belief system and not by the nature of the problem, may further suppress a minority and thus promote more terrorism. The problem may be a low level of observance of domestic law and order, and the goal to promote it, but the tactic employed – for example, exiling members of a dissident movement – may create, in the longer term, increased resistances to it.

Ideologies are put forward as statements of values and goals. It may be that they are also tactics. How do we differentiate ideologies, goals and tactics?

We have seen that political objectives are comprised of human *needs*, cultural and related *values*, and *interests*. Human needs are universal and, therefore, held in common. Cultural and other values are shared to a large degree in any society. Interests, however, separate members of societies into groupings, frequently in opposition to each other.

Within this framework the fundamental goals of different ideologies would, by definition, be similar. There might be differences in interests, and perhaps in values, but not in needs.

Indeed, this appears to be so. Communism and capitalism are both advocated in the name of an improved quality of life. The one seeks political structures that could make planned egalitarianism possible, the other promotes institutions that reward initiative and, thereby, promote increased living standards. The one controls information and expression to promote cohesion and support for the ideals of the system, the other values freedom of expression and, to some degree, of information, as a means to the same end.

The reality of shared goals and objectives, despite perceived conflictual relationships, becomes clear when parties to disputes are brought together in a face-to-face analytical dialogue, facilitated by a third party. Invariably they soon discover that they have the same ultimate goals. Greek and Turkish Cypriots discovered that neither wanted "Enosis" or "Double Enosis" (that is union with Greece or Turkey) but wished to identify with the island of Cyprus (Burton, 1984). Representatives of different communities in Lebanon discovered that all wished to identify with Lebanon as an independent Arab state if means could be found to preserve their separate identities (Azar and Burton, eds. 1986). Once it is discovered that goals are held in common, the stage is set for a search for means that satisfy all parties to a dispute.

We could conclude that if needs are universal, then philosophies and ideologies may differ only in interests and, to a limited degree, in values. However, it is not interests alone that in practice separate ideologies. Sometimes ideologies cut across interest groups. There tends to be a high correlation between support for, on the one hand, conservatism, fundamentalism, laissez-faire capitalism, socialism or communism, and, on the other, certain interest groups. There are, however, property owners, religious leaders, workers, industrialists and members of other interest groups who join in the *same* ideological beliefs. This reflects the mix of interests, values and needs that is unique to individuals, and a feature especially in societies in which there have been opportunities for individual development. It is this mix that has to be analyzed and clarified in a facilitated conflict resolution setting.

IDEOLOGIES AND SYSTEMS

System preservation is a defensive response that seems to relate far more to role defense than to interests, values and needs. The conflict between the Soviet Union and the US is not primarily a conflict over ultimate goals, or even over immediate interests. It is a conflict over systems, which are means to goals. Conflict between systems becomes acute in a power political relationship when there is any internal dissent within a system that can be exploited by rivals.

From this perspective ideologies share tactics. Socialism can be sought by revolution, or by progressive steps toward a welfare state. Capitalism can be sought by similar means. There are those on both the "left" and the "right" who favor coercive means of defense against change and toward change. They are never explicit about what it is they finally seek. Both seek to substitute one power elite for another, one system for another.

Ideologies do not allow for self-criticism. They become a value to be defended, part of the identity of the person and groups. They are to a large degree tactical, or immediate responses to longer-term problems, while greatly influenced by role defense and affected by much confusion in thought. Being tactical responses – that is, means to ends – they do not define or deal with the source of problems.

It is this combination of interests and tactics that explains why ideologies, having common ultimate goals, are so conflictual. Ideologies are, therefore, an unnecessary source of conflict. The question "what are the goals" is one on which there can be agreement. "How best to achieve a goal" is a question that causes disputes.

CONFUSION OVER TACTICS AND GOALS

The fact that similar goals are sought by different tactics raises basic questions. Can those needs that are commonly sought, such as security, identity and development interpreted widely, be promoted and preserved by authoritative controls and deterrence, by binding constitutions, and by stronger elite control? Or are threats to consensual values – that is, values held in common within and between societies – the direct result of steps taken to preserve them? Are the problems societies face due to tactics – the tactic of seeking to preserve existing institutions, without their adaptation to altering conditions and to emerging human requirements? Do *tactics* designed to preserve what is, lead to conditions in which the *goals* sought by the tactics may be destroyed?

It will be seen that unless there is clarity in concepts, there cannot be meaningful communication or analysis of the sources of a conflict. So often concepts are not perceived clearly because in practice they seem to merge into one another. But this is not because the concept is unclear. It is because there is a lack of precision in the definition of situations, with tactics and goals often being confused. This, in turn, is due to inadequate theories or an inadequate understanding of behaviors. The initial occupation of the Golan Heights by Israel was a tactic, a means of defense. Continuing to hold those heights came to be seen as a goal in itself. But security is the ultimate goal, and this could be prejudiced in the longer term by confusing it with the tactic.

One of the problems in politics is that this confusion between tactics and goals leads to non-negotiable positions and conflict. In arms control discussions certain proposals are put forward as a tactic in the negotiation. Later any modification of the proposal may be interpreted as a weakness. The proposal is promoted to the status of a goal. Sight of the ultimate goal is lost in the politics of the bargaining process.

IDEOLOGIES – IDEAL TYPES AND THE PRAGMATIC

The relationship between ideologies and human needs is one that deserves more consideration than scholars have so far given it. Ideologies emerge as the justification or rationalization of the decision making response. Fascism was a response in Italy to a set of economic and political conditions during the Great Depression of the 1930s. The response was not a planned one. Rather there emerged a corporate state as dominant interest groups sought to protect themselves in adverse circumstances. Yet it soon was claimed to be, and seen to be, an ideology to be defended in its own right. There are economic theories that lead logically to the corporate state. Other ideologies, such as fundamentalism or a return to the past, and individualism or disregard for the future, are now emerging in both developed and underdeveloped countries as unsolved problems give rise to frustration and desperation. These extreme responses are characterized by high levels of state and individual violence.

Herein is the tragedy of international conflict such as has already been experienced in the twentieth century in two world wars: those who pursue an ideological mission, whether fascism, nazism or some other, do so because circumstances have led them to respond in this way. They legitimize their often aggressive policies by reference to philosophies and ideologies that are nothing more than *post hoc* rationalizations. Ideologies are the product of circumstances, not deliberate planning. Ideologies do not address the sources of problems. They seek to justify pragmatic responses to desperate situations.

It is not surprising, therefore, that the ideology-type responses to conditions that have been made in the past have not provided the alternative civilizations have desperately sought. They have evolved as means to short-term political ends. As ideologies they have no status to justify the importance that they assume in political life. It is different responses to commonly experienced conditions, different tactics, that lead to fierce and sometimes violent opposition. Wars are fought over tactics; fierce conflict over these failed tactics is a threat to all. This is why it is important to separate tactics and goals in any analysis of public policies. But there can be no such analytical separation in the absence of clear meanings of terms and concepts based on some adequate theory of behaviors.

We should not conclude that the complexities of analysis make policy making an impossible task, and that we must, therefore, revert to the unscientific mode of the "art of the possible" with an emphasis on power as the backstop. On the contrary, it is this perspective of complexity, it is this holistic orientation, that makes possible simplicity without reductionism.

Most people are conscious of the need for clarity in terms and concepts, and the need to be as precise as possible in exposition. In the subject area of conflict resolution, however, we experience special problems of language and exposition. This is particularly noticeable when parties are interacting together, and are more concerned with making their points than hearing what the other side has to say. Facilitators have a special need to be aware of the problem of communication, and to ensure that there are not further misunderstandings brought about by lack of clarity in terms and concepts.

COMMUNICATION IN CONFLICT RESOLUTION

This detailed analysis has been made to underline the point that in complex situations such as ideological conflict – and indeed in all conflict situations from the matrimonial to the international – we require a deep analysis that examines core concepts, meaning of terms, underlying motives, shared needs and values and non-shared interests, and the costs of pursuing interests by conflictual means.

When we begin to examine the role of the facilitator it becomes apparent that what is important in any intervention is the degree to which the facilitator can promote in the parties an understanding in depth of the situation in which they are involved. This is an exercise in conceptual thinking as well as in communication.

Traditional power theorists correctly hypothesized inherent human propensities, and conflicts over scarce resources. Where they may have been wrong was in assuming that human behavior was determined mainly or solely by material benefits, and that the source of conflicts was over competition for scarce resources. Human behavior may be equally, and in many circumstances far more, oriented toward deeper concerns of identity and autonomy.

THE COMMON GOOD

Recently, gender issues, independence movements, ethnicity conflicts, employment status problems, and alienation protests, have been drawing our attention to human components that cannot any longer, thanks to conditions of modern communications and means of violent protest, be ignored or submerged by institutional devices. More and more we are being forced to acknowledge that street violence, domestic violence, terrorism and other features of modern societies are symptoms of frustrated human needs of some kind, and must be dealt with at their institutional source. We are becoming aware that this dimension, whether psychological or biological, enters also into great power relations, and regional conflicts such as in the Middle East.

There is also the more positive evidence that given conducive environmental circumstances and opportunities, with resulting valued relationships, human needs may be so satisfied that they may no longer be in evidence, despite the existence even of multi-ethnic conditions, as when economically successful members of ethnic minorities seem to live contentedly in their host society. Valued relations are themselves a human need, or at least a satisfier of recognition and identity needs. The causes or sources of conflict between individuals and groups cannot be separated from the totality of relationships, and the environmental conditions that promote relationships. Valued relationships are probably the main constraints on so-called anti-social behaviors, and institutional and social circumstances can deprive many people of them.

A focus on a human dimension, with its socially negative aspects that advise against containment, and its socially positive aspects that point to conforming behaviors through valued relationships, raises in sharp relief a core issue that has plagued classical philosophers – that is, the tension between the individual interest and the common good. Conflict resolution and provention theory throws light on this problem, for it draws attention to norms of behavior that take into account future costs and consequences of behaviors in ways not possible within settlement processes. A conflict is not resolved merely by reaching agreement between those who appear to be the parties to the dispute. There is a wider social dimension to be taken into account: the establishment of an environment that promotes and institutionalizes valued relationships. For example, agreement between some communities within a state, or between unions and management, could lead to adverse consequences for the public at large in the longer term. This important issue is discussed in Chapter 10 where we discuss the relationship between the individual and society.

DECISION MAKING

In addition to inherent drives there is another human component that has been neglected. Human beings are, of course, the product of evolution. Elements of aggression and greed, necessary to competitive survival, are undoubtedly associated with the pursuit of individual development. Human beings, however, possess the ability to make choices, to anticipate events, to cost consequences of actions, and deliberately to alter environments and social structures. Studies of problem-solving, of which conflict resolution and provention is one type, suggest that this conscious component of human behavior, which makes possible creative responses to new information and situations, may be far more significant, at least potentially, than those components of behavior that spring directly from primitive stimulus–response reactions to circumstances. We need to remind ourselves constantly of this human ability to make choices, and to control environments and relationships in order to achieve planned goals. Our problem is to find the processes and the institutionalized structures that exploit and promote such abilities. What becomes clear from an examination of trends in decision making and in the handling of conflict, which is the concern of Part III, is that there is an awareness of failure of power-oriented processes. The goal of the study of conflict resolution and its provention is to ride the wave created by that awareness.

4 The Environment of Conflict

THE DETERMINANTS OF CONFLICT

A human needs framework leads us to conclude that the incidence of conflict is the consequence of altering balances between (1) total despair and apathy due to defeat in the struggle to survive; (2), sufficient resources with which to survive plus an acceptable satisfaction of human needs; and (3), adequate material conditions by which to defeat apathy, but the denial, nevertheless of certain non-material satisfactions. (1) and (2) are conditions in which conflict is not necessarily rife: there is either apathy, or, at the other extreme tolerable satisfaction of material and non-material needs. Condition (3) provides the environment of conflict: the existence of opportunities to pursue human needs that are being denied.

Any increases in living standards that might result from scientific innovation and aid programs could take some people out of (1), the despair category, and place them in (3), the protest category. Any reduction in satisfiers of needs, any reduced standard of living, would necessarily take people out of (2), the satisfied category and throw them also into (3), the protest condition. The future incidence of conflict depends, therefore, on resource and opportunity availabilities and their distribution.

These are not marginal considerations. It requires only slight decreases or increases in living standards and quality of life to have extensive effects. We cannot anticipate increases in living standards sufficient to provide any reserve of physical satisfiers. There is no possibility that the majority of peoples in the global society will ever attain material standards of living that would be regarded by peoples in Western developed states as even tolerable. Projected population increases, along with energy and resource consumption increases, are sufficient to lead to this conclusion, together with the political impossibility of introducing a sharing and equitable global economy. Mere survival is and will remain the important material goal for most people. For many in developed societies, and for the majority of peoples in the undeveloped world, the important struggle is and will continue to be to maintain, regain or acquire certain non-material

49

satisfactions in addition to minimum physical well-being. Increases in quality of life are even more elusive. These include the opportunity to live in a sharing society, the enjoyment of close bonded relationships, and a sense of personal identity, dignity and security.

THE ESCALATION OF CONFLICT AND VIOLENCE

There has always been conflict at all societal levels, evidenced in murders, communal conflicts, revolts against oppression, religious wars and territorial expansion. Despite high costs they have been accepted as an inevitable part of the pattern of human interactions, along with zones and periods of peace in which many individuals and societies have prospered. Traditional controls and containment policies, including incarcerations, death penalties and foreign interventions have been regarded as reasonably successful means of settling conflicts, in the context of their assumed inevitability.

Now, however, there appears to be emerging, almost universally, a progressive escalation and institutionalization of conflict. This is at all social levels – in the streets, in communal relations, in multi-ethnic relations, as well as internationally. This increase in conflict has occurred alongside the introduction of progressively more sophisticated policies of deterrence that seem to be forcing a reconsideration of policies in great power relationships, for *pro*vention at that level is now a precondition of survival.

Some conflict is without violence, but increased violence is a feature of this apparent escalation. Young people now regard violence as a normal part of their cultures. It has become a major feature of entertainment. Reports of family and local violence and murders, terrorism, ethnic conflict and civil wars fill our newspapers, and are a constant feature of television.

If there could be some assurance that this is a passing phase in social evolution, or that levels of conflict and violence will not escalate further, societies might be able to live with it by improving existing means of containment so as to reduce conflict and violence to acceptable levels.

Indeed, such a view seems on the surface to be a public, and frequently an official, position. Nationally and globally a growing incidence of conflict, and the increasing levels of violence associated with it, are being accepted with concern, but with resignation, as a normal extension of past patterns of conflict, to be expected as societies become more ethnically and ideologically mixed, and more complex. To deal with it the same means of deterrence and containment are being employed.

In support of this view it could be argued that the total amount of conflict has not changed greatly, and that what we are experiencing is greater awareness of it. Certainly there is a vastly increased awareness due to television. In addition, it could be argued that we are witnessing change only in forms of conflict and violence because of changed conditions. The availability of modern weapons increases the casualties, and makes possible new opportunities for resistance and violence.

While these are relevant considerations, there are compelling analytical reasons to assume a continuing escalation in the incidence of conflict, and the levels of violence associated with it. There are reasons to believe that given present social and political trends, and given traditional means of control, there will, in fact, be at all social levels an escalation of conflict at a cumulative rate.

There are several reasons for this prediction.

First, greater numbers of members of the third world within the world society, and of the underprivileged world within developed economies, now have at least some opportunities to pursue needs of identity and to demand recognition, thanks to a measure of development, and thanks also to their possession of means of violence and their access to communications. While the inherent drives involved in human needs satisfaction do not and cannot emerge in conditions in which there is total despair and apathy, as in conditions of physical and authoritative suppression, or where there are conditions of drought or other circumstances of bare survival, some degree of freedom provides opportunities for development. Development needs once liberated are not readily controlled. The greater the liberation and opportunities for development, the more likely are struggles for further fulfillment. In the absence of increased developmental opportunities provided by society, the drug market and the gun game, for example, provide means by which to achieve needed stimulus and identity, and to find a kind of (distorted) personal dignity. So, also, at the community level in the case of ethnicity struggles and movements of nationalism.

Second, the realities of the thermonuclear age, together with the costs of modern weapons and defense system, have imposed pressures on the great powers to look beyond deterrence strategies, and to seek means by which collaboration can meet their mutual insecurities. This can lead to improved relations between them. It does, in turn, however, lead to conditions that encourage dissident behaviors and demands for reforms within great powers. Just as perceived external threat brings internal cohesion and makes possible high levels of defense expenditures, so does a decrease in perceived threat encourage internal unrest. Changed Soviet policies at the end of the 1980s had the unexpected consequence of promoting domestic conflicts within the great powers. Even more serious conflict must continue to erupt within non-legitimized nations that have depended on the great powers for their continued legal status. Gurr and Scarritt (1989) estimated (on the basis of their criteria) that 99 countries had 261 minorities "at risk" – that is, in danger of having human rights threatened, and, therefore, likely to be involved in conflict. Over forty countries had more than 25 per cent of their populations at risk in the late 1980s. Add to these those nations that are under military or dictatorial control – many of which have in the past been supported by a great power – and the future is bleak.

Third, the assumption that deviant behaviors reflect struggles that are primarily over scarce resources has diverted attention for many decades or centuries away from the human sources of conflict. Conflicts have been at best contained and managed, increasing in numbers continuously. The coercive means that have traditionally been employed to contain conflict have added to the environment of conflict.

Fourth, there are environmental, quality of life and entropy reasons to expect greatly reduced opportunities for satisfying human needs, even the most basic of physical needs. (These are two important topics for they affect the availability of satisfiers of human needs and, therefore, affect the environment of conflict. They are, however, peripheral to our main concerns. References to important studies on these topics are included as an Appendix to Chapter 4.)

EXPONENTIAL CHANGE

Societies seem not to appreciate, even after problems are out of control, the dynamic way in which the environment of conflict gets out of control. There is a phenomenon of exponential change, of which we are not sufficiently aware. Much change is of this character, but decision makers have been slow to recognize until too late the significance of such change, and the need to avoid it by adjusting to change quickly and effectively.

With exponential change at first there are imperceptible movements, as for example in population growth, environmental change, or in the introduction of some new disease. Increases in social violence are also of this nature. No special attention is given to them. Then there appears to be an increase in the rate of change which attracts attention, but only when it is too late to make adjustments. A typical exponential change curve moves along in an almost horizontal line for a long period of time before showing any marked upward shift in direction, and then once there is a significant increase in the rate of change there is a sudden acceleration until the

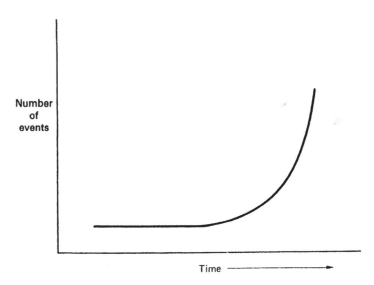

Figure 4.1 An exponential change curve

curve moves sharply into a nearly vertical direction (see Figure 4.1).

Estimates of population increase provide a typical example. General population increase in the world was fairly stable until about the time of the industrial revolution. In the mid-nineteenth century world population was about 1 billion. By the mid-twentieth century it was about 2 billion. It has doubled again in the last fifty years. Another example is energy consumption. In billion metric tons of coal or its equivalent it was about 1 at the beginning of the twentieth century, having increased only slightly over the previous century. It was about five times as much fifty years later. At present growth rates it will be 50 billion at the end of the twentieth century. Such exponential rates of increase are causally related to other exponential rates of increase – as, for example, competition over resource acquisition and environmental pollution. These, in turn, have wider consequences.

The time-span of perceptible change in any phenomenon thus becomes progressively shorter when there is such an exponential rate of change. What is hardly perceptible, what is acceptable at first, suddenly becomes dramatic and unacceptable. We are dealing in this Conflict Series with phenomena of the last hundred years, and especially of the last few decades of this century. Ethnic conflict is one example, and city violence is another. These have increased in numbers dramatically in the last two decades. They have occurred in environmental conditions that affect them symbiotically, such as rates of exploitation of resources, technological innovations such as occur in communications and which lead to shared expectations, medical advances that increase life-spans and, therefore, populations. Less conspicuously, there are other phenomena that are a by-product of such changes and, therefore, have the same exponential quality, such as numbers of socially alienated persons, and loss of personal and group identity and autonomy. These, in turn, further accentuate conflict. There thus develops an environment that promotes conflict.

Dealing with problems only as they emerge by conflict management and resolution techniques is not an answer to the kind of exponential futures societies now face. Dealing with their specific symptoms – and conflict and violence are some of the symptoms of social problems – is not an answer to their solution. There must be prediction and provention, with which we deal in Part IV.

SYSTEM CHANGE AS A REQUIREMENT OF CONFLICT RESOLUTION AND PROVENTION

For most people these issues seem of little practical interest. What have they to do with matrimonial, industrial, social, community, ethnic and international conflict? Why should any person living satisfactorily within a society move from the prevailing way of life? It is a little like smoking: if there are consequences, they are in the future.

What is raised here, however, is an important issue in conflict resolution and provention. It marks the difference between within system conflict *management* for some immediate gains, and conflict resolution and provention that looks to the future, and is likely to require system change. Whether it be family relationships or work relationships, there are structural sources of conflict, there are failures to satisfy non-material needs, that have to be tackled if conflict is to be resolved and provented, and not just settled or managed.

An obvious example lies in labor relations. Strikes occur typically over wage demands. Usually, especially in relatively high wage countries, wage demands are a disguise for other grievances relating to working conditions in which personal identity is lost. These are hard to articulate and quantify, so wage demands and strikes are a useful means of showing frustration. There is a system problem.

By dealing with any situation in a superficial way, in dealing with any particular situation merely to contain it, whether it be political corruption, deviance, terrorism or any other public policy problem, we are inviting future conflict of a much higher order. The remedy to the immediate situation must be of a kind to provent longer-term problems.

DEPENDENCY RELATIONSHIPS

Accompanying the phenomenon of exponential change, and its contribution to the creation of an environment of conflict, there is the phenomenon of resistance to change with which we will deal in Chapter 5. This relates usually to those changes that are to some degree under human control, in particular the control of authoritative decision makers in all societies. Frequently, the two are obviously related causally. Resistance to change is one reason why problems that could be solved at an early stage are allowed to reach exponential levels.

For example, despite dramatic changes in technological developments over the last two centuries, advanced civilizations have moved only superficially from feudal forms of social organization in which there were those who were in a position to exploit, and those who were exploited. The private enterprise or free-market mechanism now provides a reliable source of labor at costs less than meet minimum living standards. It thus makes slavery and serfdom obsolete, while not changing structurally many authoritative and dependency relationships, and associated perceived injustices. Indeed, it is arguable that in more traditional feudal conditions there was a dependency relationship that was mutual, and that, therefore, the powerful had an interest in the relationship, and in the welfare of the less powerful and less privileged. In modern industrial and social conditions such dependency relationships are negligible, leaving many without even this limited sense of identity and recognition, and with little sense of future security.

Furthermore, a feature of modern developed industrial systems is an increasing inequality of incomes and opportunities that is creating separate nations within states, even separate communities within cities, and increased levels of alienation. In the development from primary (agriculture), to secondary (industry), to tertiary (service) industries, at each stage the newer industries provided high returns and opportunities. A fourth stage would be required if there were to be social stability by the evening out of income and opportunity. Production structures and demand would then focus on those goods and services that would be appropriate to the stage of economic development, and not be diverted into "luxury" goods – that is, goods not relevant to that stage of development. This fourth stage has been elusive. Despite the fact that the remedy for unemployment and inflation is such income redistribution, it has not happened. Nor will it happen until societies perceive social and political costs of deprivation as greater than losses that might follow structural and economic change.

The institutions that have evolved over time have catered to the institutional needs of the system, whatever it might be, and the interests of power elites. Economics as a study and as a basis of public policy is concerned with system indicators, such as rates of interest, levels of inflation, and levels of employment. There is not within the study of economics any special concern about welfare deprivations, ethnic and gender discriminations, and other conditions that deny human needs. It no longer has (if it ever did have) a quality of life orientation. As a consequence effective social control eludes the capabilities of authorities, whose main traditional preoccupations have been institutional and system preservation. So much is this the case that authorities in many countries are now denying responsibility for the provision of human needs, leaving it to the "market" to perform this function. Already there is evidence that this is leading to increased social problems, including declines in educational standards, that will have wider consequences in the longer term.

The increase in levels of conflict, and the failure of judicial processes to cope with it, have led to privatization even in the field of dispute resolution. Courts increasingly *require* the use of private alternatives to lessen the burden on them as disputes between persons, and between individuals and society, increase in number. "Mediation" and "arbitration" techniques are among the private processes officially recognized. These conflict settlement processes supplement judicial processes. They may have a role in respect to particular disputes, but like the past coercive techniques of authorities, they are not designed to tackle the sources of conflict.

Contracting out by authorities has resulted in the powerful becoming richer and the poor poorer. This has further accentuated the environment of conflict, especially in conditions in which the poor are ethnic minorities whose educational and job opportunities do not provide means of achievement. The political control–deregulation issue that emerged in major developed states in the 1980s seems to have been addressed to the question as to whether or not there should be state intervention into the lives and systems under their jurisdiction. The question that needed to be answered was not whether there should be interventions, but the type and quality of that intervention. This is a subject to which we return in Chapter 11.

Appendix: Quality of Life and Entropy

It was observed in Chapter 4 that amongst other influences creating an environment of conflict were environmental influences affecting quality of life, of which entropy is one.

The concepts "quality of life" and "entropy" are known, but their significance is only beginning to be appreciated. They are interesting topics in their own right in addition to being relevant considerations of the environment of conflict. The following draws attention to some important and relevant studies.

DEFINING QUALITY OF LIFE

We have agreed measures to some aspects of the physical quality of life, mainly Gross National Product (GNP). GNP is estimated, according to Beckerman (1987) by adding up "the total of all goods and services that enter into "final demand." It is not "a *good* indicator of economic welfare, let alone of welfare in some wider sense." It is a measure of "the extent to which the economy is expanding or failing to do so."

In recent years – one might say at long last – there has developed an interest in the quality of life. Instead of GNP we read of QOL (Quality of Life) in an increasing number of publications. In 1973 the US Environmental Protection Agency promoted a conference study published under the title *The Quality of Life: A Potential New Tool for Decision-Makers*. At that time QOL was becoming, in the view of the participants, a subject of growing concern, but they could find no consensus on a definition. Housing, education, working conditions and many variables were taken into account, usually from the perspective of a particular discipline. Three years later "The Commission on Critical Choices for Americans" was brought together by Nelson A. Rockefeller, subsequently Vice-President of the US. Its forty-two members covered similar ground and experienced similar problems. The United Nations University (Tokyo) made a report on *Social Indicators for Human Development* (Miles, 1985). The report was commissioned in the belief that if indicators were established, there would be more attention directed to improving those conditions necessary for such human development. Other scholars have tried to clarify the concept and to find measures of QOL. (Rajaratnam, 1983; Andrews, 1986). It is significant, however, that we do not yet have consensus measures, nor is the concept of QOL widely entertained. It would seem that in the absence of some operational definition the concept now attracts less attention.

These studies did not include indices of some of the main variables relevant to QOL, especially the increased demands made on persons as a result of technological and social change: the need to have private transport, to master a computer, to shop at some place that requires private transport, to provide for child care when under social pressures both parents choose or are required to work out of the home, to obtain a technical or professional training, and the greater output in time and energy required to attain these goals and expected living standards and status. Nor did they include the increasing environment of conflict and conflict itself, arguably one of the most important variables of all, associated with these increased pressures and expectations, though the Miles study included the observation that harmonious relationships are required for the "fullest flowering of human potential."

This absence of conflict in considering QOL indices implies the acceptance of conflict as a condition about which little or nothing can be done. We would argue from a conflict resolution perspective that conflict is the product of the absence of just those circumstances QOL studies seek to reveal. A reason why no operational definitions could be found, why there has been no consensus on the contents of the concept, is that there was no theoretical framework in which to define it. A starting point could be a concentration on conditions that lead to conflict – above all, frustration of human needs. Probably no official or semi-official conference could be expected to face up to the implications of an approach which would lead to conclusions about the need for structural change.

THE PROBLEM OF ENTROPY

We have drawn attention to QOL in the context of a prediction of an exponential rate of increase in the incidence of conflict, and in associated levels of violence at all social levels. Environmental pollution, of which we are now becoming far more aware, along with the no less exponential rate of resource transformation into non-usable forms of energy, must be regarded as contributing to an environment of conflict when they lead to unacceptable pressures of living, over which the protagonists have no immediate control. Material resources and conditions are *satisfiers* of non-material human needs. Decreases in satisfiers lead to unfulfilled expectations which seem to promote conditions of conflict even more than stable conditions of deprivation (Davies, 1971).

Greater and greater effort is required even to maintain existing living standards, and this can detract from abilities to satisfy non-material human needs. One major reason why it takes greater effort to maintain existing standards is because of entropy. Entropy is largely the consequence of some economic assumptions and policies that have been followed since the inception of the industrial revolution.

In the longer term the main determinant of physical quality of life is the quality of the environment, including the availability of resources. Rifkin, in his book *Entropy*, challenges some of the fundamental purposes of economic activity – that is, the greater exploitation of resources – by pointing out their implication for energy use and, at the same time, by demonstrating the neglect by economists of non-material considerations of human development. In short he is saying that the concept of "economic man" is seriously misleading, giving rise to institutions and behaviors that are self-defeating both of physical and psychological satisfactions. Entropy is, in Rifkin's words "a measure of the amount of energy no longer capable of conversion into work." He points out that while matter and energy in the universe are constant, they can be transformed ultimately only from that which is usable to that which is unusable. Rifkin goes on to argue that the Entropy Law is not just something to be taken into account as a phenomenon in physics. It has implication for all activities and relationships in societies, especially developed societies.

Rifkin points out that while the Entropy Law deals with the physical world, there exist also non-material resources, which Rifkin terms the "spiritual world." These non-material resources do not diminish with consumption – on the contrary. We have no generic term with which to describe drives toward human development such as personal identity, recognition, values attached to social relationships and other non-material values and needs. They relate to the individual and to social relationships.

Perhaps "autonomy" is the term we need, interpreted as the full satisfaction by the individual of individual human needs (Haworth, 1986). It is this that Rifkin seems to mean by "spiritual." Traditionally we have thought in terms, on the one hand, of the state, its institutions and resources available and, on the other, of the spiritual, those areas associated with non-material resources. We do not have a term that relates to the aspirations of persons separately from systems because traditionally persons as individuals were not especially important in the scheme of things. The state and society were important, and the Church and its support for the state and society were important, but the individual had no separate status and was required to conform to the prevailing official and religious norms.

Rifkin argues that the traditional focus of economists and politicians on material welfare is at great energy cost, increasingly at an exponential rate, while the reality is that it is not this material welfare that is the beginning and end of human desires and human welfare. There are, in short, system-driven policies and trends that lead us as persons and nations to struggle for more and more material acquisition, destroying scarce resources at an alarming rate, whereas what we are really seeking is more of non-material resources, including role recognition and conflict-free valued relationships. These do not require expenditures of resource-based energy and, unlike physical resources, mostly increase with consumption.

It is these non-material needs that are discovered to be fundamental when parties to a conflict are brought into an analytical framework: their fight is not over material resources that are in short supply, but over identity and related issues that do not involve scarce energy resources. Material resources, however, may provide the means by which to pursue security, or some other goal, in circumstances in which it is denied or threatened.

In fact, the concept of economic development has altered gradually, especially in the thinking of Third World scholars, to reflect a realization that welfare is not confined to economic, that is, material goods. It will be seen, therefore, that Rifkin from his concern with the future of the environment and of resource exploitation, and we from the perspective of conflict resolution, meet at this point at which we observe that it is the pursuit of non-material human needs that is the ultimate human goal, and the denial of which is the source of deep-rooted conflict.

A CRITICISM OF ECONOMICS

In Rifkin's view, traditional thought has held that the nation that consumes most material resources, the nation that turns most resources into unusable energy, "is the wealthiest." In his view neither capitalist nor socialist systems can deal with the entropy problem inherent in such an approach to economics. Neither can cope with the interests of future generations if this is their conception of economic development.

Rifkin targets the US in particular, pointing out that its consumption of energy is far higher than other industrial countries with similar material living standards. He sees energy consumption in the US as an addiction. "The United States consumes more energy per year than all the countries of Western Europe combined, even though their populations exceed ours by 75%."

Statistics of world expenditures (Sivard, 1988) are beginning to show that developed countries, facing these escalating energy costs while still trying to maintain a high-energy consumption way of life, are politically unwilling to make the energy economies that are necessary to provide education, health and such social facilities. As a proportion of national income, these are more freely provided in less developed countries. Infant mortality, malnutrition and other significant statistics suggest that there are some major distortions emerging especially in the developed countries of the world.

PUBLIC POLICY IMPLICATIONS

Rifkin attacks economic theory and the Lockian view that unexploited resources are "waste." He regards GNP not as a measure of production, but as a measure of consumption cost, or destruction of resources.

What, then, are the public policy implications of this focus on entropy, and how does it relate to system sources of conflict, and means of dealing with conflict? Rifkin draws five conclusions:

1. It is clear that underdevelopment in presently underdeveloped countries can never be overcome. They will never have the opportunity to consume energy as the US has done. The conflict problems associated with underdevelopment cannot in the future be tackled by development.

2. Underdevelopment within so-called developed nations is also unlikely to be tackled. There can be no significant "trickle down effect" from investment resulting from income inequalities.
3. Institutional change will ultimately be forced on societies by social unrest, and this is likely to be resisted, resulting in violence.
4. Societies will become less and less rewarding, despite material gains for some, leading to alienation and its associated problems.
5. Society will become more and more conflictual internally and externally.

THE ECONOMIC PERSPECTIVE

This leads us to consider system problems, a subject that has not been explored in political science, and for the most part avoided in economics. Western economic theory is free enterprise market theory. It is about how to make the best use of scarce resources. By "best use" in a private enterprise economy is meant the quickest and the greatest exploitation of resources, the highest rate of acquisition and consumption of resources. The market economy is not concerned with how to make the best use of resources for defined human goals. On the other hand, individuals as individuals are not seeking to destroy available energy and resources. They are caught up in a system that requires this of them.

Economists have avoided this issue. Economics is not concerned with issues of justice, social and political stability, conflict avoidance or other public policy issues. It is narrowly concerned with material resource exploitation. It lends itself, therefore, to the view that the less government intervention the better, the free market or "invisible hand" being the best regulator. Pollution and waste are a necessary by-product of productivity, and in a competitive world market the costs of pollution prevention cannot be carried by industry.

Rifkin is a fitting introduction to a consideration of the economic dimensions of conflict and conflict resolution, and to a study of the discipline of economics. When we look at economics we find confirmation of Rifkin's fears, and his criticisms of economics as a subject that deals with economic man, with little or no thought given to non-material human needs, such as those on which conflict and its resolution focus.

Heilbroner and Thurow have endeavored to set out the main concepts and principles of economics (1975). For them economics "is the study of how mankind copes with the problem of provisioning itself." There are two main tasks:

1. to organize a system to assure the production of enough goods and services for its own survival, and
2. to arrange the distribution of fruits of its production so that more production can take place.

In their analysis the first is the traditional approach found in primitive and agrarian communities. This focus on survival would account for the Rifkin low percentage of time spent on production. Immediate needs having been satisfied, it is time to engage in social behaviors. The second is the approach of modern societies. "Tradition solves economic problems, but it does so at the cost of economic progress." "Economic progress" is not defined: presumably it is what is measured by GNP or, in Rifkin's terms, the amount of energy made unusable.

The foundations of economics were laid in the early eighteenth century, when Adam Smith explained to the newly emerging industrial elite how the economy worked. These were times in which there was little concern over the environment or the scarcity of resources. The thinking of most economists has changed little since. In their view the free market mechanism is still the appropriate system, and economic man provides a model of behavior on which quantitative predictions can be made. The behaviors of the real person who is responsible for events and conditions in the real world is not measurable, and for this reason is rejected by the "science" of economics.

AN ADEQUATE THEORETICAL FRAMEWORK

The problem economists have had – and also, to a lesser extent, those concerned with QOL – is that they have no adequate behavioral theoretical framework that would guide them to indices that are significant. The "economic man" hypothesis misdirects research away from the main operational indices that reflect human requirements and preferences. It has led over the years to conflict making policies, institutions, structures and attitudes.

The assumptions of strategic studies and economics, both working on the basis of their own constructs or actors, have directed consensus thinking into channels that do not relate to human behavior or ultimately to political realities. Part of the function of analytical conflict resolution processes is to question conventional wisdom, and to bring to the surface the human motivations that underlie social, political and economic relations, and lead to conflict.

5 The Influence of Tradition

PROBLEMS OF CHANGE

The traditional law-and-order system is under pressure in most societies and, indeed, in many segments of many societies it has been replaced by local mafia-type organizations. Violence is the arbiter in many conflict situations. Modern societies, under pressure for democratization and individual freedoms, could be regarded historically as in a transition stage. The tight controls of past authoritarian systems have given place to societies based on individual initiatives, but as yet there have not evolved effective social controls that are consistent with the demanded freedoms. From time to time, as and when conflict and violence escalate, there is a return to tradition and to repressive means of control, sometimes military regimes.

At the international level violence has always been the arbiter when matters of important "national interest" have been at stake. There were attempts after the First and Second World War to introduce central organizations seeking to model the international system on the domestic. Now that domestic model seems to have broken down.

What is required, what must evolve in time through necessity, is a system that combines historically emerging and sought-for personal freedoms, and whatever controls consistent with such freedoms are necessary for social organization. This seemingly impossible conjunction of freedom and control is, in fact, the foundation of conflict theory based on a theory of human needs, which we outlined in Chapter 2. The theory points to needs of recognition and acceptance, implying also elements of control inherent in the pursuit of values attached to relationships. It remains to discover the institutional means of satisfying these needs.

Our focus in Chapter 5 is on one aspect of that problem: the persistent intellectual and interest resistances to the kind of social and economic changes required for institutions to develop in ways that would help societies to avoid situations of conflict.

POLITICAL THOUGHT AND LAW

It will help to show the influence of tradition, and to set the stage for our discussion of problem-solving conflict resolution, if we note the legal conception of law and order, and its approach to conflict and its management. The following is how Lord Lloyd (1964) has set down traditional thinking with respect to relationships with authorities:

> What is entailed in the notion of authority is that some person is entitled to require the obedience of others regardless of whether those other persons are prepared to find the particular order or rule enjoined upon them as acceptable or desirable or not . . . there is something which we may call a peculiar aura or mystique investing the lord, the policeman, or the judge which arouses a certain response on the part of the other party, namely that he feels that the superior party (for so we may call him for this purpose) can legitimately give orders which he, the inferior party, feels in some sense obliged, willingly or unwillingly, to obey. This feeling of legitimate subordination is clearly one of great significance in law and calls for further explanation.
>
> Why should one person in some curious way feel himself bound to acknowledge the authority of another person and so constrained to obey the orders of that person? Or, to put it another way, what is the source of the obligation which is apparently imposed or assumed to be imposed on the subject party (the obligee)?
>
> One preliminary answer that may be suggested is that fundamentally the obligation is a moral one, in the sense that what the obligee really feels is that he is under a moral duty to obey the behest of the lord, the policeman, or the judge, as the case may be.

Traditional thinking not only postulates the right of authority to expect obedience, but also the right, and indeed the duty on the party of authority, to ensure obedience, if necessary by deterrence and coercion. Lloyd again:

> What then does experience show? Surely that at all levels of society human law has depended for its efficacy on the degree to which it is backed by organized coercion. Psycho-analysis has taught us of the unconscious factors in man's psychological make-up. Among these unconscious factors are to be reckoned, not only forces which

make for social cooperation and which exemplify Aristotle's famous dictum that man is a political animal, but also powerful drives which require to be effectively reformed in order to subject man to the needs of social discipline.

This being traditional thinking, it is understandable that the main focus of attention in explaining conflict in societies has been on human defects. Structures and institutions have been treated as givens. Persons have been required to adapt to them. If there are social problems, their source must be in the behaviors of individuals.

A FALSE DICHOTOMY

This separation of those who have a right to expect obedience and those who have a moral obligation to obey has, over time, created a false dichotomy that divides nations and peoples everywhere, to the extent that in contemporary circumstances, in which it is clear that there are problems that must be solved jointly in the interests of all, there is little cooperation between the two.

Even under an elitist system there are insuperable problems of administration. There is a "moral" sanction against any person or nation that breaks the existing rules and confronts legal norms. However, those who have the right to expect obedience are also those who have established the morality and norms to be observed. For this reason the legitimacy of rules are, in the perception of those required to observe them, always open to question. There are conventions and legal norms governing authority relations, gender relations, industrial relations, property acquisition, market mechanisms, and professional roles affecting the daily lives of all citizens. It is necessary to examine in each case the purpose for which they were designed, and in whose interests – special interests or the universal common good. Nasser of Egypt broke international rules at the close of the 1950s when he took away from foreign governments and interests their control of the Suez canal that ran through his country. Iraq broke the rules in the 1980s when it employed chemical warfare that greater powers had tried to outlaw seventy years earlier. Yet Iraq would have been within the law had it used nuclear weapons. Was Iraq employing a poor nation's tool to achieve a purpose? Was Nasser pursuing a legitimate national interest, even though defying existing legal norms? Is robbery a crime when it is the only way to survive? If rules or norms lead to frustrations, alienations, discriminations, and conflicts within society, the remedies must be in changes either to the rules or the conditions that lead to their infringement, not sanctions against reactive behaviors.

Understandably there has been a continuing tension between such traditional thinkers and leaders and those who have consciously sought and supported system change (see a two-volume collection of essays edited by Zawodny, *Man and International Relations*, 1966). It is this tension that has characterized political thought throughout the ages.

AUTHORITY AND REPRESSION

An authoritative, a divine right kind of approach, as depicted by Lloyd, implies a right, not merely to rule, but to rule if necessary by coercive measures. The intentions may be to promote a common good. This is the intention claimed by many modern-day dictatorships, military and others supported by military means. The tremendous changes sought in the late 1980s by citizens generally shocked conservatives in communist countries who saw in them reversions to pre-communist exploiting regimes. They had an arguable case in terms of goals and the promotion of a sharing society, but not in terms of processes.

Means of handling conflict have been, and are still, mainly repressive rather than investigatory or problem-solving. They are part of a long-standing tradition, for they had their early origins in past authoritative systems. Whatever explanatory theory of conflict in and between societies is offered, whatever alternative processes are suggested, they must stand the test of political realism. By this is meant that either they must relate to this long-standing tradition of repression or coercion as the means of control, or offer an alternative that makes sense to members of societies who live within this tradition.

From this perspective it is clear that change in means of handling conflict is an unlikely possibility in the absence of a widespread realization, not only that existing controls are failing, but also that the costs of an alternative, which might seem to threaten interests and institutions, will be significantly less than the costs of social disruption in the future. We return to this cost assessment in Chapter 16 and in the concluding Part V where we observe that nothing will suffice short of a clearly articulated theory of behavior and social organization, and a detailed exposition of decision making processes that can be seen to evolve from present conditions, that are meaningful to members of societies, and from which they can predict the future escalation of conflict and its costs.

This ambitious definition of the problem area is far wider than is usually associated with the treatment of specific conflicts. The problem area of conflict, its prediction and provention includes a political philosophy, and the as-yet undeveloped, and still suspect, study of institutional change.

THE LEGACY OF TRADITION

Our starting point must, for these reasons, be an acknowledgement of tradition. Tradition in all cultures has held that members of societies could be socialized into conforming behaviors. This quite fundamental assumption is now in doubt. Furthermore, experience seems to suggest that more repression, and more incarcerations, do not, and perhaps never did, act as a deterrent sufficient to cope with failures in the socialization process, and progressive increases in unlawful and anti-social behaviors.

At the international level colonial and imperial-type controls can no longer be a means toward domestic stability. If "natural law" was a first major stage in human social evolution, and if "positive law" was a second stage, and perhaps an institutionalized reaction to it, we seem now to be witnessing "human law", a third stage in which human aspirations and needs are proving resistant to socialization measures, and even more powerful than institutional constraints. But even so, in the absence of clear explanations, convincing predictions, and acceptable alternatives, traditional containment approaches will persist despite increasing costs.

No doubt the present condition and its climate of conflict are a consequence in part of greater complexities in social organization. There are, obviously, increased demands on reduced physical resources created by increased populations; there are systems of privilege which leave many in desperate plight; there is an increased availability of means of protest and violence; there is alienation, and an erosion of autonomous sharing social systems such as prevailed in "primitive societies." These and other influences are the background conditions of increased conflict at all social levels.

But there have always been such social and environmental changes. In the absence of any evidence or reason for hypothesizing any unusual rate of change there would be no compelling reason for departing from traditional explanations, predictions and policies. Even in conditions of extreme violence, homelessness and other conditions that create an environment of conflict and social disruption in localized areas of some developed states, elections are fought on platforms that maintain that there are no pressing problems that cannot be overcome by business as usual.

To a large extent we live with the past, its institutions and its structures, and see no reason for change. Industrial relations in many countries provide a clear example of an extension of past systems of authoritative controls. We have a language of democracy, freedoms, rights and justice, and we sometimes fail to place these concepts in the context of their origins – that is, a reaction against repressive systems, the essential structures of which we have inherited.

The harsh realities of living even in the most developed of countries is sometimes excluded from our thinking, at least in the absence of constant and distracting examples. For example, a major air manufacturing company in the US only a few years ago was found to be subjecting technicians to doses of radiation that led to, and was known would lead to, forms of cancer. Another major firm sacked workers after they acquired "repetitive motion syndrome." Because of conditions of unemployment others could be found to take their place. These publicly known examples took place in a modern industrial society, reminding us that the links with a feudal and oppressive history are still strong. It is well to have in mind examples such as this, as well as conditions of malnutrition and poverty, unemployment and lack of acceptance, and lack of freedoms of many kinds in many nations, for it is in this national and international environment that we are studying conflict and its resolution.

Furthermore, the past controls our thinking. Most of our thinking is based on an acceptance of the present as being the product of inevitable evolutionary forces. For example, it is the powerful who have acquired the right to rule. We label this as "power political realism." In this perspective, power becomes the legitimized and final determinant of social structures, and personal and group relationships. Change that would prejudice the immediate interests of the politically powerful is not usually on the political agenda of a society. In so far as societies accept such traditions it is unlikely that there can be a predictive concern, or a basis for an understanding of the nature of conflict and how to resolve it. At most there will be, as there has been, a revolt and revolution, which changes one power elite for another, but which does not necessarily or usually solve the underlying problems of social relationships.

The study of conflict, its resolution and provention must accept, therefore, as part of the problem area, the past history and consequences of authoritarianism in all social and political relationships, whether it be colonialism or its domestic counterparts. Unlike traditional studies, however, it assumes (and we discuss this in Part III) that human decision making has, given appropriate concepts and insights into the nature of social problems and their future costs, capabilities that can and do influence future evolutions. Given theories with predictive capabilities, and theories of alternatives, it may be that decision making can be oriented toward the future, rather than reactive in the defense of immediate interests.

MAN, THE STATE AND WAR

We need, however, to understand the nature and sources of traditional thought to assess its contemporary influence, and the way in which it might be developed constructively.

Political and social thought naturally reflect, or are a reaction against, present circumstances, including those of existing structures and processes of control. It is not surprising, therefore, that the traditional means of dealing with conflicts has been deterrence through punishment and containment, rather than on transforming conflictual relationships into more creative ones. Throughout the evolution of civilizations it has been accepted that there are those who have a right to expect obedience, and those who have a moral obligation to obey – a consensus usually shared no less by those who are required to obey. In this view, conflict should be contained within any system by the observance of existing social and legal norms as determined and enforced by authorities.

This view of the role of authorities applies not only to relationships between administrative or government authorities and their subjects. It applies to all authority relationships: in the family, in the school, in the factory, and in communal and international relations. The result is that authority relationships have been and still are essentially power relationships. The consensus theory of social relations acknowledges the role of power, thus placing conflict management at all social levels, both in and between societies, within a power framework.

Man, the State and War was the title of a book written by Kenneth Waltz in 1954. The title describes three models, or explanations of behavior then current. The first dealt with "the evil born in man," the second with the nature of the state and its power, and the third with the "political reality" that the state finally has to determine its own policies, and this could mean domestic repression and legitimate war. The general thrust follows the thesis that conflict is the direct outcome of human aggressiveness in the competitive acquisition of scarce resources, and that, therefore, there must be powerful authorities to control the behaviors of persons and nations. The acquisition of power should be, therefore, the main goal of state authorities.

It is still widely asserted that "man is aggressive." Dealing mainly with the world society, Morgenthau, one of the most widely read of writers in the field of politics, argued in 1948 that "political realists" see that the world "is the result of forces which are inherent in human nature." These inherent forces were, in his view, essentially malign, being characterized by "selfishness, pride and corruption in human nature." He and others were prepared to modify their language, and to point out that it was not necessary to argue that there were some natural human evil attributes. Their case was made by arguing that competition to acquire scarce resources necessarily led to aggressive behaviors. People were merely responding to environmental circumstances (Morgenthau, 1948 and Waltz, 1954).

This traditional conception of humanity certainly justified the acquisition and employment of power by authorities, which the power theorists advocated and continue to advocate. It also justified concerted socialization measures designed to ensure individual conformity with institutional or legal norms. This power approach to conflict has the effect of distracting attention from any further consideration of the nature of human behavior. It also has the effect of placing the blame for conflict on persons and groups, thus eliminating from policy consideration any alterations to institutions and policies.

This underlying assumption of malevolent human greed and aggressiveness, associated with assumptions regarding class and race differences in morality and intelligence, are not now usually articulated as a justification for authoritative controls. In contemporary circumstances it would contradict precepts of democracy, in which all persons are in law supposed to be treated as equals. But the assumption of social immorality or personal inadequacy persists as part of political belief. There is evidence of such viewpoints in many forms of self-perpetuating discriminations, even legal discriminations, on the basis of race, religion, gender and class.

THE IMPORTANCE OF MODELS AND LANGUAGE

We have already pointed out how much thinking is influenced by language, and the necessity of accurate use of language and clarity on concepts in arriving at any theory of behaviors. We should not miss the influence models and language have on perpetuating attitudes and policies. The models, terms and concepts that we have inherited lurk in the back of our minds, frustrate the development of alternative theories, and distort our perceptions of the present. Sometimes models become conclusions and explanations of events. Boethius's "wheel of fortune" seemed to be not just a metaphor, but also an explanation of why there were good times and bad times. This was an explanation that counselled acquiescence and endurance rather than understanding and corrective action.

In the area of international relations policies have been based on the "billiard ball" model of world society (Wolfers, 1962). This describes relations *between nations*, implying that events *within* nations are not causally related to events between them, and can be studied separately. According to this model, nations are in contact with each other at their boundaries, and what goes on inside each is solely its own concern.

This metaphor has trapped scholars into power explanations of relationships. The greater the size and momentum of one billiard ball, the more it can influence the direction of others with which it comes into contact. The model became a sufficient explanation of events, a sufficient basis for policy, at least until there were false predictions with costly consequences – as, for example, when great powers were defeated in war by small powers. Even then there was emotional confusion and rationalization rather than a change in thinking, because of the influence of the model. Vietnam did not fit the model; but in the absence of another model there could not be another explanation. One rationalization was that this example was an anomaly because the US chose not to employ all the power that was at its disposal.

By contrast, another model, the "cobweb" model (Burton, 1972), draws attention to system transactions – that is, interactions of all kinds, communications, transport, trade, cultural and all others that flow within and between nations. Domestic and international transactions become one. Whereas the billiard ball model invites defensive policies, the cobweb model draws attention to the need, in the interests of the stability of domestic systems, to preserve system relationships that are wider than the national. It focuses thought on the totality and complexities of relationships. While, however, the cobweb model draws attention to the transactional relations in international relations, it has its own severe limitations for it does not take into account all manner of behavior dimensions such as led to the final outcome in Vietnam. It does not offer an alternative theory or explanation of events. No model can do this.

These are two of the many models that may be in our minds when we think about situations, and that affect behavior and policies. There are many others. Increases in arms can be justified by reference to the "balance of power," even though the major states have an over-kill capacity, and even though no accurate measures can be made of the "power" – military and economic – that is to be balanced.

Models are abstractions and exclude many variables. Models merely reflect the main variables that are in the mind of the thinker. They also help communication between thinkers. No model, however, can depict deep-rooted human motivations. This requires a conceptualization that goes beyond the capacity of models to describe. In some ways the use of models, drawing attention only to some features of relationships, is misleading, and certainly no substitute for a full analytical exposition.

It is not only in thinking and exposition that these considerations are important. When parties to a conflict are interacting within a facilitated framework, it is these problems of thinking and communication of which the facilitator must be aware. It is these complexities that must be brought to the surface.

LANGUAGE

So, too, with language. There are few concepts that relate to social and political life that can be defined in any precise way. Each requires a total social theory in explanation.

We constantly have bitter international debates involving the ambiguous term "democracy." "Democracy" is a concept just as "seat" is a concept. A seat can be a bench, a chair, a stone. "Bird" likewise is a concept covering all kinds of birds. But frequently we think "democracy" is a particular system of government – perhaps our own system that others should imitate. The true meaning of the concept is lost. Few systems could be less representative than the majority rule, political-party system that leaves substantial minorities unrepresented. This kind of democracy has serious consequences when it is introduced into a multi-ethnic society. There are many conflicts taking place in which minorities are repressed in the name of "democracy."

"Development" has changed its meaning over the years. It once referred to the stages of growth from agricultural, to industrial, to service industries (Fisher, 1935). After independence was granted to colonial areas, development took on the connotation of "industrial" development and "modernization." Then when developing countries became aware of the consequences of foreign influences, it acquired the connotation "liberation" (Goulet, 1973). More recently it has acquired the connotation of a condition in which there is freedom for the full development of the person within a society (Burton, 1984).

There are many terms that have no precise meaning, but which are used frequently to justify policies. Foreign policy is conducted on the basis of the "national interest." However, this notion reflects the subjective judgement of decision makers. What they claim is the national interest may not reflect the views and opinions of other advisers or of people generally, still less the longer-term interests of nationals. The term is used in a context which implies an obligation to give support to some authority or policy with an implication of disloyalty if not given. In practice it often hides the real motivations of policy. The use of the term is all the more influential when accompanied by a claim that decision makers have secret or additional knowledge not shared by others, a claim that is often a deception, and that obviously cannot be tested in most cases.

Adversarial politics involving competing nations makes use of the concept "human rights." The term is sometimes used to refer to minority rights accorded by majorities under a constitution. These are more a denial of rights of participation than a guarantee of participation, for they do not allow the minority an effective decision making role. Societies accord some rights and deny others. Sometimes human rights include, for example, the rights not to be tortured or arbitrarily incarcerated, but do not include rights to be educated and to develop, to be employed, and to be free of poverty and malnutrition. Human needs would be a better term, leaving "rights" to signify different rights in different nations and cultures.

Reference to "freedoms" is similarly used for political purposes and subjective definitions are given. Freedom to walk the street without danger is a freedom that should be accorded to all citizens in all countries so that relationships are freely promoted. Freedom of the press has little meaning when few persons can express their views through the press, and when even a free press is subject to all manner of hidden constraints. Most societies accord some freedoms while denying others, and comparisons often reflect political bias and ignorance of cultural differences.

The basic terms employed in political philosophy, such as "justice," cannot be given any precise meaning unless an assumption is made that the decision as to what "justice" is finally rests with authorities. Then the term does not mean justice, but conditions that some people in powerful roles wish to define as justice. It may not seem to be just for some people to be very wealthy while others are poor, but it could be argued that this is just and, furthermore, in the national interest, if justice is defined in terms that take into account needs for economic incentives, and what might be asserted is the aggregate good.

THE MISINTERPRETATION OF DATA

Related to problems of language are problems of interpretation of data, to which we have already referred. The social and political sciences have gone through an adolescent stage characterized by an attempt to emulate the natural sciences. Measurement became important during the 1960s, an intellectual period named the "behavioral revolution." Social and political scientists then, far more than previously, collected data, but often without an adequate theoretical framework in which to select and interpet it. Furthermore, they collected it largely to support their preconceived beliefs, not to refute or to discover.

It was not fully appreciated that the "scientific methodologies" of the natural sciences that were being copied, were the ordinary run of the mill researches that can be carried on in laboratories in a trial-and-error way. When natural science is confronted by complexities and unexpected anomalies, there has to be the same thinking through of assumptions by deductive logic that social sciences require. The behavioral revolution, with its emphasis on empirical work and quantification, fits into the Kuhn (1962) concept of normal science, and by itself is insufficient to deal with the complex value and behavioral issues that are of special interest in social sciences.

The result has been, in addition to a burden of imprecise language, a burden of inadequate method. Statistics can show that there are some nations more developed than others. These are statistics of GNP, or of proportions of populations engaged in manufacture and service industries. The implication is that all backward, sharing, village-based societies need to be "developed" – that is, industrialized. It can be shown by comparative statistics that the incentives of the private enterprise system lead to higher output per head. It can be deduced that all forms of socialism must fail and that, therefore, all forms of welfare and support such as are given within a welfare-capitalist state are detrimental to development. QOL does not come into such calculations.

It is these issues of language and meaning that demand attention if we seek policies that will preserve that which we seek to preserve, and policies that will achieve those goals which we set for ourselves. It is these considerations that become a major part of any interactive dialogue between parties to disputes and conflicts.

CHOICES, INTERESTS, VALUES AND NEEDS

Our failure to differentiate by language those motivations that are transitory from those that are basic carries the implication that all human motivations are regarded as being behaviorally equal, meaning that with sufficient inducement or deterrence, all can equally be controlled. There is apparently no widespread concept that separates those drives that cannot be suppressed or compromised from those that are subject to some control.

When parties to a conflict interact, there is invariably bargaining over interests, the one party being aware of its own non-negotiable concerns, but not aware of any that the other party might have. If the other party does not accept a compromise, then it is thought to be irrational or unreasonable. In the absence of a clear understanding by the parties of the differences between negotiable and non-negotiable issues, a facilitator has difficulty in helping to conduct meaningful communication.

Yet it is this distinction between negotiable and non-negotiable issues that is necessary when any attempt is made to analyze a conflict, and to promote meaningful communication between parties to a conflict. It is a distinction necessary also when policy makers determine their strategies, for without such a distinction coercive policies are likely to be pursued in situations in which they must fail.

Conflict resolution, which seeks to deal with non-negotiable issues, is, as we have suggested, a recent notion. It is to be distinguished from settlement, which is possible only when there are negotiable issues. In an interactive situation conflict resolution, unless explained, conveys the notion of some form of control, perhaps external controls. Inventing new words does not help: they merely take understanding of conflict resolution outside the area of public knowledge, as are many specializations in science.

Let us take a specific case, the issue of "independence," that affects US policies and relations with other countries, especially in neighboring regions. It also affects relations with the Soviet Union, a country that has been invaded frequently and is sensitive to the issue. Judging by public responses and public policy decisions, it would seem that in the US there is little conceptualization of the notion of independence. The American War of Independence is history. The post-war independence movements in Asia and Africa – which were of long standing but submerged under colonial rule – were interpreted as being due to Soviet or Chinese influence. The US could imagine no other explanation without an understanding of a struggle for post-colonial independence. In the late 1980s the US had its first taste of Japanese economic invasion, and this became an issue in elections. Lacking the conceptualization of independence such as exists in many small countries that have long been subjected to greater power interventions, this experience was not appreciated as relating to the experiences and feelings of smaller states in Central and Latin America that had been struggling for their political and economic independence from the US.

Since the post-Second World War period there have been many ethnic conflicts and identity crises in gender and role relations generally that point to motivations and behaviors that cannot readily be controlled by authorities or contained within an unresponsive law-and-order framework. It thus becomes important politically to consider individual motivations or drives that appear not to be subject to authoritative control, or to compromise. In the absence of some conceptualization of these behaviors, reflected in and helped by a more specific language, there is little prospect that public policies will reflect insights that are emerging out of thinking and research.

Even within the academic community there are major difficulties in communication. Those engaged in strategic studies and those concerned with conflict analysis do not hear what each other are saying. But a recognition that the problem exists is a first step in guarding against some of its consequences.

The language of social sciences and the language of politics have not adapted to the insights into behavior that we now have. There is a widespread recognition of the increased role of the individual, but so little attention has been given to the nature of that role that we have no common expressions with which to communicate what it is.

On the contrary, the challenge to authorities throughout the world, in multi-ethnic communities and on the streets, far from being perceived in the context of human development, is usually still described as an aberration or form of deviant behavior to be suppressed, and is labelled accordingly. Republican terrorists in Northern Ireland, separatist terrorists in Sri Lanka, and Palestinian terrorists in the Middle East, are labels that suggest the absence of any conceptualization of the problem.

Similarly, labeling, rather than explanatory terms, is used to describe domestic deviant behaviors, for example, "street people" and "drop outs." Various labels are applied to different types of non-conformists or criminals whose motivations and abnormalities are not understood.

BELIEF OR INTEREST?

We have dealt with two traditional influences, interests and habits of thought. It is difficult in retrospect to assess the extent to which thinking about human behaviors reflected, on the one hand, an honest belief that human beings were of a malign nature and, on the other, the extent to which this was a justification for the exercise of power by power elites. In a longer-term historical context it would seem that this assessment of the human being was to a large degree a defensive response on the part of established elites. The history of civilizations is a history of challenges to existing structures and institutions, and of forced changes, reflecting the continued pressure of human resistance to authoritative systems and regimes.

At the international level, the virtual end of formal structures of colonialism after the Second World War was evidence of this challenge. Now there are challenges to the post-colonial authorities that assumed jurisdiction over the former colonial areas comprised of many different peoples, all seeking their own autonomy. The process is an on-going one, and the incidence of conflict seems to reflect, on the one hand, tensions between human struggles for development and, on the other, institutional sources of frustration to the pursuit of development. Whether it was a defensive response or a genuine belief about the nature of the individual, the power political theory directed attention away from this unchangeable and complex human person, to institutions of containment and their preservation.

Scholars are essentially reactive to the contemporary political consensus. They have built on this foundation not only traditional legal studies, but also other social studies, especially sociology which, like law, has reflected the philosophies of contemporary politics. There has been a special interest in the socialization of the individual. Even psychology and psychiatry have tended to focus on the inadequacies and maladjustments of the person. As late as the 1930s psychology was frequently taught on the basis of reflexes and instincts, and the implication was clearly one of primitive reactions which needed to be controlled. "Instincts" did not include the positive connotation of the pursuit of inherent developmental needs. In a historical perspective it is interesting to note that there has not emerged any scholarly discipline that has focused on problems of change and adjustments to change to meet the requirements of the human being.

There were many psychologists and others who attempted to break away from this deprecating approach to human behavior. Dollard as far back as 1939 linked aggression to frustration. In 1950, Klineberg gave support to the theme "No peace without mental health." But these approaches were more directed toward problems with leadership of nations than with any general theory of human behavior, and certainly did not focus on the positive issues of human development that would have implied institutional means of promoting development instead of containing aggressive behaviors.

It was not until 1963 that there appeared to be a shift in thinking. Klineberg gave consideration to "identification" and the apparent need of people to identify with a group, and with a nation. As we saw when discussing the "human dimension" in Chapter 2, altering thinking was to lead to significant changes in the study of deviance and social problems, giving rise to what has come to be known as "control theory," resting on the observation that valued relations influence or control behavior. This is the conjunction between human needs theory and control that we seek and will be exploring.

This is the historical and institutional context in which we are studying social problems and conflicts and their resolution, at all social levels. We will finally reject both "conservative" and "radical" approaches on fundamental systemic and behavioral grounds. Both are structurally based, and consequently do not require reconsideration of any human dimension. One seeks to maintain existing structures on the grounds that they are as good as any that are in the offering, despite social injustices, tensions and conflicts. The other, acting negatively against the present, seeks altered structures that are usually ill-defined, and that may in practice be just as authoritarian or conflict making as those they would replace.

6 Sources and Trends in Thought

A RECENT INTEREST

In this traditional context conflict resolution is a recent concern. Indeed, it was only in the mid-1960s that the *resolution* of conflict, as distinct from its *settlement* by coercive means, was given serious consideration even by those theorists and practitioners whose role it was to deal with conflict. That conflict resolution is of such recent interest may seem surprising. Why should repression, containment and management have prevailed throughout the history of civilizations, and why only now, at the end of the twentieth century, should problem-solving alternatives to tradition receive serious consideration?

In subtle ways "natural law" in primitive and relatively small tribes, communities and societies ensured a high level of conformity with traditional norms. Sanctions were exercised, and supported both by legitimized or traditional leadership, and by ritualized interpretations of the will of deities. In the authoritative systems of "positive law," which subsequently emerged with increased populations and family claims to properties, and which affected all relationships in due course from the family to the power-dominated international society, it was sufficient and possible for the powerful to declare the rules, and to enforce them. *Resolving* conflicts in either type of society would have been a challenge to existing norms, institutions and structures, and regarded, therefore, as threatening and subversive of existing social relationships, elite interests and values.

Conditions in the second half of the twentieth century, however, challenged tradition. Authorities, including the greater powers in the international society, could no longer ensure the observation of their norms, suppress dissent, or contain individual and group drives for role, recognition and resources. There remains, however, a reluctance to acknowledge that institutions must adapt to the fulfillment of human aspirations or needs. Tradition leaves it to the social and economic markets of society to exercise controls, and also punishments, such as unemployment, homelessness, ill-health and social segregation. The result is the division of societies into those whose

83

needs are being fulfilled, and those who become ever more under-privileged, with consequent increases in conflict and violence.

THE EXPERIENCE OF SOCIAL WORKERS

Some early signs of the need for changed approaches were seen by social workers. While policies relevant to conflict situations remained within the traditional authoritative law-and-order framework, social workers were sharply divided on the question whether it was their role to work within the system and to help in suppressing conflict, or to try to promote changes that would remove the sources of anti-social behaviors.

Their profession places social workers between the demands of society and the human needs of those for whom they are required to care. The two are frequently incompatible: it is the everyday experience of social workers that their duty to authorities and their duty to their clients is at variance. The structures, institutions and policies of societies create an environment in which the behaviors of some people will be outside the legal norms, and in which conflicts between persons or with authorities are promoted. Social workers are, in practice, located where problem-solving conflict resolution could be a continuous process.

While social work must operate within a traditional social–political framework, one result of its critical position has been that major contributions have been made within the social work discipline to an understanding of the deeper problems associated with conflict, its resolution and provention, at all social levels. The concern of social workers was with the conflict between institutions and human needs that could be solved only by an analysis of the problems that gave rise to anti-social behaviors.

In 1958 Boehm described the problem-solving function of social work, and emphasized that a society achieved its democratic goals only to the extent that it made possible the realization of the full potential of all its citizens. The National Association of American Social Workers in 1958 referred to "human needs common to each person." A book by Charlotte Towle in 1973, commissioned by the United States Bureau of Public Assistance, had the title *Common Human Needs*. In Britain Mia Pringle (1974) of the National Children's Bureau argued that children had certain needs of love, security and recognition if they were to develop into responsible citizens.

INDUSTRIAL RELATIONS

A second area that provoked consideration of problem-solving was industrial relations. Industrial relations consultants, however, also found themselves confronting tradition and established interests. The early endeavors reported by Blake and his colleagues (1964) showed how both sides of industry turn their backs on any problem-solving approaches to their disputes, interpreting any such interest by the other side as a trick, or alternatively as a sign of weakness in negotiation, in much the same way as great powers are inclined to do today. As is the case with social work, little progress has in practice been made in this area. There have been few adjustments in structures that would deal with the problem at source.

HIGH LEVEL CONFLICT

There has been even less shift in thought away from traditional assumptions and practices at the community and international levels where conflict is widespread and violent.

The traditional power politics approach as applied at the international level was articulated after the Second World War had commenced and had demonstrated the breakdown of the system of international law created by the League of Nations. This was done by two scholars, Schwarzenberger (1941) and Morgenthau (1948). They were disillusioned by the failures of the League of Nations, and reacted by advocating national power dominance as the means to security – a return of pre-First World War thinking. The text of Hans Morgenthau, *Politics Among Nations: The Struggle for Power and Peace*, dominated international studies for many decades. It reflected the policies of great powers. It claimed to be "political realism," not just for this reason, but more particularly because of the demonstrated breakdown of the international legal system created after the First World War.

There were variations on the theme. The general theory of power politics was a justification of whatever policies were thought to prevail at any given point of time. It was argued that Britain and the major European states had traditionally been engaged in a balance-of-power strategy. Balance-of-power was a plausible system, at least until it was examined critically. It probably never existed. It is most unlikely that any state would switch its support from one side of a possible conflict to another, casting aside differences in ideologies and traditional trade and other linkages, just to give effect to some notion of power balance. Britain and its allies in the Second World War hesitated before giving support to the Soviet Union when it was attacked by Germany. A Western European NATO state is not likely today to transfer support to the Soviet Union just because the US is thought to have a military superiority. Furthermore, there was no reliable means of calculating power, or power balances. The notion was more an intellectual construct than a political reality (Claude, 1959).

There were other constructs of this order, reflecting the ideologies of the time. There was collective security, by which was meant the coming together of some major powers in order to confront others. This was more in line with empirical realities, but not in any sense a solution to problems of international relations. Probably unrealistic, but an interesting intellectual creation, was the idea of "world government" (Clark and Sohn, 1960) – that is, a virtual monopoly of power possessed by some international institution. Intellectual expositions, such as gaming models, tended to be rationalizations of policies and used to justify the policies of decision makers which were otherwise difficult to justify and to describe (Rummel, 1970), or to make possible some quantitative precision even at the expense of realities. The same gaming tradition has been inherited by contemporary strategic studies.

TRIVIALIZING PROBLEMS

Through the use of power and coercion it is possible to achieve a predetermined outcome without going into the complexities of the problem concerned. With force the complexities of any human dimension in a conflict can be overriden, in the short term, and the situation can be reduced to the simple dimensions of institutional preservation. This is an attraction for those who have political responsibilities.

There are inevitably longer-term consequences, and even situations such as, for example, street warfare, get beyond this type of control. Defeat in Vietnam of a great power by an indigenous population whose main strength came from commitment rather than arms came as a shock, not merely to peoples in the US, but also to power theorists, everywhere. It forced a reconsideration of the simple power notion. There were, obviously, more complex factors to be taken into account. But, once again, the reconsideration was within the boundaries of traditional thinking on human behavior and its controls.

Relationships, whether they be at the international or some other level, have inherent complexities which at the time are not taken into account. The breakdown of the League system was not just the outcome of Hitler creating an aggressive state. There were post-First World War provocations for the developments that took place in Germany, accentuated by the depression policies of other Western powers. Japan had very little option but to seek its own co-prosperity sphere in the light of British and other protectionist policies throughout their Asian and African colonies during the 1930s depression period. In November 1941 the US Secretary of State, Cordell Hull, made a proposal to Japan that it be accorded equality of treatment, but there was no support from Britain, and no effective guarantee (White Paper, Australian House of Representatives, December, 1941). Power politics was designed to make simple issues out of these very complex problems. By the exercise of power it was thought possible, in the short term at least, to ignore the complexities, and to attempt to force other states to accept the status quo.

IMPLICATIONS OF POWER THEORIES

In the literature on the subject, and in popular understanding, the application of international power politics has been separated from domestic politics. There being no international constitution, or agreed norms that define defense and aggression, the power political framework has seemed more applicable at this level. However, fundamentally they are the same. Both at the international and the domestic levels there is the same choice, either to treat problems simplistically by repressive means, or by problem-solving, that is by analyzing the issues at stake within the framework of an adequate theory of behavior.

It is because coercion by national authorities is legal, and within constitutional limits, and because there are no agreed norms of resolution at the international level, that power theories developed in particular in the international relations literature. It can, therefore, best be understood by reference to that literature, though we need always to relate it to domestic problems and policies.

In this tradition the nation is the unit of analysis. What was called the "billiard ball model" has persisted (Wolfers, 1962): relationships across national boundaries are down-played in international relations theory. The "cobweb" or transactions model (Burton, 1972) and its implications are pushed aside as they are not compatible with the assumptions inherent in deterrence theories. The idea that international conflict may be largely a carryover of domestic problems (as was probably the case with respect to the origins of the Vietnam war in a period of intense anti-communism in the United States), is incompatible with the assumption of the aggressiveness of other states.

It is to be noted that within a power framework "the proper training of the practitioner is never analytical or intellectual; presumably, his proper role is simply to apply known principles to individual cases." There is a tendency "to turn attention away from structural alterations in the international system itself." Referring to various happenings, "It is not that we failed to predict the exact moment or event; it is that we were neither politically nor psychologically prepared for them to happen at all" (Rothstein, 1981).

THE "RIPENING" THESIS

One conclusion of power theories is that there can be no peace making until conflicts have "ripened," that is until costs have escalated to the point at which parties are prepared to settle. This in practice seems to be so. A question arises as to whether this is due to traditions in power political thinking.

In the nuclear age, and with modern weaponry for waging ethnic and other national struggles, such a ripened stage obviously has to be avoided. Furthermore, negotiation in such circumstances is unlikely to result in a *resolution* of the problem, and any *settlement* arrived at is likely to last only so long as the power relations make the absence of war possible: alterations in power relations would lead to further conflict while the sources of conflict remained.

The power approach is, therefore, a jumping off point for problem-solving conflict resolution in the sense that the consequences of such thinking provoke a search for an alternative to the costs and consequences of "ripening." Problem-solving conflict resolution seeks to make possible more accurate prediction and costing, together with the discovery of viable options, that would make this ripening unnecessary. The same analysis applies, of course, to domestic problems, such as violence, gang warfare and others, which need to be anticipated and dealt with before the social and personal costs escalate.

This review of trends in thought and practice will show the persistence of traditional thinking and the recent nature of thinking that provides an alternative to traditional containment or strategic thinking. It helps, therefore, to explain the widespread confusions and contending approaches that are still current in the wider fields of conflict studies. Problem-solving conflict resolution, the subject matter of this Conflict Series, is a conception that has emerged, despite a universal and long-standing consensus that favors deterrent strategies, not as a moral reaction to such strategies, but as a consequence of an analysis of human behaviors and institutional frameworks in which humans behave.

Strategic planning, whether domestic or international, must take into account not only the realities of conflict and violence, but also the human dimensions that make some repressions dysfunctional and some wars unwinnable. The problem is to find that framework for policy that relates the two apparently contending approaches, hopefully providing some prospect for the ultimate ascendency of conflict resolution.

For two thought systems to be harmonized it is necessary for both to be within the same logical framework. This has not been the case in the past, especially at the theoretical level. Power theories and conflict resolution theories have, if anything, further diverged.

There are several reasons for this.

First, in the separate discipline approach to knowledge, studies of power-political decision making have been isolated from insights that might challenge its assumptions. International relations, for example, has been a separate study, even though it is required to deal with aspects, such as psychological aspects of perception, decision making, institutions and others, that relate to other disciplines. Its power-political assumptions remain unchallenged by any developments that take place in the understanding of behavior.

Second, given power, there is little interest in, or even awareness of, a significant human dimension. Opposition is taken care of by some coercive means.

It follows, third, that to the extent that the philosophy of power politics, and the tradition of power elite dominance from which it was derived, is accepted consensually, each separate discipline adopts an institutional and non-behavioral approach to decision making.

Fourth, it has to be appreciated that a paradigm shift of the order required, from a theory based on power defense of existing institutions, to a theory that acknowledges the political realities of human behaviors, is challenging both to practitioners and to scholars, and takes many generations to reach a consensus stage.

The present intellectual task, to which hopefully this Conflict Series contributes, is to make the present a transition stage in a paradigm shift, so that these two approaches may provide a constructive problem-solving approach to relationships alongside a fallback defensive position. Translating into the domestic scene, it is police repression of gangs accompanied by intensive endeavors to deal with the social and economic problems which lead to gangs.

Interactive, analytical problem-solving processes of conflict resolution may be one step toward solving this problem of social evolution. Problem-solving in the specific situation can suggest processes and norms acceptable in other situations, and which can have a general application. The resolution of a particular street gang conflict, or an ethnicity conflict, for instance, points to the specific conditions needed to eliminate and provent the problem of street gang warfare and ethnic conflict in general. Success in the specific context can pave the way for acceptance of similar measures applied more widely. This fearful dilemma of change is one to which analytical problem-solving can make a special contribution (see Part III).

It is here that we have the connecting link between *resolution* and *provention*. The resolution process applied to particular situations is socially insignificant in proportion to the number of specific conflicts that emerge in societies. It can, however, act as the creative and validating process in theory building or explanation, and, therefore, in provention. It can, by establishing new norms in particular situations, initiate an acceptable change process.

TRENDS IN THINKING ABOUT A HUMAN DIMENSION

Positive Law, accompanied by a high level of enforcement, is now being seen, in retrospect, as a diversion, albeit a persistent one, from the main stream of development of processes that cater for the interests and requirements of the unit members of societies. The emergence of interest in the individual as the independent unit focuses attention on the lack of legitimacy of modern societies, and the way in which elite norms have prevented those changes that would allow cultural norms to reflect individual interests. It gives some insights into why class and multi-ethnic societies, including those societies that have authoritative bureaucratic classes, are inherently unstable.

The individual emerges as the independent variable despite a persistent belief that the individual adapts to, and is socialized into, social organizations and social norms. The same conclusion could be deduced from *The Logic of Collective Action*, to use Olson's title (1965). The idea that a person seeking to maximize cost-benefits will act in accord with social norms on the grounds that through adherence to them a person's interests will best be satisfied, an argument on which classical theory heavily rests, cannot be sustained. The individual unit, person or group, will pursue self-interest regardless of the social interest.

The individual was, clearly, never out of the picture entirely. Marxists, following a classical tradition, always claimed that the essence of humanity was in free creative activity, in full and free expression and development. Marx quite deliberately made a clear distinction between "alienation" and "estrangement." Alienation, especially alienation at the work place, was his preoccupation because of changing industrial conditions. However, the term did not explain the human response. Clearly there could also be alienation due to social and political conditions – the absence of participation and of a sense of control, and the absence of identity for minorities, just to give two examples. Marx was well aware of this ontological element. "Estrangement" was his term to apply to conditions that affected biological human nature. Positive Law found its legitimization in the common good through which the individual would benefit most. But the means were organizational, and in the circumstances structure inevitably reflected class and not necessarily common-good interests. The current return to the individual as the unit of analysis is far more in accord with the Natural Law notion; but it is a return to Natural Law in a scientific age. The reference point is no longer a notion of natural justice based on some mysterious divine social norms. It is based on needs that range from the physical to the psychological. These must be met if the unit within the social system is not to malfunction and be destructive of society itself. The organization–behavioral debate is being resolved by a synthesis, by a focus on the individual unit to the extent that the needs of this unit determine the effective operation of the social system of which it is part. The goal is the Positive Law goal of a harmonious society in which the unit adapts to the changing environmental conditions, but within the limits set by the satisfaction of human needs. The means of this interaction between changing conditions and the requirements of the units within society are the Natural Law processes by which organizations and political systems are adapted to the evolved and evolving needs of the participants.

THE RECENT LITERATURE

A human dimension was always included in studies of relationships. Until recently, however, they seemed to focus more on problems of perception, implying that if there could be more accuracy in perception, problems of conflict in relationships would be less likely to occur (Burton, 1972). While of course relevant, this behavioral aspect dealt only with a superficial problem. In all disciplines scholars have now begun to rely increasingly on assumptions that imply the probable existence of universal needs.

Sites, in his book, *Control: The Basis of Social Order* (1973), meaning control by the person, not by authorities, argued that given the opportunity an individual will attempt, against all odds, to be in control of matters of human importance. "Control Theory" is based on "attachment." "'Attachment' refers to the observation that deviance is subjectively available [in other words, a likely response] to us unless we develop relationships with others who are then able to provide us with a reason for not deviating" (Box, 1971). Attachment can, of course, be to authorities as well as to persons. The insight that control theory provides is that external constraints, decisions taken by others, are not effective in controlling behaviors when human needs are denied.

James MacGregor Burns (1977) looked for the "Wellsprings of Political Leadership" and found them in "the vast pools of human energy known as wants, needs, aspirations and expectations." Sir Leslie Scarman (1977) asserted that "there is a natural law springing from man's own humanity which must be incorporated into the positive law of the state." Barrington Moore (1978), when trying to define the notion of justice, was driven to observe that "it is obvious that human beings do have something that can be called innate needs." He tentatively drew attention to non-physical needs such as needs for respect and recognition, for identity (which he called "distinction"), for the absence of boredom or for stimulus, for control (which he related to freedom of inhibitions to be aggressive against dangerous targets). He concluded, "As a working hypothesis, I propose a conception of innate human nature, innate in the sense of being *prior* to any social influences but not necessarily immune to them, for which not only physical deprivations are noxious but also psychic ones; specifically, the absence of favorable human responses, boredom, and the inhibition of aggressions." In the field of comparative politics Peretz (1978) argued in his contribution "Universal Wants: A Deductive Framework for Comparative Analysis" that the future of comparative politics as a study rests on the assumption that there are some wants that are constant across systems.

Psychology has been slow to shift from organizational to motivational explanations. Weiner (1979) somewhat reluctantly included in his wide-ranging review of approaches to human motivation a final chapter on "Humanistic Theory and Personal Constructs." Psychology has been greatly concerned with what Weiner terms crippled people, whereas the so-called humanist school, he suggests, studies healthy people.

This reluctance of many psychologists to break with tradition, and the explanation of deviant behavior within a normative law-and-order framework that suggests that any individual who does not conform to social and legal norms is in some way crippled, is now being attacked by some sociobiologists. Wilson, who wrote a comprehensive review of sociobiological literature in 1973, contributed a Preface to a book *Sociobiology and Behaviour* by Barash (1977), in which he said "To understand evolutionary history and the contemporary biogram that it produced is to understand in a deeper manner the construction of human nature, to learn what we really are and not just what we hope we are, as viewed through the various prisms of our mythologies. Assisted by sociobiological analyses, a stronger social science might develop. An exciting collaboration between biologists and social scientists appears to have begun."

Haworth writes of *Autonomy: An Essay in Philosophical Psychology and Ethics* (1986) to make the same points. His concern is with the "autonomous person," the person who has self-esteem and a sense of competence that is socially recognized. Autonomy is close to the Sites concept of identity and recognition.

What these scholars and others have been saying is, in essence, that organizational approaches have been too superficial. The sources of alienation, for example, are not necessarily associated more with one type of system than another. As Scruton (1980) argues, "If a factory labourer is compelled to view his activity as means, then this is so whether or not the final product lies in the hands of the individual, the collective, or the state." Alienation occurs in any system if, in practice, participation and identity are denied.

Many scholars who did not adopt a needs approach consciously, yet rested on it by implication. In 1970 Gurr wrote a book with the title *Why Men Rebel*. He was referring to all people, at all times, in all societies, with a strong implication that there are some basic human needs to be fulfilled. Weiner (1979) pointed out that all individuals learn – learning is a universal trait, an inherent and ontological part of human and animal behavior. In fact those who have succeeded best in defining human needs in precise terms, adopt a learning framework: the needs defined are those that are fundamental to the process of learning and individual development.

In short, there appears to be a persistent trend from a focus on institutions to one of persons and groups; and from the study of overt behavior to that which is hidden.

Twentieth century experience has persuaded writers that the individual may be an independent variable, that there may be no institutional devices, rule-governed norms or organizational influences that can contain the ontological propensities of the individual. Generalizations, explanations and predictions are possible once universal patterns of behavior are discovered. Behavioral science is, in these circumstances, no different from natural science. Both have universality, both are governed by empirically observable patterns of behavior, both require at some level of analysis hypotheses concerning the unobservable reasons for overt behavior, and these require experiment and testing.

HUMAN NEEDS AND CONTROL THEORY

We have still not defined the individual, as distinct from the economic, legal, psychological, organizational or ideological "person." In particular, we have not been specific in defining the needs to which reference has been made. We are probably a long way from doing this, but some progress is being made, as the book in this Series, *Conflict: Human Needs Theory*, shows.

There is still little agreement on terminology generally or in particular when reference is made to universal variables. Needs, wants and values are sometimes used interchangeably. Pirages (1976) distinguishes needs from wants: "Basic human needs are physiologically determined while wants are socially determined." James MacGregor Burns (1977), in trying to define the role of leadership, uses the terms "needs" and "wants" in the opposite senses; but the attempt to differentiate is clear. Wants is an economic term, and can be defined in terms of market demands. Perhaps the term should be so confined. Needs can probably be defined best empirically in a similar way: that is, in terms of the behavioral frustrations experienced when not fulfilled.

In defining our terms, however, it is preferable not to start from ambiguous empirical evidence. Even the market definition of wants may not reflect wants other than those influenced by the market mechanisms of persuasion. The needs to which many social scientists are now drawing attention cannot be determined by examining the overt behavior of the individual. This leads only to labelling: aggression, frustration, violence, anti-social behavior and others are descriptions of observed behavior and have no explanatory power. As already indicated, the means by which non-observable behavior and needs must be specified is a deductive – or, more precisely, an abductive – process by which fundamental hypotheses are assessed. If learning and social development require consistency in response, security, identity and recognition, and if human behavior is characterized by learning and social development, then humans pursue consistency in response, security, identity and recognition as a condition of their learning process. It is reasonable to argue, further, that organisms have a genetic drive to learn, for existence depends upon learning. These learning needs *will* be fulfilled. If recognition, identity of self, and some measure of control over the environment are human needs, then the absence of their fulfillment will lead to adaptations that restrict development and perhaps create abnormalities in behavior, or lead to anti-social behaviors.

It is in this area that Sites has made his main contribution:

We have demonstrated the emergence of eight needs in the individual: a need for response, a need for security, a need for recognition, a need for stimulation, a need for distributive justice, a need for meaning, a need to be seen as rational (and for rationality itself), and a need to control. The relationship among these various needs is extremely complex. The last four needs emerge because the first four, which emerge out of the necessary dynamics of the socialization process, are not and cannot be immediately and consistently satisfied (1973, p. 43).

This quotation, however, does not do justice to the insights which led to the assertion of these eight "needs." "Control theory," which Sites advances, provides a synthesis of organizational and power theories, on the one hand, and of behavioral theories, on the other. Sites argues that the concept of power is indispensable to all existing theories of social and political behavior. He attempts to synthesize apparently contending theories around the notion of control. His initial proposition is that if individuals and groups attempt to control their environment, there must be a reason. He further hypothesizes that the reason is to obtain gratification of needs, including the need for survival.

The needs which he hypothesizes are independent of any particular culture or society: they are universal and genetically inherent in the individual. They are ontological. This is not to say that the individual and group will not use, as tools, the cultural and other norms of their society to gratify their needs.

Sites freely admits that human needs are no more observable than the atom and its particles; but this should not daunt social scientists any more than it does physicists. His belief, based on anthropological and other studies, is that the influence of individual needs is "many times stronger than the influence of the social forces which play upon man." (p. 9). So strong are these influences that "individuals step out of the 'real' world into a world of their own in an attempt to find fulfilment of more basic needs or at least to escape their complete frustration" (p. 10). The individual's most fundamental drive is to attempt to control his environment in order to meet his needs. Society never completely conquers the individual. Culture and societies must be viewed as being in a continuous evolution – a gap always existing between human needs and the interests and values of power elites. It follows that the individual uses the norms of society as tools to the extent that they are useful in the pursuit of human needs. If not useful, more appropriate ones are invented: "if needs cannot be met by being honest, the individual tries something else."

Control or Needs Theory, whichever one wishes to term it, is wide ranging. Such a framework provides at least part of the explanation of the behavior of underprivileged delinquent gang members, middle-class adolescents who experience a sense of lack of control over their own lives, revolutionaries who are those awakened to the possibility of a changed society, but who have no opportunities of participation in the decision making process of society.

As Sites argues, there is here a potential explanation of a great deal of "deviance" at all social levels. It follows that, once the individual is adopted as the unit of analysis, there are objectively determined guides to policy, bases on which goals and policies can be assessed and predictions made as to success or self-defeating consequences.

Box, who deals more specifically with "deviance" adopted the same approach. In his view "social structures may be 'legitimized' or 'institutionalized' for only a minority of the members of that system" (1971). Deviant behavior is nothing less or more than rule breaking: only sometimes for some people can needs be satisfied within the framework of legal norms. For him it is a matter of surprise that there is not more "deviant" behavior – he asks the question, "Why don't we all break the law?" His answer is that there are values attached to relationships, *not* that there is a fear of deterrence. Most individuals establish social bonds, "the remainder of the population are free to engage in delinquent behavior."

Control Theory is an explanation of normal, ordinary, conforming behavior. There is the abnormal aspect. For example, deprivation frequently leads to overreaction, and the individual goes beyond the normal pursuit of needs satisfaction. A person (or a communal group), deprived of rewarding relationships, recognition, security and identity over long periods, will tend to have a chip on the shoulder, to perceive injustice and deprivation and to be aggressive even in circumstances that do not require it. Totalitarian political and social leadership roles tend to attract such individuals. Or there may develop a personal paranoia that attracts persons to intelligence services directed toward possible enemies. Control and power for their own sake are not a part of Control Theory as such; but such a theory demonstrates how aggression can be created by circumstances, thus pointing to the long-term costs and consequences of needs deprivation.

AN ASSESSMENT OF CONTROL THEORY

We have been discussing and relying on trends in behavioral sciences, the experiences of those engaged in research and consultation, and the hypotheses to which they have been led. We have arrived at a hypothesis that asserts the existence of specific human needs that have a bearing on social organization.

In modern industrial society the application of Positive Law is beginning to require such an extent of coercion, rather than reflecting any habit of obedience, that it and the authorities which impose it are being challenged, especially in developed societies. Human needs are being frustrated on a large scale in all modern societies, and the more law and order is enforced to control frustration the more the frustration. There is now a widespread concern regarding the legitimacy of even the most seemingly legitimized authorities. The members of protest movements of many kinds in many different societies, and the terrorists who spring from relatively privileged classes, are demonstrating that there are features of societies, of all political types, unacceptable to a significant number of the people that comprise them.

THE CONTEMPORARY LITERATURE

Social and political science literature is responding to political realities with altering concepts, changing emphases and wider orientations, giving rise to alternative paradigms. These changing concepts reflect an interdisciplinary approach. The whole individual – not separate economic, legal, psychological or ideological constructs – is being analyzed.

The vocabulary of contemporary social science focuses on concepts such as alienation, autonomy, change, conciliation, deprivation, development, deviance, discrimination, elitism, ethnicity, feminism, freedom, functionalism, identity, independence, justice, legitimization, levels of analysis, minority rights, needs, participation, privilege, problem-solving, protest, rebellion, reform, repression, resolution, revolution, role, structural violence, terrorism, transformation, unit of analysis, values, and violence. The words are not new; but the concepts represented by the words played only an inconspicuous part in traditional approaches that dwelt on authoritarian structures, and normative and coercive processes.

These conceptual notions form sets. For example, legitimacy, law-and-order, coercion, obligation, and many others form a set relating to authority. However, to a significant extent the sets in which such notions are placed reflect trends in thought and discourse. Depending on pre-theories, notions such as "rights" can be in a set with authority and majority rule or, alternatively, and implying a different meaning, in a set dominated by the notion of universal needs. This is the nature of changes in thought and paradigms shifts. There are shifts in meaning. A developed terminology is necessary to remove ambiguity and to enable communication. For example, "rights" and "needs" are sometimes used in the contemporary literature interchangeably. However, *rights* are traditionally referred to within majority–minority constitutional relations, while *needs* are now more and more referred to in the evolving literature as universal requirements. The difference is important in relationships. No one culture or system can require observation by others of what it regards as "right;" but "needs" satisfaction can be regarded as a universally required condition for harmonious relationships.

Classification of conceptual notions (the logical process), and the analysis of trends in the literature (the analytical process), suggest sets of concepts that seem relevant to behavioral relations. There are sets based on, for example:

1. Authority.
2. Institutions and structures.
3. Responses to authorities.
4. Individual human needs and values.
5. Growth and change.
6. Processes in dealing with conflictual relationships.
7. Methodologies in arriving at theories and conclusions.

The authority set is concerned with law-and-order, the role of authorities, sanctions, norms and management. It is institutionally-oriented. The relevant actors are governing elites. The response literature deals with reactions to authorities. It is change-oriented. The relevant actors are the governed.

Some contributions, however, approximate to an interdisciplinary status, and in doing so provide the beginnings of another set – an interdisciplinary set in which the whole of a topic is analyzed, not its parts. This developing literature is clearly different in kind from all others. It contains contributions that embrace assumptions and methodologies that are currently regarded as controversial. For example, many authors move freely from one social system level to another, and indeed from one culture to another, for they assume that there are fundamental behavioral patterns common to all.

THE INTERNATIONAL LITERATURE

At the international relations level David Mitrany had speculated about *A Working Peace System* (1944) based on the notion of functional cooperation. A Center for Research on Conflict Resolution was established in 1959 at the University of Michigan, publishing the *Journal of Conflict Resolution*. There was a Peace Research Institute in Oslo publishing the *Journal of Peace Research*. There were misgivings being expressed about deterrence approaches. In 1962 Osgood observed that "The policy of mutual deterrence includes no pfovision for its own resolution . . . It is a game without end the attempted solution of which becomes the problem." In the same year Burton wrote *Peace Theory*, trying to deal with problems of change. There were debates as to whether there could be more than analogy in linking conflict at one social level (for example, the domestic) to another (for example, the international). In 1963 a Conflict Research Society was created in Britain, and in 1964 a Centre for the Analysis of Conflict at the University of London. In 1963 Deutsch pulled together many strands of thought in his *The Nerves of Government* in which he placed the whole area of conflict in a decision making framework, on which we seek to build in Part III. In 1965 Kelman, a social psychologist, edited an important set of contributions on *International Behavior* in which he sought to bring together in one volume, though not into one synthesis, different aspects of the general problem of conflictual relationships.

An early attempt to bring together different social levels and to analyze conflict and its resolution within a generic framework took place at a conference held at Windsor Park, just outside of London, in 1963. This was followed by a symposium convened at the CIBA Foundation in London. The resultant publication must be regarded as an important review of thinking at that time (CIBA Foundation, de Reuck and Knight (eds), 1966). In it Lasswell examined leader-follower relations, Boulding pointed out the need for long-sightedness and realistic images, Rapaport argued that the contemporary strategic theories, reflecting the thinking of Clausewitz, were theories of those who wage war, and not theories designed to avoid war. He suggested as an alternative the *analysis* of *issues*. Burton stressed the need to cost decisions, and especially their consequences over the longer term. Karl Deutsch stressed the need to recognize the realities of interdependence.

In those days there was a great interest in conflict in primate society, and the study of monkeys and apes in their competition for food and territory, and for rank order. This was the beginning of a conscious search for some theoretical framework in which to analyze conflict. While a major interest was misperception as a source of conflictual relationships (Burton, 1972), there were at the same time the beginnings of a theory of human needs, especially those identity needs evidenced in "nationalism."

These were the early beginnings. There were inputs into thinking about explanations of conflict, doubts cast on contemporary strategic thinking based on game models, and some consideration of problems of perception and interpretations of behaviors. At the end of the 1960s reports were being published on means of bringing parties to disputes together in an analytical framework (Burton, 1969).

Book 3 in this Conflict Series is intended to make readily available some of the more important contributions of this period. It was intellectually an important one. The initial interest in conflict resolution of the 1960s was, however, short lived. The small groups engaged in these inquiries were swamped in the 1970s by those who were responding to the circumstances of the Cold War. Strategic studies dominated. At this global level, the heightened East–West tensions then dominating thought, unsettled post-independence regional conditions, and a scientific fascination with nuclear technologies and power strategies, pushed aside this new area of interest (Banks, 1984). Scholars, reacting to the political environment, joined the "military–industrial" complex spoken of by Eisenhower. Deterrence theorists adopted without question the prevailing ideologies of the "cold war" period, and their ideological assumptions. The theories of international relations that were advanced were theories likely to appeal to those who were professionally engaged in preparations for war, or the deterrence of war by threatening it. War was still casually treated as "the continuation of political intercourse by other means," after Clausewitz, or as diplomacy in another form. The only policy advocated was deterrence by the mutual threat of total destruction (see Rapaport, "Models of Conflict", in de Reuck and Knight (eds), 1966). Grant-giving foundations were caught up in the same environment, and their funds were diverted to strategic studies. The question whether deterrence in practice deters when fundamental needs and values are at stake was not often addressed.

There was also the reaction of peace activists, and peace studies evolved. These were confined to international issues, and there was no theory that related domestic and international conflict. Conflict resolution remained no more than a segment in some courses in international theory studies. The history of thought in most disciplines reflects the contemporary political circumstances, and this is particularly so in respect to thinking about the handling of conflict within and between societies during this period (Dedring, 1976).

Conflict *resolution* is only now coming back into academic programs. It still remains outside the conceptual framework of most politicians and administrators. They continue to legislate and give effect to authoritative decisions for the suppression of the symptoms of conflicts.

What commenced in the 1960s, largely as a response to post-Second World War conditions, was a shift in thinking probably far more fundamental than had previously been experienced over such a short time-span. It is only in the last decade or so, and again thanks to the realities of human protest and the availability of the means of protest, that the nature of this shift in thinking is being studied and assessed. Whereas in the 1960s the focus was on the obvious conflicts associated with independence movements and great power rivalries, in the mid-1980s it became apparent that traditional law-and-order controls were not effective even at the domestic level, thus stimulating at least an interest in problem-solving as policy.

In the curious circular way in which events evolve, conflict resolution was conceived in the early 1960s largely as a response to international conditions, although there was some limited carryover into the domestic field, especially in industrial conditions at the domestic level, and this began in turn to influence once again studies in international relations.

Many have made contributions, and submerged contributions are reappearing (see Book 3). The quality of contributions is remarkable over a few decades. Maslow, for example, is associated with a hierarchy of human needs. But his observations on the relationship between physical and psychological development, and the relationship of this development to social cohesion and stability, are perhaps even more significant. (*The Farther Reaches of Human Nature*, 1976.) These insights are fortuitous because their origins predate any consensus awareness of crisis. The emergence of such studies of human behavior that cut across separate disciplines was a prerequisite to the development of conflict resolution.

Reflecting a change in perspectives Mitchell in 1981 made two contributions, *The Structure of International Conflict* (1981a), and *Peacemaking and the Consultant's Role* (1981b), falling well within a problem-solving conflict resolution framework. In 1987 Sandole and Sandole brought together articles by those who had been contributing to the wider fields of conflict management and problem-solving. A book in 1988, *New Approaches to International Mediation* (Mitchell and Webb (eds)), reflects these trends, especially a final contribution, "Paradigms, Movements, and Shifts" (Sandole). In another important recent contribution Coate and Rosati (1988) have drawn attention to *The Power of Human Needs*.

II
The Political Context

Chapter 7   Navigation Points   109
Chapter 8   The Legitimization of Authorities   123
Chapter 9   Multi-ethnic Societies   137
Chapter 10   The Individual and Society   147
Chapter 11   Constructive Intervention   158

Introduction to Part II

Part I was a survey of the field of conflict, its resolution and provention, and the problems to be faced in their development. Now we look to the political–philosophical underpinning, especially the relations between authorities (at all societal levels) and those over whom authority is exercised, for it is from these that we deduce the processes of conflict resolution and provention. It is this wider subject matter and greater depth that is important in the training of facilitators. This is the prerequisite to knowledge of processes and experience in qualifying the facilitator.

Furthermore, it is these political–philosophical considerations that hold the facilitator within a facilitation role. In practice there is always a temptation to favor certain values, to be prejudiced against some behaviors, and to be influenced by empirical evidence that appears to contradict deductive conclusions. A strong theoretical, logical and philosophical framework is the guard against this happening, and against possibly destructive pragmatic interventions.

The focus on individuals and their ontological needs provides some objective navigation points in thinking about relationships that were missing in classical political philosophy. We lay this foundation in Chapter 7 and discuss the question whether the domination of interests in politics at the expense of problem-solving has been due to an absence of objective policy guidelines.

The greater objectivity in political analysis that needs theory provides, enables us to examine what is perhaps the core problem in human conflict, the legitimization of authorities (Chapter 8). Because multi-ethnic societies raise some special issues of legitimization, we then give consideration to legitimacy and conflict in these societies (Chapter 9).

We have touched several times on the topic of the relationship between the individual and society. The focus on the individual, to which we are led by a study of deep-rooted conflict, raises this classical problem in a different context. After all, the debate between *settlement* or *resolution and provention* of conflict revolves on a judgement whether or not it is expedient to repress conflictual behaviors. From street warfare to conflicts in ethnically divided societies, authorities adopt a pragmatic and usually coercive stance. We must deal with the issue in a politically realistic way, and we seek to do this in Chapter 10.

In this wider context we come to the problem that is of contemporary significance, that of intervention by authorities into personal and social relationships: when is it desirable, when not, and what form should it take if societies are to be peaceful and stable (Chapter 11)?

7 Navigation Points

In Chapter 7 we put forward two propositions: first, that problems of conflict could be tackled more analytically and realistically if there were some objective "navigation points," some agreed explanations of conflict, and a consensus philosophy that pervaded all theories and policies in much the same way as power policies have up to the present; and second, that needs theory provides this objective basis of decision making.

INTEREST POLICIES VERSUS CONFLICT RESOLUTION

It will be recalled that in Part I we dealt at some length with the problem of exponential change, taking population and energy, and also entropy, as examples, and pointed out that personal and public decision making by authorities, by contrast, tended to avoid change and adjustment to altering conditions, thereby leading to conditions conducive to conflict.

We then suggested that the reason for such a reluctance on the part of authorities to adapt to changing circumstances might be, not so much the influence of interests, which certainly appears on the surface to be a major reason, but the absence of any clear alternatives. If there were clear policy guides, clear and known solutions to problems, then it would be more difficult for interest pressures to prevail. If, for example, there are no clear-cut solutions to problems of unemployment, it is difficult for politicians to resist pressures to approve possibly unnecessary defense contracts. Unless it can be shown clearly that juvenile gangs may be a direct consequence of breakdowns in family relations due to an inadequate social infrastructure, then it is difficult to have resources diverted towards education, housing and community development and to tackle the problem at what might be its source.

In the 1980s in countries such as Great Britain and the US there were strong tendencies toward economic and financial policies that had the result of benefiting the already rich, and prejudicing further the already poor. (Some evidence of this is contained in child poverty statistics; see the US Census Bureau survey of incomes analysis as reported in the *New York Times* of 28 February 1989.) Conditions of poverty lead to local violence, theft and social conflict. Such policies could be justified or opposed by contending economic theories. Contending theories usually reflect different value systems and economic goals in addition to differences in analysis. There was no objective basis on which these theories and the policies they suggested could be assessed. In countries where there are already ethnicity discriminations, however, economic and related policies that accentuate existing long-standing class–minority divisions are likely to promote protracted conflicts, whatever their merits might be from the point of view of economic growth.

Where there are divided nations, as in Sri Lanka and Cyprus, or major racial conflicts as in South Africa, there are contending approaches, but policies predominantly reflect a continuing resistance to change by those in control. The continued dominance by those in power, despite the costs of suppressing the activities of those seeking change, suggests an absence of known alternatives by those in power by which they could preserve their legitimate needs.

At an international level there are many examples of military interventions by major powers into situations that they have wrongly defined, and that have resulted in the escalation of international tensions and acts of violence, leading to the need for further costly interventions.

There seems to be an inevitable progression: the emergence of social problems, reactions by treating symptoms in the absence of an understanding of the nature of the problems, the exploitation of the uncertain situations by interest groups, accentuation of the problems, leading to political divisions and ideological–interest stances and pressures that finally destroy the democratic decision making process and any possibility of problem-solving on an objective and analytical basis.

THE SUBJECTIVE AND CONTROVERSIAL NATURE OF POLITICS

To reiterate, the labelling of conflictual behaviors as aggressive, deviant, terrorist, irrational or in some other pejorative way reflects an absence of understanding of the problems concerned. In the absence of understanding of a social problem and how to tackle it, only symptoms can be treated. Even more serious from a policy perspective, if there is no understanding of the problem there is no basis for agreement on policy, and even the treatment of symptoms becomes a matter of controversy. (For example, there was in the late 1980s in the US a superficial controversy whether to treat the drug problem by law enforcement or education about drugs.)

This leads us to conclude that there can be a problem-solving approach only if there is an adequate explanation of conflict, and only if, furthermore, it can be pursued on a non-controversial (that is, non-ideological) basis. Does needs theory provide an explanation of conflict that could be the basis of agreed proventive policies, and of a problem-solving process for the handling of conflicts that do emerge?

The traditional view, which most scholars presently hold, is that politics is necessarily subjective – that is, there are no objective criteria by which norms and policies can be assessed. While there are some commonly held aspirations, such as the greatest good for the greatest number, and equality before the law, there is no means of assessing what is the greatest good, what is the best means of attaining it, and what constitutes equality. As a result, there is no means of assessing whether, for example, the welfare state or the private-enterprise corporate state is any better or worse than any other form of economic organization, or what policies need to be followed to achieve consensus goals within these systems. In the absence of any objective guides, there is no means of defining or determining what policies are just or in the national interest – or, indeed, what meaning can be given to terms such as this. There is no basis for assessing any policy until it has turned out to be a success or a failure.

In no area is there more confusion and less agreement than in the area of conflict management, resolution and provention. The traditional and least controversial approach is, as we argued in Chapter 2, to attach responsibility to those involved, the members of street gangs, or the leader of some state defined as a terrorist state. Their behaviors being the obvious symptoms of whatever the problems are, they as persons must be blamed and punished.

We are led, therefore, to the core problem of politics. If there is a physical phenomenon, such as a flood or a fire, there are investigations out of which agreed policies emerge to deal with the present and, if possible, to prevent future catastrophes. In conflictual relationships, as in policy matters generally where there is a human dimension, including economic issues, there being no agreed explanations of events and behaviors, decision making is inherently controversial. Contending theories provide an opening for ideological and interest differences to emerge and to become the basis of political argument and decision making. Where there is no basis for any agreement, treatment of symptoms is the most that can be expected.

One consequence is that in even the most participatory of societies there is an uncomfortable consensus that, while there can never be agreement among different ideological political parties, there needs to be tolerance of each, the electorate being persuaded by media processes to side with one or another on the basis of some short-term interest. Indeed, a virtue is made of necessity. The multi-party political system is deemed to be a hallmark of modern democracies, despite the fact that it has its origins in subjective disagreements over methods to be employed to bring about even agreed goals – law and order, the greatest good for the greatest number – that are commonly shared.

This is clearly an important issue in the study of conflict, its resolution and provention. How can there be a *science of politics*, or a problem-solving approach to conflict and its provention, and related issues of politics, and how can there be a problem-solving approach to any situation, if there is no objective basis on which an analysis can be made of the issues at stake? Should we not conclude that this is one area in which conflict has to be played out within a power and coercive framework? If we can tame potential conflict by constitutions and conventions, using authoritative power as a back-stop, so much the better. If not, as is the case frequently with class, communal and international relations, should we not expect and prepare for violent conflict?

In accord with this traditional view, that politics are essentially subjective and, therefore, conflictual, authorities – regardless of how established – will, if they are farsighted, cater for human aspirations as much as they think possible. But ultimately it is up to them to decide, from their particular interest or ideological point of view, what is best for all, and what is in the national interest, and to enforce their decisions even at the risk of domestic and international confrontations.

AN UNCOMFORTABLE DOCTRINE

In this traditional perspective of subjective assessment we have to conclude that any one state must be regarded as being led as well as any other, even though we might not like what is going on in some country that has a repressive regime. Many did not like what went on in Germany and Italy in the 1930s, but in this perspective there could be no grounds for criticism. There were, on the contrary, legitimate arguments that could have been used to advocate negotiation rather than war, for example, that the German economic plight that led to a dictatorship was a direct consequence of post-First World War Western policies. There were scholars and allied nations, furthermore, who tended to side with Germany on ideological grounds. Germany was for them a welcome defense against socialism and communism. There was no objective basis on which they or German leadership could be criticized.

In the absence of any agreed basis of assessment, it has to be accepted that it is up to the state authorities to decide policy within their own jurisdictions from their interest and ideological positions, especially if they are duly elected authorities. In this perspective it is necessary to accept repressive regimes as legitimate, perhaps implying that they should be given external support against internal dissent which, indeed, happens extensively in the contemporary world society. Aggressive foreign policies have to be treated as being in the national interest as perceived by policy makers. We have no basis for criticism. Leadership elites have the right and duty to act as they think fit.

In applying this thinking at the international level we must conclude that Morgenthau (1948) was right. A state that has the opportunity to acquire economic and military power should accumulate as much of it as possible, and use it to enforce its will, promote its interests, and prevent any damaging competition or threat, even though this means being aggressive in self-defense. Decision making becomes the straightforward task of acquiring and using power to attain an immediate goal.

Applying this thinking at the domestic level, from family to industry, we must conclude that those with role power should exercise that power to the limit in the pursuit of what they believe to be in the short- and long-term interests of themselves and those over whom they exercise authority.

So we have a problem. On the one hand politics involves subjective decisions, and we should respect the judgements of elites and leaders. On the other hand, in many cases we do not like what we see and experience. Moreover, we witness daily many examples of widespread corruption of authorities or of resistance to authority, posing the question whether opposition is legitimate or not, and in what circumstances.

How do we judge between a benevolent dictator and a coercive elected government? How can we determine when authorities should intervene in the affairs of others, and when not? How can we criticize any government that seeks to dominate in strategic weapons? How can we be analytical and apply conflict resolution or analytical problem-solving processes to a situation that is governed by subjective judgement, and controlled by power?

In trying to deal with this problem there have been many shifts in thought. There have been shifts from so-called "political realism" – that is, unequivocal control by power – to some measure of consideration for politically organized human responses. But these variations remain within what is essentially a power political framework.

There will be a major shift in thought, a genuine paradigm shift, only when there is a movement away from authoritative power as the main focus, for it is this that is the essence of traditional thinking. But is it possible to find another focus, another theory of politics, one that does not rest ultimately on relative power? Is it practical? Are there any trends in this direction?

EMPIRICAL EVIDENCE OF A HUMAN DIMENSION

It does seem that there is a kind of power more influential than the power of authorities, specifically the power of the individual or identity group to resist coercion by authorities. We are aware of confrontations in Sri Lanka, Northern Ireland, Cyprus, Fiji, South Africa and elsewhere, in which the military power of state authorities is successfully confronted by identity groups, even in some cases by groups that are militarily weak. Experience – defeats of powerful regimes, defeats of powerful states, failures of central authorities to control community conflicts – suggests that it is this kind of "power" that is greater in the longer term, and constitutes a more genuine political realism. Parents, teachers, police and industrialists know of this "power," no less than central authorities who struggle to control minorities.

In confrontations, individuals and identity groups also resort to coercive power. As we have seen in Part I, the individual will use all means at his or her disposal to pursue certain needs. Thus we have state violence, held to be legal, confronting unofficial violence, usually labelled by authorities as rebellion or terrorism.

The question that we pose is whether this condition is something societies, including the world society, have to try (against obvious odds) to live with, or is there some way out of this condition? Is it possible to avoid the confrontations of politics by understanding them and adapting institutions and policies accordingly?

SOME RECENT WHISTLE BLOWING

The shifts in thought referred to above have occurred as the result of experience. Now warning whistles are being blown: hold everything, we may have got it wrong. There are limits to effective state or authoritative power.

There is a dynamic in state politics that we do not wholly understand. Authorities could govern with elite control when they had a monopoly of violence. Even slavery was possible. Colonialism was possible, but it is possible no longer. Now even control of the streets within the territories of the nation-state itself is impossible. The exercise of administration by a central authority in multi-ethnic societies is beyond its capabilities. Britain cannot maintain law and order within Northern Ireland. The Soviet central authorities must use force to control demands for autonomy by ethnic minorities. Families, schools, police and communities cannot control widespread drug abuse and violence. There is, in short, a widespread failure in law-and-order policies within and between nation-states.

Where are we if we find that the individual and the identity group are the real locus of power, and the only effective instrument of control? What do we do when we find that politics is not simply the allocation of resources at the discretion of an elected authority, but an allocation that must reflect some specific individual aspirations? Sometimes these aspirations will seem to authorities not to be in the industrial, social or national interest. How are the different viewpoints to be balanced? A different political ball game is involved. Does it require different systems, different decision-making processes, greater decentralization, and different philosophies?

These questions stimulate more constructive thinking. The same empirical evidence that suggests that an erosion of state and other levels of authority is widespread directs attention to individual and group behaviors. It also suggests that some guidelines for authorities are emerging, some rules by which they can operate that may enable them to regain legitimacy and their authoritative role. If these guidelines were to be the basis of policies, societies might be able to move toward a more comfortable and more orderly social system.

There are now scholars in all disciplines blowing the whistle. They warn that we are being led to dangerous and self-defeating policies within and between states because we have been working on a false set of assumptions, some false theories of the nature of politics.

They have been blowing whistles for a few decades now, but have rarely been listened to within their own disciplines or by society generally. Typically, few hear the early whistles because few want to hear. The earth remained flat in the general perception for a long time after it had been found to be round. What the whistle blowers have to say in the field of politics is very threatening to those who follow traditional thought, and who have not studied and understood the changes in thought that have taken place, or the nature of alternative approaches (Banks, 1986).

The result is that elites and the societies they lead hold to their assumptions. They seek to get on with the job even after costly failures have been experienced. This is particularly the case in the handling of complex issues such as those involved in foreign, strategic and economic policies.

THE NEED FOR AUTONOMY

The whistle blowing is across disciplines and in relation to all areas of human behavior. The message is the same: we have assumed the human organism can be forced into molds required by institutions and ideologies, we have assumed that sufficient coercion reliably produces the results sought, and that deterrence deters. We have assumed, furthermore, that the physical environment can be exploited almost indefinitely without harm to living conditions. We have been proved wrong on all these counts.

The reality is that attempts to promote the greatest good for the greatest number of individuals have been based on a false concept of the individual. Policies have suited a small minority of persons who seek material and role gains. The greatest good has been designed for hypothetical individuals, economic and legal "man" and others, leaving the real person alienated and frustrated in most societies.

Whistles are blowing especially in public policy matters, but also in industry, in family relations, in gender relations, in teaching, in *all* authoritative relationships. The warning is that we are on the wrong track. The message is to look at our assumptions and get them right, especially at the international level, before it is too late.

We are not here referring to differences between communism and capitalism, or to differences in ideologies. These are superficial compared to the issues at stake. The whistle is blown to urge that we re-examine assumptions that are being found to be false in *all* authoritiative relationships. The communist–capitalist conflict includes a politically convenient diversion from the more fundamental domestic problems that neither side is able to resolve.

FROM SUBJECTIVITY IN POLITICS TO OBJECTIVE GUIDELINES

If there is simultaneously great ferment in the home, the school, industry, society and world society that cannot be curbed by authoritative coercion, we can deduce that there are some non-random human behaviors at work. If we can discover what these are, then we can discover guidelines for policy, for leadership, for authorities, for interactive behavior generally. We may not know precisely what the ontological human needs are that have to be met, but we do at least know that some exist, and their general nature.

If ontological needs exist it follows that the traditional belief that politics is subjective is false. It is this discovery, this deduction, that is at the core of the contemporary shift in thought. Policy can no longer be justified as arbitrary, determined by ideologies and interests. It is possible to assess 'isms, leadership and systems generally by reference to these needs. We can predict the consequences of policies. If certain human needs are not met, there will be trouble. In some cases there will be political instability and change, in others behaviors that are anti-social and disruptive, including protest violence and frustration addictions such as drug abuse.

POLITICS NOT INHERENTLY CONTROVERSIAL

If politics are not subjective – if, that is, there are some guidelines or navigation points – then politics are not inherently controversial.

Let us dwell for a moment on the thought that politics are not inherently controversial. It is easy to label persons or policies as "conservative," "liberal," "socialist" or something else. There is no need then to try to get at the root of a disagreement. Ideologies provide a convenient way of avoiding thinking about differences and analyzing conflicts. We may be tolerant or intolerant of others who have different ideologies. We do not try to find out where we differ or why we differ, let alone whether we differ on goals.

If, however, we hypothesize the existence of human needs of some kind that have to be satisfied, then we have a basis of analysis. We are no longer justified in saying we differ because of different philosophies or values. That becomes superficial. The more fundamental questions are, do we differ in our definition of the needs that are to be satisfied, do we differ in our means to achieve policy objectives, or do we differ just because we have different interests at stake and would rather not be too analytical?

THE CHALLENGE

Let us see where we are. We are conscious of failure in high policy. We have discovered – to the dismay of authorities at all social levels – that the individual is not infinitely malleable. We have been led to hypothesize the existence of certain human needs or drives that seem to be ontological. We are led, therefore, to believe that there are objective criteria on which to assess systems and policies. This means the end of subjectivity in politics, and theoretically the potential end of controversy in politics. Controversy in politics is then shifted from subjective judgements to controversy over what are the navigation points: what are the guidelines, what are the individual needs that have to be met? We are only at the beginning of this quest (see Burton and Sandole, 1986, in Book 2 in this Series).

So here is the challenge. If there are such guides to policy, such navigation points, then we are forced to substitute analysis and problem solving for authoritative decision making and coercion. This is required at all social levels, from the home to the world society.

It is a challenge because we are forced to be thoughtful and not just ideological. We have to work our way through, step-by-step, questioning assumptions, being clear on the terms and concepts we use so that we are sure we are logical and clear. In theory, if this is done carefully, politics becomes no more controversial than any other situation in which a problem is to be solved!

In this context labels like "liberal," "conservative" and others are irrelevant. The only distinction that can usefully be made is between persons who are prepared to question, to think and to be analytical, and prepared to shift positions in the light of discovery, and persons who are not.

However, there is one applied difference that needs to be noted. It emerges in this transition period in which the nature of politics is not understood. This is the difference between those who wish to use violence to promote change, or to preserve what exists, and those who are prepared to employ problem-solving and conflict resolution processes as the means of change or preservation.

Let it be noted that those who seek change and preservation by violence are the vast majority. All argue that they are responding to the violence of others, and thus justify their own approach. Blacks and whites in South Africa and Basques in Spain take the view that dialogue with state authorities is subversive of their causes. American foreign policy, for example, has been a violent one over many years; covert and overt military aid has been a major ingredient. In none of these situations is there evidence of deliberate analysis, planned problem-solving. This is in accord with traditional power politics beliefs that are widely spread, nationally and internationally. If persons concerned are not aware of any thought system or process other than power thinking and its application, this dedication to violence is understandable.

A QUESTION OF PROCESS

When we assume that there may be some objective basis for public policies leading to the adoption of agreed options, then the important consideration becomes the nature of the processes required to arrive at these options.

In Book 4 in this Conflict Series there are set out procedures to be followed when parties to disputes interact in a problem-solving setting. These assume that a thorough analysis of the situation, leading to an agreed definition of it, can lead to deduced options that would meet the needs of all concerned. The justification for this assumption is that there are needs held in common which are not of a kind to require a win–lose outcome.

The processes required in public policy making are not dissimilar. Indeed, little-by-little, many societies are moving toward them. The growth of joint parliamentary committees, served by staff that investigate problems, public hearings at which specialists give evidence, and public enquiries leading to professional reports, are part of the analytical process. Depending on the integrity and professionalism of those concerned, interest groups are less likely to exercise influence than is the case when public policy decisions are taken merely as the result of debate behind closed doors, or by the exercise of political party voting.

This is a small beginning, and organized pressure groups find means of exercising their influence. For the process to go forward it would be necessary for adminstrators and advisers not to be appointed for political reasons, for this prejudges issues prior to analysis, but to be chosen only on the basis of their knowledge and experience in their own areas of specialization, and on their abilities to respond to analytical interactions. Unfortunately there appears to be a movement in the opposite direction as policy failures increase, giving rise to more and more interest and ideological pressures.

These considerations open up even wider areas. The need to upgrade public administration so as to attract the best of advisers, the need for far more emphasis on the nature of problem-solving at schools and universities, the need for ongoing non-governmental monitoring of events by scholars, the media and private bodies across national, class and cultural boundaries, the need for research into human behaviors, are just some of the background requirements of public policy making that would help to reduce the environment of conflict, and to tackle existing conflict situations analytically.

THE TWO-TRACK APPROACH

This anti-power approach is not adopted for ideological or value reasons. It is for reasons of political realism. Promotion and preservation of whatever ultimate goals we seek to promote or preserve are most surely and most economically achieved by problem-solving procedures that state goals precisely and take step-by-step moves toward them. Violence has unforeseen consequences. It is costly and inefficient, and frequently dysfunctional in terms of goal achievement. We are concerned with how to make the practice of politics more predictable and more realistic.

The approach could be termed radically conservative: the attempt to preserve values, societies and civilizations through non-violent and non-costly change. As will be seen, the focus is, therefore, finally on change within systems by decision making processes, rather than on system change brought about by external forces.

This is not to argue that institutions of defense, police, courts, etc., which are all within the power paradigm, are irrelevant. Rather, the approach involves two tracks. Track 1 is the formal one, the official one, the law-and-order one. Defense, police, controls, regulations will always be necessary even in the most efficient of systems for there is always the need to protect the public interest and safety in the here-and-now.

Track 2 is the analytical track that explores options and feeds into the first track. Once a street riot occurs it probably has to be handled by police on the streets, but simultaneously there is a need for direct contacts with those with the causal grievances. The Northern Ireland conflict could be handled better by interaction between the parties leading to a better understanding both of grievances and possible options, rather than by policies that discourage interactions and which keep the parties feuding.

THE SEPARATION OF SYMPTOM TREATMENT AND PROBLEM SOLVING

This kind of track 2 is only beginning to emerge. In the meantime, and for historical reasons, there is a separation of the two in training and in practice. The United Nations peace-keeping forces of Cyprus are equipped to keep the peace, but not to try to resolve the local conflicts that are symptoms of the wider problem. Police are not trained to do more than treat symptoms. Defense departments are required to send military advisers to assist a threatened government, but not to give the kind of advice that would reduce the threat.

These two tracks cannot come together until there is a changed consensus, some widespread understanding of the nature of conflictual behavior, and of problem-solving processes that are relevant. But the importance of policy navigation points is even greater for conflict provention. The major challenge that societies face is not the resolution of conflict, but its provention by institutions and policies that are not themselves conflict making.

THEORY AND PRACTICE

We give attention to navigation points, to the possibility that there may be some objective basis for public policy making to be derived from an adequate theory of behavior, as the appropriate opening of this exploratory Part III. Those working in the field of conflict studies tend to be preoccupied with process, and very largely with pragmatic means of dealing with particular situations. This is important in some situations. Having in mind, however, the exponential rate of growth in the incidence of conflict at all social levels, from family violence to international conflict, it is an unproductive focus. It is the environment of conflict that needs to be tackled.

The two approaches are not incompatible in practice. If administrators in industry, in local government, in central government, in national and international institutions, and if political leaders also were aware of analytical problem-solving processes as a viable option to power negotiation, bargaining, containment, coercion and other traditional practices, each would be contributing to the wider process, probably to the advantage of those to whom they were responsible. This is the deduction to be made from the hypothesis that there are objective points of reference on which to base policies.

8 The Legitimization of Authorities

Whether because of the influence of interests and ideologies, or because authorities see no solution to problems with which they are confronted, their failure to make possible the satisfaction of human needs and aspirations leads to loss of legitimization of their authority. Once this occurs authorities have no option, other than resignation, but to be more defensive and more oppressive. Situations of conflict, even interpersonal relations, typically reflect role behaviors that are defensive–aggressive because they lack a legitimized foundation.

THE CONCEPTUALIZATION OF LEGITIMIZATION

The legitimization of roles is a precondition of cooperative and harmonious relationships. The absence of respect and reciprocal relationships almost defines a conflictual relationship. Yet, for reasons we shall discover, legitimization has not featured in the study of conflict and its management.

Let us look as this term and its origins, for once again we can then obtain an appreciation of the way in which tradition and institutions have controlled our thinking, and prevented alternative conceptualization of issues fundamental to our concerns with conflict and its resolution.

The term "legitimate" goes back to the fifteenth century, and its original meaning is clear: that which is legal, normal, regular, conforming with law and consensus norms. "Legitimate" as a verb means to make legal. Then comes "legitimitize," to make legitimate. In the nineteenth century "legitimize" came into use, as a substitute for legitimitize.

We do not find "legitimized" as an adjective used to describe whether a "legitimate" authority had, in practice, the support of those over whom the authority was exercised. Indeed, even in contemporary writings "legitimization" is rarely given this meaning. We may hear of repressive governments, but their legitimacy, that is their legality, is not put into question.

An authority has a legal status when, (1) it is seen to be in full control of those over whom it exercises authority, and when, (2) it is recognized as the legal authority by other authorities. While these principles apply generally to all social levels from the family to the international, they find formal expression in International Law that defines the legality of states in terms of their effective control and their recognition by other states.

From an historical perspective, effective control and recognition by others of this control are principles that could be expected to emerge. Societies have evolved in competition with neighboring societies. Effective control, including an ability to defend, and recognition of this by others, remain the main criteria of legality.

It is understandable, in this historical perspective, that it has not been, and is still not, a requirement of legality that authorities have the support of those over whom they exercise authority. Whether respected or not the parent has a legal control over children. Even when resisted by a significant proportion of the population, the national authority and its police and army have a legal role. Despite the objections of some countries in special circumstances, and their attempts sometimes to observe elections, it is not necessary for a government to be "legitimized" in order to be accepted by the United Nations as the "legal" representative of the country.

THE CASE FOR LEGALITY

In practice the need for legitimization is not widely accepted by authorities at any social level. The parent who exercises control in a coercive fashion justifies this by reference to superior knowledge and experience, social obligation and the responsibilities and rights of parenthood. State authorities in the global society – including members of the United Nations – include a large number of military dictatorships and externally supported regimes that maintain themselves in office by repressive measures. Leaderships and elites operating in these conditions frequently argue that this is in the national interest. In this view, the ordinary people do not have either the knowledge or the common interest perspective that are required for government.

While this issue has been debated throughout classical political philosophy, it has not been an important political issue while control has been effective. In contemporary times, public opinion polls tend to be rejected by leadership when they conflict with leadership policies on the grounds that elites know best. This may well be so. It is a proposition that needs to be examined, and one to which we will return later. Let us merely note here that the status of "legality" traditionally and currently does not require "legitimization" – that is, the support of those over whom authority is exercised.

Indeed, there are many occasions on which authorities claim the right to govern even when the recognized tests of legality itself are not met. Once established and recognized, authorities tend to retain their legal status, even when they lose effective control. At the time of writing the Government of Cyprus is not in control of the Turkish areas in the North, and the Government of Sri Lanka is not in control of Tamil regions. Yet they still claim to be the legal authorities, and are still recognized as such by the international community. These governments are the members of the United Nations representing all peoples on these islands, even though they cannot exercise political control over a proportion of them.

It has always been the case that authorities recognized as legal have difficulty in maintaining effective control without the employment of at least some force. In classical terms, central authorities have a right to the monopoly of force because it is an assumption of classical theory that some coercion is necessary and justified for purposes of the common good and the preservation of law and order.

As a consequence a tolerant view has always been taken of effective control for the reason that all authorities are vulnerable. The UK Government is not in control of areas in Northern Ireland, and after dusk authorities in the US are not in control of sections of some cities. Indeed, there are few, if any, governments in the world society that claim unqualified control, yet they claim to be, and are recognized as, the legal authorities. While international law maintains the principle of control as a prior condition of international recognition, in practice the world society accords recognition even though there is not effective control.

In reality, therefore, control is not a necessary test of legality. Legality is accorded to governments that are not in effective control despite their widespread use of military policing and violence.

CONFLICT AS NON-LEGITIMIZED RELATIONSHIPS

In the world society there are no defined limits to the force that legal authorities may exercise. As a result the employment of intimidation, surveillance, coercion, violence, terrorism, torture, incarceration and exile by legal authorities is in practice tolerated by the international community of states. Those who are responsible are not only formally "recognized" by others, but frequently they, as the legal authorities, are also supplied with the means of repression and assisted in eliminating organized oppositions.

An erosion of authority – that is, challenge to effective control – is a symptom and precondition of conflict, likely to be violent, between authorities and communities, and among communities and their members. A growing erosion of authority within many states has been prompted by the aftermath of colonialism. Colonial boundaries, especially those drawn as the result of wars, in many cases cut through tribal boundaries, and these divisions have sometimes been accentuated by forced migrations. Many post-colonial states are, therefore, multi-ethnic states. There are currently many post-colonial situations in which authorities have been accorded formal "recognition," but in which no reasonable observer would attribute effective control by the legal authority.

Conflict, therefore, can meaningfully be defined as a situation in which authority or power is being exercised without the sanction or approval of those over whom it is being exercised. This definition applies to all social levels, parental authority, industrial authority, religious authority, communal authority and state authority. It applies even to some forms of interpersonal conflict, as this often involves attempts by one person to exercise some unacceptable control over another.

The notion, legitimization of authority, brings to attention a phenomenon that is as old as civilizations, at least as old as positive law, but which has been pushed aside by lawyers, by ruling elites and by the powerful. In any conflict situation, whether it be matrimonial, industrial, communal or international, there is this core problem of legitimacy of roles. The matrimonial partner, the parent, the business manager, the chairperson of a meeting, the political leader, are all enacting roles based on tradition, selection or functions that carry with them some degree of authority. Harmony and discord depend on how these roles are enacted, in particular on the degree of reciprocity experienced between those exercising authority and those over whom it is exercised. If those affected value the mutual relationship it will be stable. If there is no experienced reciprocity there will be an erosion of authority. Workers, for example, may tolerate repressive authoritative management if there are adequate rewards and no alternative job opportunities. In due course, however, resistance and instability in the relationship are likely.

In analysing conflict, and seeking its resolution, therefore, we clearly need a term that conveys the condition of reciprocity, or its absence, between authorities and those over whom authority is exercised. We need a term that distinguishes authority based on reciprocity from pure legality, because reciprocity is such an important element in human and political relationships. Hence we give these special meanings to "legitimized" and "non-legitimized."

RECIPROCITY AND LEGITIMIZATION

Legality, a concept that relates to an authoritative role, one that seeks to preserve institutions, is a static concept. Legitimized status, on the other hand, is a description of the quality of authority, the quality of reciprocal relationships between authorities and those over whom authority is exercised. Because of constantly changing political circumstances, legitimization must be treated as a dynamic phenomenon.

Unlike legality, legitimization cannot be maintained by force. It is continuously eroded by change as environmental conditions and reciprocal demands alter, and can be maintained only by the dynamic process of change and adjustment to change. The study and practice of legitimization is, therefore, the study and practice of change and adjustment to change. The dynamic nature of a condition of legitimization is its key feature: adjustments in a continuous flow in response to continuous changes.

There is, thus, a major difference between the two concepts, and major differences in the philosophies and policies that relate to each. Legality has associated with it the traditional notions of an authority with the monopoly of violence, the right to govern, the obligation to obey, loyalty to a sovereign or formal leader right or wrong, elitism, the common good and the national interest as interpreted by elites, and the use of violence in the defense of institutions.

Legitimization, on the other hand, stresses the reciprocal nature of relations with authorities, the support given because of the services they render, and respect for legal norms when these are legitimized norms. The use of state violence is a symptom of lost legitimization and the need for changed policies.

The test of legitimization is not necessarily representation. There can be benevolent dictators, though the human need for participation (an exercise of control) would seem to suggest that such a situation cannot be permanent. The test is the reciprocity that is established, the degree to which persons will accept even laws that cut across their interests because of more fundamental values to be gained from the system as managed by authorities.

THE PHENOMENON OF CHANGE

Change and adjustment to change is not a subject that is relevant in a traditional power setting. Yet it is the key to legitimization, and, therefore, to harmonious social relationships (Burton, 1962).

Change is of two types. There is *primary change* – that is, change over which there can be little or no human control, such as the weather, population increase and resource scarcity. Primary change also includes human activities which are inevitable, such as discovery, invention, innovation, changes in culture and in thinking.

There is also *secondary change* – that is, responses to primary change, or the introduction of some policy that alters the political, social, or even physical environment.

The difference between the two types of change is significant for there is a far greater capacity by persons to adjust to consequences of primary change than to man-made change. There can be widespread suffering as the result of an earthquake or some other natural disaster without adversarial responses. Far less suffering arising out of a deliberate human act, such as a curb on freedom, a protectionist tariff, or industrial damage to the environment, evokes hostile responses. In secondary changes the cause or source of the hardship can be perceived and targeted.

This leads us to another concept, the *cumulative need for change* when it is resisted. A legal authority that does not have a clearly legitimized status, and that relies on coercion to maintain its legal status, tends to employ more and more coercion rather than to adjust to demands made upon it. Primary change tends to be a continuous process. It cannot be stopped. If secondary change is designed to avoid adjustments to altered conditions, the accumulation of required change that occurs grows beyond the capabilities of the system, thus forcing system breakdown and crises, and sometimes unplanned and dysfunctional change. Revolutions could fall into this category.

Secondary change can, clearly, be positive or negative in its impact.

In Chapter 12 we will be referring to restrictive and constructive intervention to signify attempts to resist change, and attempts to adjust to it. There may be an absorption of the consequences of change by adjustment, for example, the retraining and relocation of labor after some major shift in market conditions. On the other hand, as an example of negative secondary change, there may be deliberate steps taken to shift the burden of change on to others, as when protective tariffs are imposed on imports after some market or technological change. Placing the burden of adjustment on others is a form of secondary change likely to generate conflict.

It can be seen that a condition of peace in any set of relationships is a function of adjustment to change. It is not a static condition of equilibrium, for there can be no such condition except that produced over a short term by the use of force to prevent change or to prevent adjustment to change.

This observation has an important bearing on processes of conflict resolution. Traditionally mediators have endeavoured to arrive at compromises within existing role and institutional constraints. This is the *management* of conflict. Our analysis suggests that in the case of deep-rooted conflict such compromises merely put off the day of reckoning. They do not face up to the realities of the need for change in policies and institutions, and even in role occupancy. Problem-solving of this order is a far more difficult task to accomplish, and can be achieved only by processes that enable realistic costing by those concerned of the consequences of their resistance to change and of their adjustment to change.

A SHIFT IN THOUGHT

In contemporary times the authority of the state, and of other institutions, has eroded almost universally. The authority and power of the state is no longer the main reference point. The explanation of why societies have moved from systems of slavery, to feudalism, to industrial we–they relations, and why they are now moving away from all forms of dominance, including gender and race discriminations, is not to be found in the lack of coercive power of authorities. It is to be found in resistance by modern technological means to authorities that do not have legitimized support.

In other words, the explanation of historic trends, and of current situations, is to be found in the drives and needs of individuals and the groups with which they identify to achieve their full development. It is the individual struggle for identity, for personal security, for recognition, for stimulus, for distributive justice, that has in the past, and is now to an even greater degree, thanks to the availability of means of violence and of communications, eroding the power of non-responsive institutions and authorities.

It is in this framework that we should be analyzing the defensive posture of nations, and their fears of one another. The sense of absence of control, the sense of lack of direction, the sense of system failure and impending change, that are the consequence of the inexorable pursuit of human needs, give rise to fears of change and the costs of adjustment to change. It creates hostile responses from those whose immediate interests are in resisting change. This is a type of resistance to change that finally contributes to the destruction of those institutions and values it seeks to preserve.

THE DILEMMAS OF LEADERSHIP

We are pointing to a dilemma leaders face — regardless of the type of society. Either they cater for human needs at the possible expense of what they interpret to be societal or national interests, or they pursue the latter at the risk of losing legitimization. Chinese leaderships, amongst others, have had in recent years to face this dilemma on several occasions. On a smaller scale it is a usual one in all societies.

The dilemma is more acute in societies in which there are organized pressure groups that have to be satisfied, sometimes at the expense of more pressing welfare, educational, health and other developmental needs. Leadership is caught between its own notions of the national interest, the pressures of interest groups and the longer-term responses of the electorate at large.

Even though individual drives may have been behind the erosion of authority over the ages, we cannot assume that non-legitimized authorities have no moral and philosophical justification for asserting their authority, by force if necessary. Whether it be a rationalization or not on the part of elites, the fact is that the majority of political elites in democratic systems assume that it is their moral duty to enforce law and order and to ensure conformity with certain moral values.

Authorities presiding over change have an additional and special dilemma: risk the consequences of their repressive policies, or risk failure to consolidate the new or altered system. In the case of Poland in the 1980s, workers and unions who opposed aspects of the centralized system, were not necessarily in opposition to a planned economy, or some welfare-state form of political control. But they did resist the restrictions that were being imposed on their freedoms of all kinds. Authorities, on the other hand, fear that such freedoms would lead to system change, even change that those resisting do not desire.

In all cases of sudden and far-reaching system change, both interests and values may be destroyed. Inevitably there are endeavours to regenerate or repossess. This is the case even when the change is from some repressive feudal system to a more liberal one, as was demonstrated in the Philippines after the fall of President Marcos. The change to a new system itself requires unrelenting control until institutions are consolidated and until those whose interests have been destroyed accept the new system. In contemporary world conditions this takes time as some external interests are likely to give support to those who are resisting change. This is an important source of conflict. It is an inevitable consequence of revolutionary change rather than some process by which goals and tactics are defined and agreed.

The threat to authorities is apparent in South Africa and in many, if not a majority of other countries. It is no less present and real in even the most apparently harmonious of societies. As between countries, comparisons are a matter of degree and interpretation. Every state has its own legitimization problems. Each makes a case for control by the central authority of any dissident political movements that seek to promote the separate cultural identity of groups within the nation. Each can interpret international law in its support. Each can reinforce its position with some special ideological expositions that justify particular applications. What appears to be different in modern times is that authorities can no longer manage conflicts by relying on coercion as the ultimate remedy.

The major task today in almost every society is the management, by whatever means are available, of threat to the legitimization, and finally to the legality, of authority. Naturally elites seek to preserve their interests; but they also rationalize and claim to be combatting alien influences, unacceptable permissiveness and a breakdown of orderly society.

SYSTEM LEGITIMIZATION

Authorities are helped in their endeavours to maintain their own legitimization through system legitimization. There are many examples of authorities, elected to office, who pursue unpopular and widely unacceptable policies that were not mentioned in their original mandate. They are protected by system legitimization: that is, the system by which authorities are removed and others are elected is so valued that there is tolerance between elections of high levels of non-legitimization.

There are, however, limits to which authoritative role occupants can take advantage of system legitimization. We are accustomed to an abuse of role in the early stages of an electoral term, followed by compromises before an election. We are also accustomed to the employment of misinformation, foreign adventures and other tactics designed to distract attention from domestic problems and failed policies. These are usually short-lived, though sometimes very costly, means of protracting threatened role occupancy.

THE MEASUREMENT OF LEGITIMIZATION

Like many useful concepts, including justice, freedom and others, we have no measure of legitimization. We may believe that the Government of Sweden is more legitimized than the Government of Haiti. But we have no precise definition of it and no operational measure of it.

Taking an overall view of the Swedens and the Haitis of this world, and then looking at whatever statistics at present exist that could have a bearing on the notion, we find that there are some possible measures of legitimization, even though they were not designed for this purpose. For example, catering for the education and health of a population is seeking to promote some basic human needs. Education, however, tends in many countries to be primarily for the privileged: typically there is a large proportion of the total educational budget spent on a relatively few people. Health expenditure is less discriminatory and, indeed, tends to benefit the underprivileged who are those who are most likely to need health care. Some statistics available, however, do not include private health expenditures, and this makes comparisons difficult. The figures for infant mortality do seem to offer a measure that accords with subjective assessments of

Swedens and Haitis. The first ten countries in the low infant mortality league are Sweden, Japan, Denmark, Iceland, Norway, Finland, Netherlands, Switzerland, Australia and Canada. The UK is fourteenth, and the US eighteenth (see Sivard, 1988).

We could adopt a composite figure for education and health, and then we would find Sweden, Norway, Denmark, Canada, Switzerland, the US, Denmark, Iceland, Australia, Saudi Arabia and West Germany in the lead. We need some measure if only to clarify the meaning of the term, but in the meantime must be content with a somewhat subjective conception, but one based on the notion of human needs, itself lacking a quantitative or operational definition.

THE REALITIES OF THE POLITICAL CLIMATE

The perspective of legitimization helps us to define the political climate and the political framework in which conflicts are to be resolved. Unless we have a clear and realistic perspective of the essential ingredients of the political climate necessary for the avoidance of conflict, it will not be possible to be realistic about means of handling conflict in a particular situation.

The type of political system may not be an important consideration. As a system one may not be more conflictual than another. It is the type of institutions within a system that determines levels of social conflict. There is no reason to believe that a planned system is necessarily any more or less conflictual than an unplanned one. Both must adjust to change. Both, therefore, require measures of constructive intervention, and both must avoid certain types of intervention that are dysfunctional within the system concerned (see Chapter 10).

As a consequence, conflict resolution processes are apt to focus on different institutions in different systems. For example, if there were a centrally planned socialist system, with adequate controls of behavior, conflict resolution processes would have a special role in determining relationships with authorities, and in longer-term planning designed to satisfy human needs within such a centrally planned framework. If there were a free enterprise system with little central government control, conflict resolution would be far more concerned with dealing with localized disputes and, over a longer term, establishing norms of behavior that would govern relationships generally.

In practice, neither of these environments is likely to dominate in the future. They are part of the past. At both the domestic and international levels we must now anticipate further developments in local control, identity-group control, including ethnic and special interest groups and, as conditions become more competitive, even extended "family" control of the kind presently represented by gangs and mafia groups. This development is already a major element in the US, and is likely to become general as populations increase, as identity groups demand recognition, and as central authoritative controls become less effective (see a contribution by Rubenstein in Book 3).

In short, to be politically realistic we have to assume less and less central control, and more and more local and identity group influence, with a strong tendency toward short-term goals. Longer-term planning, as it affects ecology, resource distribution, equal opportunities, education, health, and other services associated in the past with the role of central authorities, can be assumed to be a past phase in political organization. While within and between states strictly functional arrangements -- for example, air traffic controls, communication agreements, ecological controls -- will increase, it will be smaller and smaller identity units that will be interacting within the framework provided. This will place a greater burden on local authorities and community organizations, and decision making at all social levels. Some consensus knowledge of "navigation points," and interactive decision making will become an essential precondition of harmonious relationships.

THE SEARCH FOR PROCESS

There are many individuals and groups who act non-rationally, that is without due regard for their own longer-term interests. They thereby may create situations of non-legitimization. This is both understandable and inevitable. In any evolving situation, the more advantaged seek to profit in the absence of strong cultural sharing norms, and these rarely persist in large communities where there is an absence of face-to-face relationships. In large industrial societies, positive law ensures that those who identify with the state and its power will prosper, even at the expense of others.

In this evolutionary perspective it is no solution to replace one elite by another. It is no solution to replace one failed system by another. What we seek is change in existing systems to policies that cater for human needs, including needs for valued relationships. It is the resultant system or systems that will predictably dominate, if the human race survives this present transition stage. They will be systems that ensure both individual development and, also, because of values attached to relationships, the collective social good.

Our problem is that we do not yet have the means of change so that the necessary accommodations can be made. The traditional law and order framework that favors the status quo is not suited to the tasks ahead, nor are the "weaker forms" of conflict management, such as negotiation and mediation, that evolved with the failure of judicial settlements. We have to move away from management of change designed to prevent change, towards a recognition of the need for change in certain determined directions – determined, not by ideology, but by the objective criterion of needs satisfaction.

Not so long ago, it was believed that there were no guidelines for policy, that goals were subjective and that ideologies could not be assessed. That was the case when the state authority was seen to be supreme, and when the preservation of the state, its ideologies and the roles of its elites were the main goals of politics. Now we are entering another phase of history. We are seeing that the individual is the unit of explanation of social and political developments. It is political realism that the individual and identity groups, not the state, are finally the locus of power. Ideologies, value judgements and subjective judgements generally of what is the common good, of what is justice and freedom, are being pushed aside by the objective fact of human needs, especially the need for identity, that will be pursued regardless of costs to self and to society. Justice and freedom must now be defined with reference to human needs, not authoritative norms. This is why the notion of legitimization must be a core concept in political philosophy.

This raises disturbing questions about the role and power of special-interest, extended family and even illegal groups, that owe their role and power to the degree to which they satisfy identity needs. They attach little value to their relationships with the wider society, or to its norms of behavior. These are in behavioral terms no different from street gangs. Like street gangs, their existence reflects a failure of society to provide means of identity and development within its framework. This is the major issue that societies, national and the international, will face in the future.

The concept of legitimization enables us to predict directions of change, to interpret empirical data differently, to give a more precise meaning to the language of politics, to assess the relevance of political institutions and policies, to determine the nature and extent of government intervention required, and to find those processes of conflict resolution that lead to peaceful change.

9 Multi-ethnic Societies

ETHNICITY AND OTHER IDENTITY PROBLEMS

Perhaps there is no more challenging contemporary problem than conflicts in multi-ethnic societies. They account for most of the protracted violent conflicts in the world society. They are not only destructive of the societies directly affected, but spill over into the international society.

These divided societies are a special case of non-legitimization, as discussed in Chapter 8. In this case the absence of legitimization is so apparent, and those who identify with organized oppositions to authorities are so united, that violence and protracted conflict is almost inevitable.

Protracted conflict is even more likely in those cases in which the minority happens to have the dominant forces with which to control the majority, as in South Africa and Fiji. Whereas a subjugated minority usually seeks limited goals, such as the end of discriminations and some limited means of cultural autonomy, a controlling minority assumes that it has everything to lose by being absorbed into a majority-rule system.

Because of the predominant notion of majority government as being democratic, the international community tends to be more sympathetic to those authorities that reflect a majority, even though they repress the minority, than with those that are minorities defending themselves against the threat of majority rule. Numbers, however, seem hardly an appropriate criterion on which to assess these situations: both are situations of conflict in which majorities and minorities have similar goals, that is the promotion or preservation of their identities. Neither is more "right" or "wrong" than the other: there is a problem to be solved, and taking sides by coercive interventions is not helpful.

Frequently one or both sides are given external support for strategic or ideological reasons, or because elsewhere there are sympathetic peoples of the same ethnic origin, as a result of the way in which colonial boundaries were drawn and as a result of past migrations. Usually there are combinations of these conditions, as is the case in the Middle East. Such protagonists often have, therefore, in addition to modern weapons of resistance, the prospect of external assistance.

The likely result is costly and protracted conflict, the disintegration of the economy as well as of the society, and finally a threat to the values that were to be preserved by the original resistance to change.

So far there has been no solution to any major multi-cultural or multi-ethnic conflict. Ethnic and cultural conflicts persist and either become an on-going part of a social–political system, or erupt, leading to violence and the destruction of the system. At best such conflicts can be contained by peace-keeping forces, such as have operated for twenty years in Cyprus. Because of migrations, world communications that report the resistances of others in similar circumstances, and the availability of weapons, the global problem becomes more, and not less, general. Why has there been this failure to deal with such a widespread, potentially universal problem?

AN ISSUE OF IDENTITY

Societies that are split by ethnic divisions are important analytically because they throw light on the nature of other identity struggles that persist in societies that regard themselves as mono-ethnic or integrated. Class conflicts within societies have the same features: there is an identity group of persons facing the same problems of deprivation and perhaps discrimination that provide some degree of security, and promote class loyalty. At the same time, placing ethnic conflict in the same analytic framework as class and other divisions within a society throws light on the nature of ethnic conflicts.

Treating class, ethnicity and other forms of internal conflicts as separate phenomena diverts attention away from their essential characteristics and causes. Members of ethnic minority communities usually experience the same discriminations as do members of less advantaged income groups. For purposes of political analysis, use of the concept of "identity group" helps to focus on the core issues involved, and is, therefore, more useful than trying to differentiate between class, ethnicity, cultural, minority, or other underprivileged groups within a society on the basis of their specific characteristics. The problems that emerge are behaviorally the same. Each case involves the individual pursuit of acceptance, sought through a relevant identity group. Furthermore, the focus on an identity need rather than on the specific features or demands of a group, draws attention to the nature of the social–political problems that are inherent in divided societies, and the non-discriminatory or separate structures and institutions that are required for their solution.

THE LEGITIMIZATION PROBLEM

Neither the preservation of majority authoritative roles, nor of values sought by minority communities, is promoted in practice by adherence to the traditional notions of majority rule, (which, it so happens, emerged in societies that were mono-ethnic). Under that system both majorities and minorities suffer, as conflict is inevitable. A far more sophisticated form of democracy is required, one that meets the requirements of legitimization, and does not rest only on numbers.

Liberal political thinkers sometimes have difficulty, as do traditional Marxists, in coming to terms with the realities of multi-ethnicity. In a typical liberal view, race and culture should not prevent societies being integrated: multi-ethnic and multi-cultural societies should not be treated as special cases. The classical notion of democracy, including non-discimination and universal representation, should prevail. Majority government should provide whatever safeguards are necessary in the short term to protect minority rights; but the constitutional framework should provide for an integrated society as the ultimate goal.

The Marxist view is somewhat more realistic in that it tends to equate ethnicity with class, and anticipates that non-discrimination and shared development will eliminate ethnic tensions. To some degree this is the case: underdevelopment promotes discrimination between ethnic communities in the struggle for existence. Unfortunately, there is little prospect of development either in the underdeveloped world or the developed world on a scale that could promote QOL to an extent sufficient to overcome problems of discrimination, and to make possible the satisfaction of human needs.

Underdevelopment, moreover, is only part of the picture. It merely brings to the fore tensions that are present in developed societies where there is multi-ethnicity. Even controlled economies cannot avoid tendencies toward discrimination. Furthermore, competitive leaderships, which are a feature of communal clashes, trade on ethnic differences.

Neither the liberal nor the Marxist view attaches sufficient importance to the realities of ethnic and cultural differences, and the sense of insecurity experienced by minorities, and the drives for autonomy. Liberalism in particular reflects middle-class values, and the relative economic security experienced by political leaders and intellectuals even in minority communities. Integration is assisted when persons of different ethnic background have had identical or similar educational and professional experiences. There are leaders and scholars in Lebanon, for example, who sought an integrated society and opposed the separate organization of communities. But integration, as a solution, is a limited possibility because it ignores the fears and anxieties of disadvantaged peoples generally who experience personal security only within their autonomous communal setting.

In practice, even when leaders and others avow integration, the dynamics of politics, supported by the classical idea of democracy, gives rise to majority policies that make second-class-citizens of minorities. Elites of the majority or more powerful group are pressured to seek to preserve their cultural values – for example, the use of the majority language as the official language. They take advantage of their majority or power role, and the legality that recognition gives them, to ensure that they are in full control. The more they exercise their authority to this end, the less it is respected by other ethnic communities, and the greater are the resistances, and the less is the legitimized status of authorities. The long-term goal may be an integrated and non-discriminatory society, but the coercive means employed in attaining this goal are likely to be destructive of it.

INTEGRATION THROUGH SEPARATION

Probably the only means of preserving cultural and consensus values, and the only means of integration in the long term, is through local autonomy in the short term. Separation promotes a sense of security from which there can be cooperative transactions between communities, leading finally to a higher degree of functional cooperation, if not integration.

This, indeed, is the process through which integration even of communities of the *same* ethnic origin is also most peacefully achieved. The Commonwealth of Australia is one example of an integration that emerged out of separate states. They were drawn together by common functional bonds, and integration ultimately presented few problems. Even now there are institutional devices for sharing between more and less economically favored states.

The political reality is that in many cases multi-ethnic societies become socially and politically divided, and it is almost universally necessary to accord local autonomy in areas that are predominantly occupied by ethnic communities. It is dysfunctional in divided multi-ethnic societies to try to impose a central authority. The US was greatly misled in 1985 in its endeavours to bring stability to Lebanon by trying to help establish a strong central authority. Governments in divided societies make the same mistake in themselves trying to enact the role of a strong central authority, as experiences in Cyprus and Sri Lanka have shown.

Local autonomy would probably not be necessary if initially there existed the conditions necessary for integration – non-discrimination in all aspects of social and economic life, including effective political roles. In practice, this is rarely the case. The majority of critical situations in the world society are a carryover from colonial days in which an external authority employed minorities in the maintenance of law and order, taking advantage of the desire of minorities to use the colonial power as a protection against the majority – a policy that came to be known as "divide and rule." With independence the majority–minority fears and clashes quickly came to the surface, especially when majority-based constitutions were imposed by the outgoing colonial power.

Attempts to make central authorities viable by power-sharing processes that give to minorities representation they might not otherwise achieve, can also be dysfunctional. Power sharing as a means to legitimization creates more problems than it solves. On the one hand, it underlines, if anything, the minority status of smaller ethnic communities and, on the other, it leaves the majority with a sense of threat and injustice. It was tried in Cyprus, and its failure led to the rejection of the constitution by the majority, and a refusal by the minority to cooperate within an altered constitution.

Yet the notion of majority rule prevails, usually at great cost. Authorities do not readily give up their jurisdictions. They employ as their support misinterpretations of Western classical political theories, emphasizing the rights of majorities to govern.

ZONAL SYSTEMS

We have made a distinction between needs that are universal and inalienable, such as security, participation, identity and recognition, on the one hand, and interests that can be traded, on the other.

This distinction suggests the nature of the political structures that might be appropriate in multi-ethnic societies. Universal needs of cultural identity and security would necessitate the separate entity of confessional (Lebanon), cultural (Cyprus), and tribal (South Africa) groups. The establishment of separate political entities makes possible the cultural security and the effective political participation even of small minorities, and the reciprocal recognition of each unit. In many cases such a cultural separation does not necessarily require separate nation–states, or eliminate free movement between separate zones by nationals of the state.

Indeed, formal separation is frequently not even desired, nor is formal integration with other groups of the same ethnic origin. Facilitated exchanges took place at University College London, Centre for the Analysis of Conflict, in 1966 between Greek and Turkish Cypriots (Burton, 1984). During these it became clear, and events since have confirmed, that the Turkish minority of Cyprus valued its relationships with the Greek majority. The problem was to find the means of preserving this relationship while maintaining a separate autonomy. Confessional entities in Lebanon valued the unique culture that evolved as a result of Lebanon being the meeting ground of Christianity and Islam (Azar, 1986). The Tamils in Sri Lanka did not seek some special relationship with Tamils in India, but were not prepared to be a minority in a traditional majority-government society. In each such case the goal is to find an alternative to majority rule, one that provides both autonomy and opportunities to pursue a valued relationship.

The game of personal and party politics will always be played. It is better played within autonomous identity groups than between identity groups, where the issues are frequently life-and-death ones. The para-militaries in Northern Ireland, the PLO in the Middle East, and other identity groups that were struggling for recognition, typically were constantly in turmoil as frustrations increased. But with local autonomy these leadership struggles are removed from the wider environment of conflict and have, therefore, limited consequences. Political separation has the effect of making possible role and interest struggles outside the wider context of ethnicity struggles.

Given such separation, there are then unlimited possibilities for functional cooperation in areas of common interest that do not impinge on ethnicity issues. What should be resisted where there are separate ethnic communities is the imposition (even by agreement between leaders) of some traditional federal structure. Such traditional federations imply representation, and inevitably the power or numbers game is played. This, as we know, is divisive and destructive of good relations between different confessional or ethnic groups.

In the international system this problem of cooperation in matters of common concern between separate groups, sometimes hostile, is overcome in a very simple and effective way by establishing functional organizations to deal with the various matters of common concern on a specialist or professional basis. Agreements are arrived at covering civil aviation, health, communications and a host of matters by the simple expedient of negotiations by specialists in the particular areas. These negotiated agreements are subject to ratification by member states. This is usually a process that proceeds smoothly, even unremarked.

It is this type of functional relationship that is likely to evolve in multi-ethnic situations. In most cases there are common problems of irrigation, tourism, foreign policies and many others, that are probably better dealt with as problems, and outside the power games of party politics. In the place of a central authority, which raises the numbers question, there are likely to evolve in such situations, a series of specialized interactions and negotiations, subject to ratification by each entity. A strong bureaucratic control that would undermine political control is unlikely for the reason that each of these specialist areas functions separately, and influence is spread amongst a large number of persons, each operating in the limited sphere.

There are some formal problems, such as a recognized head of state required to present the image of integration for purposes of membership in international organizations, and for purposes of receiving accredited foreign representatives. These are problems readily resolved, as was the case when the British Crown was designated a symbol of unity within its commonwealth of independent states.

These are possibilities once it is recognized that there are in multi-ethnic societies needs that are not negotiable, and interests that are. What inhibits movement in this direction is the liberal-minded resistance to separation as a means toward integration. In the case of Cyprus, after twenty and more years of fighting and expensive peace-keeping by the United Nations, it became apparent that despite declarations of a separate Turkish state, there was a strong preference for some continuing form of integration, but one that secured a separate identity.

The application of needs theory early in a situation can help the protagonists to deduce the kind of framework that would satisfy the needs of the parties concerned, without having to allow the situation, after costly conflict, to "ripen" to the point where a similar solution becomes acceptable.

THE PROBLEM OF MIXED SOCIETIES

Empirical evidence shows that where a minority is more than about 10 per cent, as was the case in some mixed villages in Cyprus, there is tension. Below that level there is typically less of a problem because of the total absence of threat to the majority, and above about 40 per cent there is less because of a reciprocal recognition. Once conflict occurs, however, there is a strong tendency for population movements to take place, as in Northern Ireland and Cyprus, thus creating conditions in which some form of separation or zonal system has to be applied.

There is a more difficult problem of ethnicity when different identity groups are mixed geographically throughout the total society. No zonal system or physical separation is possible. The hope and expectation is that eventually there will be assimilation. The "melting pot" theory is, however, a convenient political myth. There is typically in such cases, as in the US, more a coexistence than an assimilation, especially when the ethnic and cultural differences involve clear racial differences.

There have been "communal chambers" with some decision-making role in respect of cultural matters, as was the case in Cyprus before the constitutional system broke down. There are special boards and ministries that are supposed to cater to the needs of small minorities, as in the US, New Zealand and Australia dealing with indigenous minorities. But there has been little attention given to the more general problem of mixed societies, as in the US and the UK where it is assumed that there can be, if minorities wish it, an integrated society. The evidence that this will not happen, the evidence that there is an ongoing problem – as reflected, for example, in proportions of minorities in jails, unemployed, unskilled and unhoused – is brushed aside. The failings of minorities are treated as the inevitable consequences of intellectual or cultural problems, not as consequences of long-standing discriminations. Even as intellectual or cultural problems, they are not being dealt with by significant educational provisions. The result is that a form of ethnic conflict is beginning to disrupt these societies, being a major cause of theft, violence, drug addictions and other social problems.

In the absence of an understanding of the nature of the problem, it will probably not be faced until there has been a further "ripening" of conflict. After violence and high costs there might be an analysis of the nature of the problem, and of the options that might be available. Some difficult constitutional and social issues are involved; but as in the case of geographically divided societies, options can be deduced once an analysis has been made. In this case the options are likely to involve far greater attention to the provision of adequate educational and career opportunities.

ETHNIC CONFLICT AND LEGITIMIZATION

The above conditions describe class relations no less than ethnic relations. When minorities are spread through a society, rather than being located in particular regions, they tend to become an underprivileged class. This is particularly the case when they have migrated from an underprivileged environment to seek work and career opportunities. They may not be discriminated against, but rather treated on their merits. However, this does not explain the discriminatory treatment and role of minorities that have been within the society for hundreds of years, or were the indigenous populations. It is their members particularly who are the unemployed, and who fill the jails.

The problem of indentity conflict draws attention to the nature of the shift that is required even in mono-ethnic societies, if social and global stability is to be achieved. It draws attention to the nature of class conflict, and the way in which it can disrupt societies if accepted merely as an inevitable phenomenon in a society that expects and rewards initiative and achievement. Minorities that demand separation, as in Sri Lanka, are likely to be integrated in due course through their separation, as this gives the basis of security from which members can branch out into the wider society with which they must be associated functionally. So, too, with class. Unions have played some part in providing the separate identity sought, from which members can branch out into the wider society once their legitimate requirements are met. The curbing of unions that tends to take place in some developed societies could be dysfunctional if members do not yet feel that they have been incorporated into the wider society.

In both cases, ethnicity and other forms of identity, probably the longer-term solution is the same, adequate educational and development opportunities in a social framework that provides separate security until there is identity with the wider society.

The multi-ethnic and multi-cultural examples are useful because they highlight dramatically what goes on at all social levels where authorities and elites are exercising control in the absence of a legitimized status.

10 The Individual and Society

THE SOURCE OF CONFLICT: INSTITUTIONS OR PERSONS?

In Chapter 11 we will be considering the policy issue of intervention, that is the type of intervention that is required by some institutionalized process to provent conflict. Before being in a position to do this we must assess the hypothesis that is basic to the approach we have adopted – that the major source of social conflict at all levels is within institutions and structures, and not within the discretion of the individual, or the identity groups to which individuals look for support.

In dealing with any social problem there must ultimately be a balance between the needs of persons within a system, and the preservation of system attributes. The traditional attempt to treat symptoms of a problem, with the accompanying focus on the preservation of institutions, has not ignored human dimensions, but it has attributed to them a secondary role. Are we in this analysis overemphasizing the satisfaction of individual human needs, perhaps to an extent that in the longer term could lead to anarchical conditions that could be destructive of social organization and, therefore, of individual human needs?

It is only theories of behavior that can guide us in this necessary assessment. It is theories of behavior that have divided philosophers and social scientists over the issue of the individual and the common good. Assumptions about the nature of persons underlie philosophies, and political, sociological and psychological theories. If we wish to make progress with problems of conflict within societies, we must have a valid conception of the person involved, and especially the degree to which the person can be subordinated to the demands of society. We cannot afford to base thinking and policies on artificial constructs that emerge out of the evolution of systems, and are designed to justify the role societies impose on their members. We have to discover the real person, and from this deduce theories of behavior, and the structures and policies that are in the individual and the social interest.

147

It will be seen why at the outset we made the distinction between conflict *settlement* and conflict *resolution*, and between *prevention* and *provention*. These terms represent a "balance" between the interests of the individual and the common good, and we would argue that the shift from settlement and prevention to resolution and provention is a shift that promotes the common good by defining and satisfying those human needs that have in any event to be satisfied, and by processes that ensure the promoting of the common good.

THE HISTORICAL CONTEXT

The traditional hypothesis, that the fault or problem is with the individual, emerged out of conventional wisdom developed in feudal and class systems, and later in an international system dominated by colonial expansion. There were those who had made it by inheritance, opportunities and drive, or power, and those who had not made it for some reason or other, and who were consequently unemployed, poor, alienated, weak or otherwise disadvantaged. Without some hypothesis that lack of ability to cope, lack of sufficient drive, or perhaps lack of divine grace, was a personal and negative attribute, there could be no justification for the existing feudal or elite systems, the maintenance of existing economic and political systems of privilege, and territorial expansions, that served elite interests.

With the coming of the industrial age in Britain, for example, there was a severe unemployment problem as agricultural workers and small farmers were displaced and drawn toward new centers. In the absence of any support system during a period of structural transition, and in the absence of policies designed to deal with the problem, the unemployed were hounded from village to village as trouble-makers who did not wish to work. At a later stage when living conditions were even worse for those who had not made it in the new industrial system, law-breakers, including those who stole to survive, were hanged or deported. Unless the view were upheld that there was nothing wrong with the social system that justified such behavior, the unemployed could not be so treated. To acknowledge a problem would have been to be critical of a system, implying the need for change that in fact was being demanded by some political critics.

These were conditions in which there were rival elites, some traditionally based in agriculture, some in emerging industrial enterprises. There were also class or income divergencies. The problems created by such divisions within a society are greatly accentuated in the contemporary world by ethnic differences, and clear cases of discriminations in according opportunities based on ethnicity.

In contemporary times, whether the issue be class or ethnicity, care is taken not to articulate the sources of deviance and conflict in these stark terms that reflect upon the intelligence and morality of those who do not happen to make it in a competitive society. Nevertheless contemporary legislation in many developed countries is based on a premise that welfare problems have personal indolence at their source, and that problems of deviance have at their source personal immorality or aggressiveness. In other words, there is no recognition of a system fault.

The focus on systems inevitably leads to an ideological position: there have to be assumptions on which to construct the ideal society. These reflect stated or unstated values and interests. Given certain values and interests there may be advocacy of socialism, capitalism, communism, fascism, or some other system, justified in each case by reference to concepts of freedom, justice and others, the definitions of which can be made to fit the ideological requirements. It is not possible to assess what is the common good in such frameworks.

A PROBLEM-SOLVING APPROACH TO THE INDIVIDUAL AND SOCIETY

The starting point of problem-solving conflict resolution is the perceived reality. Faced with parties involved in some particular conflict, a facilitator, unlike a judge, is not in a position to set down norms. A facilitator helps protagonists to make an analysis of the total situation, including the values and interests of the large society in which the conflict is taking place. Any political philosophy that is implied, or that might evolve over time, emerges out of the discoveries made in the study of the conflict and its resolution, such as the patterns of behavior, the common causes of conflict, and the institutional and constitutional options that are found by the process to be relevant. In short, the contribution of problem-solving conflict resolution to political philosophy is not an alternative set of norms, or some subjectively arrived at values and assumptions, but the discovery of the realities of conflict as perceived by the parties and facilitators involved in conflict resolution. From this empirical experience patterns of behavior emerge that cut across cultures, and across social levels.

A next task is to find explanations of them, and to develop theories of behavior that explain and make prediction possible. From this empirical and theoretical study of individual and group behaviors the study of conflict resolution leads to an examination of the sources of conflict, and this takes it into the realms of ecology, politics, sociology and other influences on behavior, and finally, into political philosophy.

The values and interests of the larger society in which the conflict takes place and is being resolved are a most important consideration for students of conflict resolution, and especially for facilitators engaged in helping parties to a dispute to arrive at viable options. In the longer term, any agreement that contradicts the common good will be self-defeating of the goals and values of the parties to the conflict. In the area of interest disputes, employers and employees could arrive at agreements from which they both benefited, as happened in pre-Second World War Italy, but at the expense of the economy as a whole, and this can have unforeseen and adverse political and economic consequences for them. So too in issues of wider social significance: agreements on land rights designed to satisfy some minority insecurities can trigger responses that make even more difficult the free participation in the wider society by members of the minority and their offspring.

THE POLICY DILEMMA

The study of conflict and its resolution thus highlights the policy dilemma inherent in the common-good problem: either societies preserve interests by arguing that the source of problems is with persons and not institutions, thus finding reasons for maintaining the status quo though thereby promoting protracted conflict, or they tackle at source the problems that lead to escalating levels of conflict that will, if not dealt with, finally destroy those same interests. For the individual seeking to preserve interests, and for those responsible politically, it is a time dilemma in addition to being a human–institutional dilemma, for it involves a costing of the immediate advantages against a future loss. (In the nature of politics, immediate interests usually prevail.)

The same analysis applies at the international level. An undeveloped state seeks to free itself from the dominance of more economically powerful states, and to conduct its domestic and foreign policies in ways that are relevant to its stage of development. It seeks land reform, income redistribution to provide free education or to pursue some other community policy. To do this it finds it must exercise curbs on many in a privileged position. This provokes intervention from the more powerful states whose economic interests may be affected, and whose political philosphies are being challenged. In an attempt to justify their interventions, greater powers define the problem, not in system or indigenous developmental terms, but in terms of the threatening ideologies and characteristics of the leaders of these developing countries. Steps are taken to replace them. In the resultant conflicts both the developing state and the intervening state endure heavy costs – as, for example, has been the case in US interventions in Vietnam, Korea, Central America and elsewhere.

We cannot escape this dilemma between system preservation and human concerns if we wish to get to the bottom of problems of conflict. It is a dilemma that rests on a fundamental question, one that is at the core of conflict and its resolution. Are there, or are there not, human needs that will be pursued, and that require appropriate institutional frameworks?

If we were confronted with the odd example we could be led to psychological explanations. When we are faced with widespread and escalating conflict, crime and violence at all societal levels, then we must look to structural sources as explanations of such behaviors.

This is the topic on which debate should focus until there is consensus: where is the source of conflict, in historical traditions and systemic influences, that deny the pursuit of human needs, thus leading to social problems and to conflicts throughout societies, or in inadequate, maladjusted or misled individuals who require to be socialized and constrained by power elites? Raising this question is the contribution of conflict resolution to political philosophy and, in particular, to the discussion of the individual and the wider social good.

Whatever the answer, it is irrelevant to attach blame. The issue is not one that should divide societies, except to the extent that the immediate interests of some might be prejudiced. There is no right and wrong in the defense of systems, or in endeavors to obtain change. In so far as institutions are a source of conflict we are dealing with the legacy of history, with conventional wisdom, and with the politics of interest. If our shared goal is to get at the source of conflict, which if not remedied can destroy nations and the global society, then these issues must be examined. They can be examined by developing theories of conflict, and by the handling of particular situations of conflict, thus feeding back insights into theory and to public policy.

INTELLECTUAL CONFUSION

In the past philosophers and scholars have accepted the hypothesis that the problem is with the individual. Traditional sociology was the study of how to socialize the individual into the norms of the society. Politics has been the study of how to structure societies according to certain institutional norms far more than to meet the needs of persons. Law has been based on an assumption that there are those who have the right to expect obedience and others who have a moral obligation to obey.

Within a theoretical framework that suggests that there are human needs that are not negotiable and that go beyond the need to survive physically, the empirical as well as the theoretical evidence increasingly points to environmental conditions as the source of conflict and of deviant behaviors. Take, for example, the life history of John McVicar (McVicar, 1974), a many-times murderer for whom a cage had to be built to prevent his breaking through floors and walls. He had a most deprived early childhood in some of the worst slums of England, and was a problem at an early age. Given opportunity in gaol he became a sculptor. Ultimately he was released to become an adviser to prison authorities. There are many other such examples. At another level we have examples of respected national leaders who were wanted terrorists in earlier political life. In all of these cases the empirical evidence suggests that there was no initial fault with the individuals concerned: there were system faults that led to certain behaviors. These people were violent and aggressive in reaction to the conditions they previously faced. Dealing with their behaviors by some repressive means does not solve the problem in the particular case, and is not a remedy for the prevention of other incidents.

Where conflict resolution differs from traditional approaches is in asserting that the purpose of institutions is to cater for the needs of the person, and not the other way around. If there are deep-rooted conflicts, then within the analysis must come an examination of the institutional sources of the conflict.

In this approach to conflict resolution, the nature of the human being and the identity group is a given. The resolution of problems and conflicts is based on an acceptance of the individual and identity group as givens. With the exception of conflicts that are the result of some misperception or misunderstanding, the remedies must be, therefore, structural, institutional and environmental. Conflict is at least in large part a function of an environmental setting, not necessarily of inevitable failure in human adaption to conditions that deny human requirements.

This does not imply that there is no need for prisons or for strategic defense; it does assert that such holding strategies are not an answer to the problems that have led to their being needed. Nor does it imply that there are not individuals with serious psychological problems, including sometimes leaders of nations. In these cases treatment, and containment of some kind, may be required. What it does assert is that such exceptions should not be made the justification for an approach to deviant behaviors, and to conflict situations generally, that is repressive, coercive, and designed to ensure conformity with the norms of existing powers and institutions.

Conflict resolution, as we are treating it, rejects, therefore, the view that the contemporary and seemingly global escalation in conflict and violence, and the accompanying resistance to any form of a coercive authority – including the parent and all authorities up to the great powers – is due to a degeneration in human nature, or decline in moral values. There has always been a drive toward freedom from oppression, and a struggle for individuality, or, as Haworth terms it, "autonomy" (1986). We cannot assume that members of contemporary communities have become inherently less socially responsible, less moral, less rational and more violent than their predecessors.

Taking this a step further, we cannot assume either that persons within certain cultures, or certain groups of people that are associated with violence, are necessarily different from others. With the approach we are adopting, an approach that focuses on generic or universal patterns of human behavior, there have to be other explanations of the levels of conflict and violence that we are currently experiencing.

THE SOCIAL GOOD AND VALUED RELATIONSHIPS

There is a reasonable concern that the pursuit of human needs by the individual could be socially disruptive. But the theory of conflict, its provention and resolution argues that included in human needs is a particular need for valued relationships. This acts as a self-restraining influence on human behavior. In the absence of valued relationships there are no self-imposed restraints. Where valued relationships are absent, it is not through their arbitrary rejection. They are constantly and persistently sought. The typical street gang member is seeking out valued relationships among his colleagues within the gang. The person freed from jail seeks out others from jail. There are reasons why relationships with parents, teachers, police, society and other nations are sometimes not valued relationships. It is these that need to be investigated.

We deduce that while the pursuit of human needs cannot be contained over the long term by external coercive sanctions, that while there are limits to socialization processes, the human need for valued relationships and their preservation may be an effective controlling influence. In other words, while traditionally we have looked to social control as the means to social harmony, a more effective approach may be to provide those conditions that generate valued relationships, and, therefore, self-imposed controls.

If this is so, then it is not authoritative controls *per se* that are a source of conflict. Authoritative relationships are themselves the consequence of conditions that deny or destroy valued relationships, leading to the non-legitimization of authorities and the need for coercive policies.

Indeed, the erosion of authority to which we have had our attention drawn in recent years has its negative social consequences in that it also erodes leadership. Societies and the world society are in turmoil through lack of leadership and control. Leadership is not incompatible with reciprocal and valued relationships at any social level. Reciprocity between leaders and led creates a valued relationship.

THE DEMISE OF RELATIONSHIPS

The common-good issue is best discussed in the context of the legitimization of authorities, which we have already considered. The need for an exchange relationship between authorities and those over whom they exercise their authority is at the core of the problem of conflict and its resolution. It seems also to be at the core of the problem of the common good.

There is something more taking place than resistance to authoritative controls. We are facing the reality that workers, women, minority ethnic communities, children, the unemployed, the disadvantaged, and peoples generally of different cultures and stages of development, are all seeking, sometimes by violent means, certain conditions of identity and development. It cannot be assumed that what is being sought is freedom from controls, and the absence of well-defined political and social frameworks. There may be resistance to capitalism, communism and other forms of organization with which we have had experience; but it could be, nevertheless, that some well defined boundaries of behavior are sought. They would be boundaries drawn by respect for authorities in exchange for opportunities for individual identity, recognition and development.

We are led to a hypothesis that our present levels of violence and anti-social behaviors at most social–political levels are due, not to the exercise of authority or the lack of it, but to the prevalence of systems of control that are characterized by the absence of valued relationships. Societies in the world society are now subject to economic and political influences that appear not to be controlled by any human decision or decision maker, but by financial and political *systems*. There are uncontrolled market changes, widespread cartels, including now drug cartels, that have become actors in the international system more powerful than many nations, and whose activities the greatest of powers cannot control even within their own territories. This is a new kind of subjugation and dependency. It is new in the sense that there is exploitation, but with no valued relationships. This is *system control*, not control by any direct authority or known person with a particular role.

This absence of valued relationships on its present scale is a new phenomenon historically, but also in kind. Even the most oppressive forms of government and employment have traditionally been compensated for by the existence of roles and of relationships. If the dominant restraint on behavior is valued relationships, in their absence there is nothing to control behaviors, and violence becomes unrestrained.

This impersonalization of relationships is encouraged by many related policies that are becoming more and more widespread. Deregulation, privatization, lessened government responsibility for health and education, the belief that the unemployed are more likely to find jobs if left to themselves, that the market mechanism is the best regulator, and other such thinking that is a characteristic of modern industrial societies, could lead to attempted remedies to current *economic* problems that do not take into account adequately human dimensions of relationships and systems and, therefore, may be a major source of escalated conflict and violence.

(There is a practical problem concerning values attached to relationships viewed as a human need. They provide, as we have noted, the effective control mechanism promoting social behaviors. It is reasonable to suspect, nevertheless, that a high value attached to relationships could inhibit personal growth and development. So, too, at a societal level. Wholly legitimized authorities – for example, a charismatic personality – could lead a society in ways that curbed individual and social development. This is a problem tackled by some of the contributors to *Conflict: Human Needs Theory*.)

WHAT ARE FUTURE GOALS?

While there can be no return to the past and its unacceptable features, the goals of a desired future still escape us. The problem we face is that neither those promoting change, nor those resisting it, have any clear concept of future goals, still less any clear notion of the processes of change that can provide a smooth transition from the current point *A* to a desired future point *B*.

Societies are in a stage of transition, not just in the sense of change, but more importantly in a primitive evolutionary sense. They are drifting – or evolving – from one stage to some non-defined other. They are not evolving as a result of conscious planning, that is by tackling their problems analytically and deliberately. Ultimate goals have not been articulated, and means of moving toward them have not been researched and adopted.

It is this perspective that beckons an analytical problem-solving approach that involves all parties concerned, whether it be in the context of parliamentary decision making, a matrimonial dispute, an ethnic dispute, a conflict between persons and authorities, or whatever. We are here concerned with a generic theory of behavior, leading to processes of decision making that are generic. To make them available at all social levels is still a major task before societies and the world society.

THE COMMON GOOD AS COMPENSATION

Pulling these arguments together, it should be observed that the classical concern with the common good was a compensatory response to early elitist and authoritative systems. The concepts of justice, fairness, social values of many kinds, so-called democratic institutions, along with many religious beliefs, were all the product of repressive systems. None would have emerged had there been a system that was just and democratic in any real sense. So also with the common good. Had there been a perfect system in which the individual developed fully in perfectly free conditions, in which valued relationships were promoted and led to the observance of social norms, the common good and individual development would have been as one.

This ideal-type context is relevant because it points to a confusion we have with terms and concepts. Within a power framework the individual and the common good is a relevant topic. Within a needs theory framework there is not this separation. The full development of the individual *is* the common good.

We are at an early stage in thinking about these issues, but the conclusion is important that within a needs explanation of behavior, the pursuit of individual needs and the common good are one and the same thing.

11 Constructive Intervention

From the outset we have made it clear that the scope of this study of conflict goes beyond the study of process – that is, of how to deal with specific conflicts as they crop up in an organization or society. We are concerned no less with provention – creating the conditions that ensure the conflict does not occur. Indeed, the more we examine the problem area, the more it appears that conflict provention is, like the provention of illness, the area in which resources may most effectively be expended.

We have adopted the position, also, that if conflict is to be provented or resolved, institutions and environmental circumstances generally must cater as far as is possible for the needs of persons and groups – and not primarily the other way around. On this basis, the study of conflict, its provention and resolution necessarily leads us to consider the environment of conflict – the ecological, social, political, economic, historical and other aspects of the total environment of behavior that can either exacerbate or reduce levels of conflict.

The role of authorities at a national level has traditionally been treated as being primarily concerned with defense, and with internal law and order. Legal thinking has held that authorities have a legitimate monopoly of power, and the exercise of this power for these purposes has been regarded as their main responsibility.

Similarly, tradition has been that authorities at all other social levels, from the parent, to the teacher, through to industry, have had a power role to fulfill. The handling of conflict within their social systems is their responsibility. In short, authorities are associated with power, and with the enforcement of relevant norms of behavior.

Within this traditional framework, the implication of our approach to conflict, its resolution and provention, is that there is a special responsibility on leaderships and authorities generally to promote conflict-free environments in the interests of the societies for which they are responsible.

We wish, however, to examine the assumption that there is necessarily this high level of responsibility on authorities and, if this is not a valid assumption, to consider what are the alternatives or supplementary sources of intervention.

158

We are led, consequently, to three major political question: first, in what conditions is intervention required in social relationships; second, what is the nature of the intervention required; and third, what is the nature of the apppropriate intervening agency?

THE QUALITY OF INTERVENTION

Needs theory would seem to imply the necessity for some kind of institutionalized devices in all societies, and at all societal levels, from the family to the total world society, to create conditions in which there can be individual development and the pursuit of human needs. The necessity for some form of intervention is there because persons and nations, pursuing their daily and systemic lives, do not as individuals or groups have either the knowledge or the incentive to cater for the needs of all others, especially the needs of others in other communities, and of others in the longer-term future. There must be interventions, first to protect the individual and society from special interest pressures and from each other, and second, to protect the person and group, especially the person and group that will comprise future societies.

In the ideological debates about intervention by authorities into the lives of peoples and their societies there has been a confusion between two separate issues. These are (1) the degree of intervention, and (2) the quality or nature of intervention. The debate has been whether or not there should be intervention, especially the interventions of central authorities, rather than the quality and nature of interventions. Schools of economists, troubled by unwise or interest-inspired interventions, have favored leaving the free-enterprise market to determine futures, and some political leaders, daunted by the political problems associated with environmental and other controls, have gone along with them. The result has been progressive decreases in the QOL, increased entropy and an escalating environment of conflict.

This separation of the two issues, whether and when intervention is required, and the quality of intervention (including consideration of the relevant intervenor), helps to focus on the main issue, that is the relevance and quality of intervention. If the quality of intervention is high, that is if the type of intervention deals effectively with the problem being addressed, the degree of intervention required is likely to be acceptable and probably low in terms of altered personal and group relationships and conditions. If the quality of intervention is low, that is if the measures taken do not accomplish their goals, more and more intervention will seem to be necessary in an endeavor to make it effective. We are familiar with progressive increases in government controls as policies fail, and as resistances to authorities increase. An intervention designed merely to contain a current situation can end up being a permanent exercise of police or military power.

The quality or form of intervention is, therefore, the key element, whether it be a private enterprise or a planned system, and regardless of societal levels. In order to discuss quality, we need to introduce the notions of *restrictive* and *constructive intervention*.

Restrictive interventions, controls of various kinds that apply domestically and internationally, refer to policies that intervene in systems transactions for some immediate reasons, in ways that threaten the system, and the changes and adjustments that would be made if the system were to operate freely. For example, when an industry is in difficulties, demands are made for subsidies or tariff protection as a means of avoiding adaptation to altered conditions. There will be some circumstances, as we note later, that can justify some such restrictions. But when there are high levels of such restrictions to which others cannot accommodate, the consequences can be catastrophic, as when Japan in the 1930s was denied access to colonial markets. Falling into the same category are other restrictive responses to complex situations, such as containment of dissident and deviant behaviors without dealing with their sources.

Constructive intervention, by contrast, refers to policies that seek to assist in processes of adjustment to change, for example, the redeployment and retraining of labor when industries are running down for technological and related reasons. Interventions to improve health so as to decrease health costs in the future, to promote education to improve productive capacities in the future, and to prevent discriminations so as to avoid class and ethnicity tensions, are within this category. Included, also, are interventions by various authorities and agencies that protect the environment, and generally ensure the long-term conditions that are in the general interest, which short-term interests tend to ignore. Examples are not hard to think of, for example, interventions that are required by parents, teachers, and others in educational roles.

A NEGLECTED SUBJECT

There is virtually no literature that deals with the nature and quality of intervention outside what are clearly ideological expositions favoring either free-enterprise or planned economic systems. The criterion on which intervention must be assessed is not in economic development, but QOL, including, as we have emphasized, an absence of conflict and the full development of the person. The traditional focus on institutions rather than the development of persons has prevented a thorough non-ideological exploration of the question whether the development of the individual is best achieved by allowing individuals to operate freely with the least possible intervention, or whether a significant level of planned intervention in certain activities and relationships is necessary.

This question of intervention by authorities has a special significance for private enterprise systems. The psychological assumption of classical economics is that the greater the freedom, the more likely it is that individual enterprise will increase innovation and productivity, and thus promote the GNP. This, however, takes no account of long-term consequences of current behaviors, consequences for the environment, for social relationships in the future, or quality of life generally.

There being no consensus regarding levels and types of government intervention in Western-type political systems, changes in governing political parties give rise to cycles of greater and less intervention. These cycles appear to be self-perpetuating. Unnecessary and inappropriate intervention on the part of authorities representing some ideological or interest groups leads to reaction and withdrawal of interventions, to be followed by growing needs and demands for them. Controls on industry to maintain ecological standards, or to ensure competition, are followed by demands for deregulation, to be followed by conditions that require control. Such cycles are a feature of the interest-dominated party-political system, affecting even defense. Such cycles could be regarded as part of a healthy system of checks and balances. In practice, however, costs are high when neglect of the environment, or the promotion of an unnecessary defense system, affect the future of a society and its relations with others.

NEEDS THEORY AND INTERVENTION

So accepted has been the tradition that authorities are concerned primarily with their use of their monopoly of power in the areas of law and order and defense, that any debate about the measure of intervention by national authorities has been confined largely to the economy, especially in private enterprise systems. It came to the fore in Britain and the US in the early 1980s with policies of deregulation, and it has since spread to other countries. As suggested above, this proves to be an on-going debate because deregulation in the due course creates conditions requiring intervention.

Furthermore, unforeseen circumstances raise the issue. The issue of intervention preoccupied economists during the depression period that led up to the Second World War. Economists like Lord Lionel Robbins argued strongly for the greatest possible freedom. He held that enterprise and rewards for enterprise were essential, and taxation and other social policies should be formed with this as a consideration. The by-products, such as inequalities, were a mixed blessing. They promoted, for example, cultural development and the arts (Robbins, 1936).

The advent of war required government intervention on a large scale, as did post-war reconstruction. And now the pendulum has swung back. In the 1980s, US President Reagan made this a key theme. He opposed more progressive taxation on the grounds that encouragement had to be given to private enterprise in the interests of all. He believed in the "trickle down" process. It was through increased incentives and productivity that poverty would be reduced. Economic indicators have measured some success. Social indicators, on the other hand, suggest failure: poverty increased while GNP and other indicators showed increases.

It is this same issue of the quality and quantity of intervention that separates free enterprise and planned economics. Those defending capitalism argue that the increased productivity that the free enterprise system sponsors, along with freedoms of speech, of the press and of criticism, more than compensate for the human and social costs of unemployment and elements of distributive injustice. Those defending planned systems argue that the right to work, to economic security and to distributive justice compensate for reductions in incentive and productivity and in some civil liberties. Both acknowledge their problem areas and endeavor to take care of the underprivileged, on the one hand, and to promote productivity, on the other, but only within the limits imposed by the nature of their systems.

This economic systems perspective, however, does not take into account human dimensions. It provides only one guideline to the quality of intervention. Another is the provision of opportunities for the pursuit of human needs. Identity through occupation, stimulus through acceptable employment and incentive, distributive justice through reasonably equitable income distribution, and rules that prevent gender and race discrimination, are amongst the means by which intervention can promote the pursuit of human needs.

It could be that system transactions, and the economic benefits from them, have to be sacrificed for some pressing human needs. For example, there may be cases in which developing states need to protect traditional cottage industries for cultural reasons, to provide time for adjustments to changing circumstances.

There may also be cases in which security and recognition must be provided in conditions in which a system denies these to persons. For example, where there are discriminations in employment favoring the ethnic group of major employers, thus creating massive unemployment for another ethnic group or groups, as in Northern Ireland or with Afro-Americans, there may be reasons for intervention to prevent ethnic conflict, and, finally, system disruption.

The concepts of constructive and restrictive interventions relate to certain definable goals and questions: what is the purpose of the intervention, what values are to be preserved, what are the immediate human costs and burdens of change that would justify restrictive intervention in the preservation of existing conditions?

These are questions that are separate from any notion of liberalism or conservatism. Ideologies are not directly concerned with the degree of control by authorities, though their differences are often defined in this way. Both seek the promotion and conservation of particular values. Sometimes this may be effected by non-intervention, sometimes by high degrees of intervention. It is the quality or kind of intervention that is the important issue.

THE RELEVANCE OF QUALITY INTERVENTION

Here we return to the issue of goals. Modern free-enterprise industrial societies seek the greatest possible exploitation of resources, the highest possible GNP, regardless of income distributions, social relationships, and consequences for the future ecology. This is a concentration on living standards at the expense of QOL. These economic goals are the kinds that have guided modern civilizations (though members of other cultures, such as Islam, may claim other values, such as a sharing society, as a prime goal).

Narrow economic and interest-based goals are so much part of the consensus that they influence and confuse thinking in most areas of political concern. Let us assume that objectively there were no threat to the US from the Soviet Union, that unilateral arms reductions had been made by the Soviet Union that removed the need for many weapon systems, and that there was, objectively, no need to maintain existing arms levels. There still could not be significant arms reductions without extensive planned intervention into the economic system of the kind that was required by post-Second World War reconstruction. Resource reallocations would be required, taking workers out of defense industries, probably into technical training, and into housing, health and other social services that were run down during the arms build-up of the 1980s. These are not adjustments that can be made by industry alone without widespread social disruption. The interest-group pressures against this would be tremendous, and they would be based, not on rational argument, but on ideological argument, to justify a continuation of existing levels of defense. Political and public support would rally by reason of the numbers of persons involved, including those engaged in research at universities.

The need for quality in intervention becomes apparent. In the absence of planning to cover fields other than those immediately concerned by some specific legislation, there can be detrimental consequences.

INTERNATIONAL INTERVENTIONS

We have focused so far mainly on interventions by authorities within the national system. Intervention by one nation into the affairs of others is also an area in which guidelines are required. In the global society there are large numbers of domestic situations of conflict in which greater powers seek to intervene.

The two situations are related. Intervention by greater powers seeks to take advantage of conflicts within nations to promote their own ideologies by intervention. An apparent anomaly is that a commitment to non-intervention in national affairs does not usually carry over to non-intervention elsewhere: on the contrary, there is persistent intervention by great powers who oppose it nationally to ensure that others follow their non-interventionist ideological commitment.

There appears to have been little discussion between great powers on principles of intervention in the affairs of third countries, despite the fact that it is over such interventions that they confront each other. Within a power political framework in which rivalries are between planned and private-enterprise societies, other countries are potentially friendly or hostile depending on their internal intervention ideology, that is, whether or not there is a large element of central control.

Attempts to impose a system on other nations prove costly and frequently fail, as both the US and the Soviet Union have discovered. Even when they seem to succeed, success is short-lived when the imposed system does not take account of human dimensions and the need for change. In the 1980s the US labelled opposition in El Salvador as communist intervention, and provided the government with military advisers as an alternative to changes in land use, political participation and social–political changes. Such intervention, taken without due consideration of the human dimensions involved, must lead to protracted conflict that is ultimately costly both to the US and to El Salvador. Similarly, the Soviet Union labelled Afghanistan a case of American intervention. Sending military support for the existing regime was not a substitute for working out the problems that existed in that tribal area.

In a conflict resolution perspective, the type of system is something to be determined by the peoples concerned, and if there are divisions of opinion, as there usually are, these are to be resolved by analytical costing processes, probably assisted by a third party.

If for humanitarian or other reasons there is to be foreign intervention, it would be constructive if it took the form of encouraging problem-solving processes. If such an approach were to be adopted, it would lead to agreements amongst great powers not to intervene, not to back one party against another, or to supply weapons, at least unless there had been conscientious attempts to resolve differences by these means.

These are not considerations that have so far entered into the study of economics, or even of politics, let alone their practice. It has not been within the concerns of these separate disciplines to adopt such a holistic view of social problems. But such problem-solving considerations are the essence of face-to-face interaction in a conflict resolution setting. Indeed, it could reasonably be argued that the trivialization of politics will be reduced in the longer term only by the employment of more analytical practices in interaction at all social levels between authorities and those over whom authority is exercised. What is learned and practiced with success on one level would then have its influence at others.

THE PROBLEMS OF PUBLIC POLICY MAKING

In all systems and at all social levels authorities, whether self-appointed or elected, are subjected to interest pressures. They are ideologically-oriented – that is, they have their own definition of the common good, and their own preferences for satisfiers by which to attain it. As a consequence, longer-term societal interests are frequently of little political interest to decision makers. Their concern is with maintaining their roles, especially in the immediate present. Short-term perspectives tend, therefore, to govern policies. So far civilizations have not invented a component of decision making that ensures the costing of the future consequences of policies. When decision making processes fail in their future costing of policies, the goals and values, and probably the interests of societies also, are pursued in ways that are likely to be self-defeating.

Political philosophers and political scientists have accepted that authorities are finally responsible, and have tended reluctantly to accept as an inevitable fact that short-term views and personal interests of decision makers are the unavoidable deformities of a political process.

There is a school of economists called "Public Choice" that seeks to break away from this tradition. It advocates built-in constraints on political decision making that would limit the scope of authorities, especially their decision making abilities to expand resources, and thus help to prevent political responses to pressure-group lobbying, and to local electoral processes. Such constraints, however, would tend to limit decision making generally, and thereby prejudge the principles of intervention. This school of thought is consistent with a philosophy that hands over decision making to corporate bodies and the market place. This may solve one problem, but it creates another. There is no longer an intervention possible that would protect the society and its members, now and in the future, from the influence of interest-dominated short-term decision making (see Buchanan, Tollison and Tullock, 1980).

PROBLEM-SOLVING PROCESSES

Can problem-solving conflict resolution make any contribution to thinking about this universal problem?

Problem-solving conflict resolution is an intervention into relationships, as are political economic policies pursued by authorities and by market interests. It seeks changes, not only in behaviors to the degree that these may be possible, but also and mainly in policies, norms and structures that affect the relationships to be controlled. Whether the relationships in question be in industry or over ethnic discrimination nationally, resolution must include whatever changes in structures or policies that might be required. (In Chapter 18 we examine the notion of second order change, that is system change, and try to assess the extent to which it is in practice in the social good.)

Conflict resolution is also concerned with costing, especially future costing, so that parties to a conflict will not arrive at agreements that are in the longer term dysfunctional to them directly, or indirectly by reason of adverse effects on the wider society in which they exist.

There is thus, ideally, this common goal in the formal role of authorities of all kinds, including those in the market place, and the role of conflict resolution processes: both are concerned with the environment of conflict, present and future, and means of removing sources of conflict. Conflict resolution, however, adds a dimension missing in political and economic decision making, that is the interactive process, involving parties affected, in which there is an analysis of problems, including their human dimension, and also longer-term costing of options available.

Sometimes the necessary changes in a conflictual relationship can be made within the system concerned, for example, the kinship group, the industry or the local community. System change is not then required. Frequently, however, interventions may be required at a national or even an international level. Here the type of intervention required can best be determined as the result of the insights gathered from analytical problem-solving processes, and also from conflict resolution cases, and theories of behavior that are built on such cases.

PRINCIPLES OF INTERVENTION

So it is with interventions at all system levels: they are there to provide a forum of communication, but they are there also to ensure that the longer-term interests of those concerned, including future generations, are protected.

There are certain principles that can be deduced.

First, there is the need to promote and preserve legitimization. Legitimacy is a function of valued exchange relationships. Whether at an interpersonal level, in the family, in the classroom, in the factory, at the local government level, or at the national level, legitimacy is a precondition of effective influence.

Second, because legitimized relationships are a precondition of conflict avoidance, decision making processes must be such that human needs are identified and satisfied, again at all levels of interaction. Personal relationships in business and industry can be harmonious, while structural relationships and decision making processes can at the same time create conditions of alienation and frustration.

Third, in order for needs to be identified and satisfied, there is probably a need for decentralization of decision making in most organizations and societies, together with means to influence decisions at other levels.

Fourth, the social system, acting through authorities or through other sources of intervention, must provide for basic needs for which the individual cannot assume responsibility, such as health and education, in ways that ensure their general availability, and furthermore, their equitable quality availability. This is an area in which inequality has longer-term social consequences. Education includes retraining as social and industrial demands alter. Protection of the ecology also is clearly a matter for intervention, probably at an authority level.

Fifth, the provision of readily accessible problem-solving institutions at all levels of interaction is a necessary back-stop in all societies.

Sixth, foreign interventions raise their own special problems, and must be regarded as subject to the same kind of obligations and constraints.

CONFLICT RESOLUTION AND PROVENTION AS PROVIDING AN ALTERNATIVE SYSTEM?

At the outset of Chapter 11 we observed that once the problem area is defined to include conflict provention, the whole field of political philosophy becomes relevant. Drug-related conflicts and murders can possibly be contained to some extent by police action. Education about the dangers of drugs might help to discourage consumptions and trading. But the more the problem is investigated the more far-reaching are the policy implications. So it is with class, ethnic, religious and all other types of conflict. They are the symptoms of underlying and environmental circumstances, and it is these that must finally be treated. It follows that the study of conflict, its resolution and provention becomes a general study of societies and their organization and administration, a study that is the necessary intellectual background of all persons with social responsibilities.

It is in this sense that the study and practice of conflict resolution and provention is far more than process. It becomes the source of political philosophy by reason of the insights that are gained from analytical interaction between parties to conflicts. It is by these means that the fundamental goals and requirements of human development are revealed. In a circular fashion, the political philosophy so generated provides the principles of conflict resolution processes: analytical, problem-solving, option exploring, future costing, with wholly value-free and neutral attitudes towards contending parties whose behaviors are ontological responses to experienced conditions.

Facilitated conflict resolution is an intervention into relationships. It is to assist parties to a dispute or conflict to be analytical about their relationships. But it is more than this. Assuming the facilitator is working within the framework of a theory of behavioral relationships, based on a theory of individual behavior, the role of a third party is also to point out consequences of behaviors and decisions. For example, if there were a third-party intervention in the South African situation, it would be compatible with its neutral role to point out that a one-man-one-vote system would create the type of conflict that prevails in multi-ethnic societies. The parties would be encouraged to explore more widely to find constitutional systems that were democratic, and which did not prejudice the needs for autonomy and security of minorities within the system. The role is to assist communication, but at the same time to protect against decisions that could be dysfunctional in the longer term.

As conflict resolution processes are more widely applied, the insights and input from conflict resolution cases into policy making at all levels will increase. Already they are altering the confrontational processes of courts when there are conflicts that involve a human dimension. Legal scholars, lawyers and non-lawyers are forming mediation panels. These developments are, however, still within a quasi-legal framework, whereas the non-fault interactive processes of conflict resolution would better reveal the sources of the problems and prevent future incidents, rather than merely punish in particular cases.

There is, however, developing a new industry of conflict control and resolution, in which there are many different types of firms producing different products. Their impact has not as yet been assessed, but it is clear that all societal relationships, from interpersonal to the international, are being affected more and more by it.

III
Conflict Resolution

Chapter 12   Decision Making   173
Chapter 13   Trends in Conflict Management and Resolution   188
Chapter 14   Conflict Resolution as Problem-solving   202
Chapter 15   Culture   211
Chapter 16   Acceptability of Conflict Resolution   217

Introduction to Part III

Conflict resolution is an extension of decision making. In this Part III, dealing with Conflict Resolution, we commence by tracing out developments in decision making (Chapter 12), and then see the way in which conflict management and conflict resolution has evolved (Chapter 13). We are then in a position to deal in some detail with conflict resolution as a problem-solving process (Chapter 14). Before concluding the decision making analysis there are some considerations of culture that should be noted (Chapter 15).

We then assess the acceptability of the process (Chapter 16). Questions we shall examine include: does the distinction we have made between, on the one hand, disputes that are negotiable and, on the other, conflicts that involve deep-rooted issues, justify the further distinction we have made between *settlement* and *resolution*? May it not be, despite these differences in the nature of interests and needs confrontations, that traditional power processes are more effective in preserving consensus social and political values and stability? Conflict resolution as an alternative to a power political philosophy cannot rest on a value judgement that there *should* or *ought* to be an absence of coercion and violence in the control of conflict. Its justification must be in relation to efficiency and acceptability in reducing the incidence of deep-rooted conflict by means that at the same time preserve legitimate goals.

12 Decision Making

CONFLICT RESOLUTION AS DECISION MAKING

In Part I we outlined the history of "power political realism" in the management of conflict, which has gradually given place to thinking and practices that tend to take human responses more into consideration. In Part II we placed this shift in thinking in its political context. Now we seek to translate this shift in thought and practice into a framework that helps to explain, and to anticipate, future trends both in conflict management and problem-solving conflict resolution.

In tracing out past thinking within a power politics framework, followed by a transition period, we have actually been reviewing alterations in decision making. Policies at all social levels, personal policies and national policies, are pursued as a result of decision making processes. Leading to decisions are the assumptions, the knowledge, the philosophies, the ideologies, and the interests that give rise to them. By tracing out decision making experience and decision making theory, and the parallels in conflict *management* and *resolution*, we will discover the background assumptions which take resolution beyond conflict management.

Many writers both on conflict management and resolution recognize that they are, in effect, writing about decision making, and vice versa. Janis and Mann call their book *Decision Making: A Psychological Analysis of Conflict, Choice and Commitment* (1977). Fraser and Hipel use decision making as their framework in *Conflict Analysis: Models and Resolutions* (1984). Patchen in his *Resolving Disputes between Nations* has a chapter on decision making (1988). In their preface to *Managing Public Disputes* (1988) Carpenter and Kennedy say that their book is designed for decision makers, thus recognizing that conflict management is a core topic in decision making. Fox reminds us that conflict resolution is part of the process of decision making, as is also problem-solving. The title of his book is *Effective Group Problem Solving: How to Broaden Participation, Improve Decision Making, and Increase Commitment to Action* (1987). Lawrence Haworth (1986), dealing with the need to satisfy *Autonomy* if conflict is to be avoided, sets down the main tasks of decision making.

REACTIVE AND INTERACTIVE DECISION MAKING

In Chapter 12 we will show that early decision making models depicted power and reactive decision making, and were indeed reactive in that there was no analytical consideration of the behavioral responses of those affected by decisions. Theorists constructing models of decision making on the basis of their observations and experiences were not initially concerned with behavioral aspects of decision making itself, outside perhaps some problems of perception. This has been reflected in conflict *management* (Chapter 13).

Decision making as an activity has its unconscious origins in reflex responses and instinctive reactions to external stimuli. The reflex action in pulling away from something that burns or gives a shock is a crude form of decision making. Such responses give rise to habitual responses, which may be no less reactive and unconscious – that is, made without thought or awareness of consequences. Some such reactions may be learned by example, and may reflect tradition and social norms. Some may be influenced by religious beliefs, and by political philosophies. The bulk of our daily decisions, perhaps not consciously taken, are the product of such reactive responses and habits.

Decision making, even at high political levels, is greatly influenced by unconsciously held prejudices, belief systems and what are called "values," that guide decisions, even though not subjected to analysis. In politics those leaders who are "decisive" and "forceful," that is reactive, are frequently those who most readily obtain electoral support when opposed by leaders who are contemplative, logical and analytical, suggesting that people generally respond more readily to stimuli that elicit reactive responses.

Such a perspective is relevant to our conflict resolution concerns. Participation by the parties concerned is widely held to be a desirable feature of conflict management and resolution; but we should note that for the reasons given above, this participation is likely to be no more than reactive responses unless carefully controlled in an analytical framework so that there can be the consideration of all available knowledge.

A shift from the reactive, hierarchical type decision making processes to interactive ones in which decisions emerge from the interaction of all affected parties is, clearly, a profound one. Decision making in these two modes are really different phenomena, as different as reflex actions and considered responses. The history of decision making theory suggests that such a shift is of recent origin. Within a previous power environment consideration of responses of those affected – family members, workers, servants, minorities, and others – was not relevant. The full implications of this shift, the way in which it is affecting institutions and social relations generally, are not yet fully realized. We will trace out this shift and the added insights that have emerged step-by-step, for in this way contending approaches to conflict management and resolution are better placed in their evolutionary perspective. As indicated, we will begin in Chapter 12 with the most simple conceptions of decision making. In Chapter 13 we will examine their applications to unilateral conflict management.

THE POWER INPUT–OUTPUT MODEL OF DECISION MAKING

The traditional and still prevalent power-political decision making concept was modeled by Modelski in 1962. He presented a simple input–output model of unilateral decision making. The inputs are the power inputs provided by resources and populations that are available to decision makers. The outputs are the distributions made by them

Stimulus   Response

Figure 12.1 Power inputs and allocations

of the available power (see Figure 12.1).

Modelski was concerned primarily, and almost exclusively, with international relations. We must remind ourselves, however, that decision making is a generic phenomenon, and shifts in thinking, as represented by different models, have a universal application.

The input–output model is clearly an authoritative and elitist model: the assumption is that there are, in any organization or set of relationships, those whose job it is to supply the resources or inputs (the stimulus), and those whose job it is to make allocations (response) according to their goals and interests. A focus on resources that provide power and allocations of such resources assumes that there is no decision making process as such required. Given power an authority can make these decisions in an arbitrary manner with little thought to consequences. It was in this context that politics was once defined as "the authoritative allocation of values" (Easton, 1981). It is for this reason, also, that the legitimization of authorities becomes a key topic in political thought: legitimacy provides the exchange link between the two roles, those supplying resources and those allocating them.

So much has there been a focus on authoritative elites and policies that in this Modelski model the actual decision making process is not represented: it is not even conceptualised. The preoccupation is with the quality and quantity of resources available for distribution, and the allocation of these resources, not as a decision making process by which the allocation is made, but as a perceived result. Given power and authority the actual process of allocation, that is the process of decision making, is assumed not to present difficulties or call for attention.

By the early 1960s, however, it was appreciated by those in situations in which there is closer interaction than in international relations, such as is the case in industrial relations, that the decision making process itself is the critical part. The "black box" between stimulus and response was the focus of attention: how inputs are recorded, processed, assessed, filed, retrieved and so on (Snyder, Bruck and Sapin, 1962; and Blake, Shepard and Mouton, 1964). Efficiency in process could compensate for lack of power in some

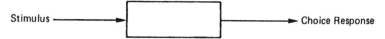

Stimulus ⟶ [ ] ⟶ Choice Response

Figure 12.2 Reactive decision making model

circumstances (see Figure 12.2).

More and more complex models of the decision making process emerged, and systems analysis helped to promote these considerations. The input or stimulus, and the output or response, were no longer the only components in conceptual thinking. The visual models drew attention to processes that take place within the "black box" of decision making. More and more complications were inserted as experience and awareness directed attention to other details. The cybernetic or feedback process loomed large after the invention of electronic self-steering and self-correcting devices, such as were introduced into aircraft during the Second World War. They provided models on which cybernetic thought could be based (Deutsch, 1963).

This cybernetic conception was still within the power framework. It recognized that there could be savings in the use of resources, that is in power, if there were processes by which problems could be foreseen and circumvented, just as navigators change course when radar provides feedback showing a storm ahead, and can reset a course to compensate for the altered direction. The feedback can be into the decision making process, or into the initial perception or

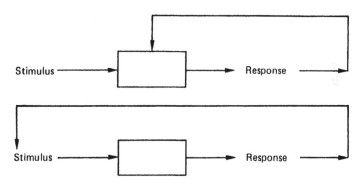

Figure 12.3 Cybernetic models

stimulus that provoked the response (see Figure 12.3).

In due course further complexities were introduced to take account of evidence that different stimuli sometimes produce identical responses in different persons and systems, while different responses are sometimes produced by the same stimulus. Values, motivations, and individual behaviors generally, had to be taken into account – which was not the case with the simple power input–output models (see Figure 12.4).

All of these models, however, from the simplest stimulus response to the most complicated decision making process, had in common those features that had been inherited from a classical tradition. They all depicted unilateral and reactive processes, and they all assumed a major power element in decision making. By implication the cybernetic model acknowledged the existence of human responses and the need to circumvent them, but none of those models dealt in any depth with the values and motivations of those affected by decisions.

They were, in short, all models of power elite responses to environmental conditions and to changes in these conditions. The

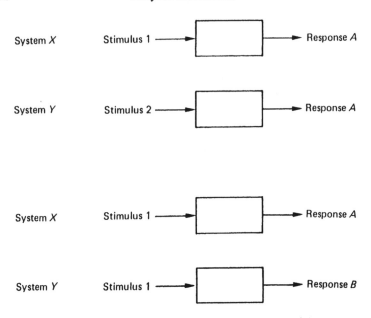

Figure 12.4 More complex stimulus–response models

classical assumptions that had dominated legal thought, that there
was a power elite right to expect obedience, and a moral obligation
on the part of others to obey, were implicit in all. All were in a
framework in which it was assumed that it was negotiable interests
that were in conflict, that these interests were primarily material, that
relative power could determine negotiation outcomes, and that power
bargaining and authoritative coercion were, therefore, the relevant
decision making processes.

To the extent that any human element entered into decision making
theory it was limited to problems of perception. There was an input
from psychology into international relations and other studies which
demonstrated how empirical data and perceptions generally could be
misinterpreted because of problems of perspective, and also gestalt
or image formation problems (see Burton, 1972).

MAKING PUZZLES OUT OF PROBLEMS

The traditional decision making process, being power-oriented, was
assumed to be a vertical process, commands coming down from the

apex of the decision making pyramid that comprises a small elite, to the mass of those who have the obligation to obey. In so far as there is any protest response communicated upwards, it is dealt with within the power framework that this structure implies, at least to the extent that available power makes this possible.

In this traditional system of authoritative relations, which applies to industry and even to family relations in many cases, no less than to political life, it is seemingly expedient and efficient to employ power and coercion as a means of eliminating non-compliant behavioral responses, and as a means of ensuring discipline. Countervailing behavioral pressures are curbed, at least temporarily.

This effectively makes puzzles out of complex problems. A puzzle has a known outcome, as does a maze. For example, in dealing with a riot it is possible to bring about a known outcome by sending in the police to quell it, without any interest in its origins and causes. A problem, on the other hand, has many possible outcomes, many leading to new problems as the result of transformations in relationships.

Resolving problems of conflict in human and organizational relationships is an on-going process. For this reason the strong and understandable preference in decision making is to make puzzles out of problems. There is a political and personal preference for certainty, for decisive leadership, and an institutional need for firm agreements. Wherever there is an effective power capability, complex behavioral and organizational problems can be simplified into puzzles. Dissident and deviant behaviors can be suppressed without finding out their causes, or resolving the underlying problems.

In the short term, authoritative decision making, especially in politics, is effective and widely admired as positive decision making. In the longer term there are frequently adverse effects because important variables have been ignored or suppressed. For example, minority problems, defined as rebellion, are frequently dealt with by suppression. In the longer term ethnicity, autonomy, and identity factors emerge, often leading to protracted violence. Experience is leading us to believe that, to be effective, decision making must take into account all behavioral variables, regardless of the complexities in analysis and in procedures.

LEGITIMACY

It is when puzzles are made out of problems that a legitimacy problem emerges. We have seen that in classical and traditional thought, authority and leadership were derived from tradition, legality or charisma, or some combination of these. In all cases they were concerned with we–they relationships, that is relationships which assumed class divisions. Legality was defined pragmatically, by reference to effective control over society, and recognition of this control by others.

There is now, however, as we have shown in Chapter 8, a distinction emerging between that which is legal or legitimate, and that which is legitimized. Legitimized authority is that which is self-supporting, being derived from those over whom it is exercised. There can be legitimized authorities even within a power–authority framework. In a legitimized relationship there is a valued exchange relationship between those in authority, and those over whom authority is exercised. There is no implied coercion or manipulation necessary. There is an implied reciprocity in relationships. While there can never be a pure form of legitimization, any more than there can be any ideal type, it is possible to observe and to make judgements about relative legitimization. There are in world society, and within nations, many authorities that are legal, but which have little legitimization.

Once this distinction is made between that which is legal and that which is legitimized, there is revealed another source of authority, role differentiation as distinct from hierarchical roles. Legitimized role differentiation is the choice of one among imputed equals to carry out a role of limited authority. An example would be the designated chairman of an informal parents' meeting at the local school, or the speaker in a parliament. It is possible to conceive and to model an interactive decision making process that has such a legitimized foundation, as we shall see later in this chapter.

DECISION MAKING AND IDEOLOGIES

Decision making processes themselves limit options and determine in advance the range of outcomes that are possible. For example, courts make judgements within the boundaries of legal norms: "equity" courts cannot arrive at decisions that could in their view be "just" if the law provides otherwise. Mediation seeks compromise:

the mediator, regardless of the justifications for opposing claims, tries to obtain a compromise or reasonable agreement. Bargaining confines negotiation to a set of proposals. Arms control negotiations do not include discussion of the reasons for arms. In such processes the outcomes are likely to reflect the bargaining power of the contestants, not agreement on the key issues at stake.

The invention and the selection of these processes reflect definitions of the problem in advance of knowledge of it. A communal conflict, occurring in a "democracy" defined as majority government, is defined as rebellion. Police and military coercion is the appropriate remedy on the basis of this definition. The facts that there are identity and recognition issues, that there is evidence of discrimination against the minority, that the minority has no effective voice in decision making, are given little weight – even though, in practice in the longer term, these influences prove more powerful than military coercion.

Policies and remedies thus reflect ideologies. The invention of processes, their selection in particular cases, and the definitions given to particular situations, arise out of assumptions, frequently false, made about the behavior of persons and the role of authorities. These are not assumptions held just by a few or by decision makers. They are often inherent in popular consensus, and in elite thought and philosophy. There are many of these assumptions that are widely shared: conflictual relationships are "win–lose;" nations, even multi-ethnic societies, are, or should be, politically integrated units; institutional and social values are more important to the preservation of societies than are human values.

Societies have come to the end of the line with these reactive practices of decision making, based on assumptions that do not take into account the human responses of those affected. No matter how sophisticated, they do not seem to be effective in solving policy problems in industry, in domestic politics, or in the world society. As we shall see, when applied to conflict management these reactive decision making processes are equally limited.

DECISION MAKING AND CONFLICT RESOLUTION

What we seek in conflict resolution are decision making processes that do not prejudice or limit outcomes in advance of a wide and deep exploration of the situation, including the human dimension.

These processes seek to promote the search for and consideration of discoverable options. In short, what we seek are realistic definitions of situations, from which would flow insights on which to base decisions. It needs to be emphasized that the definition of a situation, its nature and source, is the end product of analysis, and not a first perception on which to base decisions.

Instead, therefore, of a unilateral reactive power model of decision making, such as we have described, let us now consider a multilateral interactive model. It remains essentially a stimulus–response model, but between stimulus and response there is an interaction between all parties who make decisions, or are affected by decisions, in any particular situation.

Such a model implies a set of assumptions that are distinctly different from those that underlie traditional authority relationships. First and foremost is the proposition that the issues that appear to be the source of conflicts are not of a win–lose character, as is so often assumed to be the case by protagonists operating in a traditional power framework. Once perceptions, value hierarchies and costing have been explored and analyzed, the definition of situations alters. Those issues that appear to be win–lose or zero sum often turn out to be means to ends. The ends being held in common, and not necessarily of given size or in short supply, the issues are seen to be negotiable.

The presence of non-negotiable needs does not, therefore, necessarily mean that conflicts cannot be resolved. Their presence does mean, however, that decision making processes are required that transform what appear to be win–lose conflicts into positive sum ones by separating out non-negotiable human needs from strategies and tactics.

Such processes of decision making are far removed from stimulus–response reactive decision making. They must take into account problems of perception, choices available, problems of overloading of decision makers, politically relevant time-spans, crisis behavior, costing of consequences, and a host of other aspects of analytical decision making. Such non-adversary and analytical decision making opens up options not available to traditional adversary-type courts, parliaments and industrial institutions of decision making (Burton, 1969; Kelman, 1972; Wedge, 1971; Kelman and Cohen, 1976).

INTERACTIVE MODELS OF DECISION MAKING

Looking at decision making from this point of view, there are two models. There are, first, those that make puzzles out of problems. They are interactive, but nevertheless still lie within a power framework. These are the cybernetic models that we noted previously, and they are the link with reactive models. Second there is a problem-solving model. It rests on analysis and seeks outcomes that are positive sum, satisfying the values of all parties.

This second model usually must rely, as is argued below, on a third party who is non-judgemental, non-directive, non-manipulative, and who seeks to ensure an effective analytical interaction between parties (see Figure 12.5).

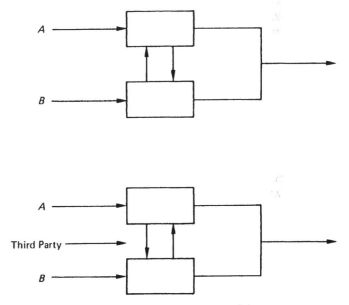

Figure 12.5 Interactive models

In the seven situations depicted in Figures 12.6–12.8, both *reactive* and *interactive* models are described in more detail. The pay-offs to each party, the nature of the decision making process, and the dynamics of the interaction are described. They are in three sets, power reactive models (Figure 12.6) transition models (Figure 12.7), and problem-solving models (Figure 12.8).

In the first set, the power models, there are three models. The first

Model No.	Puzzle or problems	Model	Pay-offs	Description	Dynamics
1	Complexities ignored: puzzles	A → Perception of situation → Power → A's goal	$A = +x$ $B = -x$ where $x = 1$	Reactive Power model: win–lose outcome	A determines outcome, e.g. war or compulsion: settlement enforced
2	Complexities ignored: puzzles	A → Trial-and-error cybernetics → A's goal	$A = +x$ $B = -x$ where $x > 0.5$	Win–lose, but in less extreme proportions	A influences outcomes having experienced B's responses: settlement enforced
3	Complexities ingnored: puzzles	A → Analysis of many complexities in relations from ascendancy viewpoint → A's goal	$A \sim B$ (indeterminate)	Paternalistic model	A takes into account B's goals and influences outcome: settlement enforced

Figure 12.6 Reactive power models

Model No.	Puzzle or problems	Model	Pay-offs	Description	Dynamics
4	Transition	A → As above from A's position → A's goal; Direct negotiation; B → As above from B's position → B's goal	Stalemate or $A + x$, $B - x$ where $x > 0.5$	Perceived incompatible goals; but recognition that relationship are based on relative power and both sides must participate in decision making	A cannot determine outcome and must compromise: <u>settlement agreed</u>
5	Transition	A → As above → A's goal; Third Party; B → As above → B's goal	$\dfrac{A + B}{2}$	Incompatible goals; but acceptance of mutual need to accept the third party norms or compromise	Compromise mediation: <u>settlement agreed</u>

Figure 12.7 Transition models: interactive power models

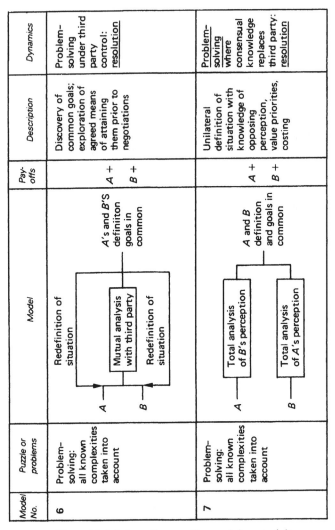

Figure 12.8 Interactive problem-solving models

is a straight power model of the stimulus–response type, taking no account of the reactions of other parties. The second is one in which there is an element of trial and error, or cybernetic decision making, in which the more powerful concedes something. The third is one in which the powerful party endeavors to take into account some of the needs of others in a paternalistic mode.

These reactive models are presented merely to show the limits of such decision making notions: within a power and reactive framework, this is the limit beyond which reactive models cannot go. This is the point reached today by many authorities in politics and in industry: there appears to be no further step that can be taken within the philosophies and conceptions that are at the base of reactive notions of authority.

The second set, in which there are two models, is a transition set – transition from power to problem-solving. It depicts negotiation with other parties; but still within a power framework. Alternatively there is third-party mediation introduced to assist negotiation. In both cases the outcome is likely to be compromise, neither party being satisfied, with potential conflict written into the settlement. However, it is an advance on what is possible within a purely reactive model.

The third set is the interesting one. Here there are two models, one in which a third party enacts a role to assist in problem-solving – a special role not to be confused with arbitration or mediation. The other is a somewhat unrealistic and idealistic model, yet a logical extension, that assumes that the parties themselves have the professional knowledge of a third party in a problem-solving context, and have the willingness and ability to apply that knowledge to their own situation.

It is not wholly unrealistic or idealistic. If there were an adequate theory of behavior, and if there were a widespread understanding and knowledge of it, parties could work out their relationships without the assistance of a professional third party.

This is the decision making framework in which we wish to survey the field of conflict resolution. It is a framework that enables us to place all other processes in an appropriate place, according to the degree to which power, coercion, manipulation, participation and other ingredients are present or absent.

THE EMERGENCE OF PROBLEM-SOLVING

It is at this point that conflict resolution breaks new ground by branching off into a different direction, the direction of interactive problem-solving, based on a deep analysis of the conflict, and of the longer-term costs of outcomes imposed by relative power. The earlier diversion from reactive decision making to authoritative decision making having failed, we are witnessing a movement toward interactive decision making in which the responses of peoples affected are taken into account *before* decisions are taken.

13 Trends in Conflict Management and Resolution

We have traced out some changes that have taken place, over the last forty years, in unilateral and reactive decision making processes in industry, government and authoritative relations generally, and changes also in our understanding of them.

We would expect to find similar trends in the development of conflict management and conflict resolution. If we can discern clearly what these trends are, then we will have an understanding of the nature of conflict management, where it has failed, and the directions in which it is heading.

THE EMERGENCE OF THE THIRD PARTY

It is to be noted that when the parallels are drawn between decision making generally and conflict management and conflict resolution, a third-party role emerges. A third party is not necessarily a part of conflict management, but when policies and decisions lead to conflict in practice there is frequently recourse to a third party of one kind or another.

It is the role of the third party that is the main subject of debate when conflict management and conflict resolution processes are discussed. As we shall see, it varies greatly. In some procedures there is a high level of authoritative decision making, in some there are mild forms of influence, and in others an endeavor to be neutral, and to make no inputs of substance, merely helping to find a consensus.

CHANGING MODELS: DIRECT POWER CONFRONTATION

We will deal with conflict management and conflict resolution processes separately, as they are substantially different.

In conflict management, as in decision making generally, there are three components which are significant. *First*, there is the degree and quality of participation by the parties to the dispute. This includes the bargaining power available, influence on the decision making institution or forum concerned, knowledge and negotiating skills available, and other power attributes of the participants. *Second*, there is the degree and quality of communication between the parties. This includes their perceptions and understanding of the situation, abilities to receive information and to communicate it. *Third*, if there is a third party involved, there are the degrees of decision making power, degrees of neutrality, levels of analytical skills, and other attributes of third parties.

It is useful to represent these three components diagramatically so that the essentials of change and trends over time can be perceived and conceptualized readily. For example, a profile of a direct conflict situation would be:

```
Participation      ————————————————————————————
Communication      ————————————————————
Third Party        –
```

Translating, this means that between parties in direct conflict there is total participation, a high level of communication, even if it is only shouting at or dropping bombs on each other, and usually no third party involvement.

The traditional means of handling conflicts within a society have been authoritative controls such as court settlements, police interventions, and other processes associated with the notion of the maintenance of law-and-order. This form of control can be modelled thus:

```
Participation      ———
Communication      –
Third Party        ————————————————————————————
```

Interpreting, this means that in a judicial setting the parties have very little participation, their cases being represented by counsel, and the arguments being based on precedents and legal norms rather than on an analysis of the values and needs of the parties. There is little or no direct communication between the parties concerned. The role of the third party is decisive.

Even when the dispute is between parties within a nation, that is, when they are subject to the jurisdiction of the same authority, experience is that authoritative decision making is not effective whenever there are important human concerns involved. This has been demonstrated in the many multi-cultural and multi-ethnic conflicts that have taken place within nations since the Second World War, of which Cyprus and Northern Ireland are widely known examples. Less conspicuously, such means of controlling conflict fail in industrial and even family relationships when important personal needs are at stake.

When authorities are themselves in conflict, as in international relations, no settlement procedure is possible in the absence of some overriding authority – which would have the effect of placing the parties in one political system. The result is that there are no means of settlement short of a power confrontation. It is this that, at the international level, the world society has sought to avoid. For these reasons there evolved forms of judicial settlement with the creation of an international court, or mediation through the United Nations in which parties were expected to accept the recommendations of the mediator.

Judicial settlement and obligatory processes, however, have not been effective even within the same domestic political system. It was probably a mistake to try to model the international system on the national: courts and enforcement processes are even less likely to succeed in dealing with differenct nations and cultures, where separate identity and sovereignty are important values.

Failure of coercive measures nationally and internationally has led to what lawyers call "weaker" forms of conflict management – that is, less and less decision making and coercive power by an authoritative exercise of power through the courts. In fact, the history of conflict managment, or mediation if we use that term in the popular sense, is a progressive movement toward "weaker" or less judgemental forms.

The next form that is slightly weaker than court jurisdiction is quasi-judicial arbitration, where the parties each nominate someone to represent them, and these nominees may nominate another to preside. Virtually the same legal procedures apply. The parties may be more comfortable because they participate more by having had some say into the selection of persons who will make the decisions that affect their fate. There is a little more participation, but no more communication between the parties, for argument remains within a legal and confrontations framework which includes a decisive third party role.

This form could be represented thus:

Participation   ————

Communication   –

Third Party   ——————————————

Mediation, used strictly to denote the process whereby an agreed third party is asked to make decisions after consultations with the parties (usually separate consultations), is the next "weaker" form. There is more participation by the parties, some indirect communication, but the third party role is still dominant. It may be depicted thus:

Participation   ————————

Communication   ————

Third Party   ————————

There evolved another form of mediation in which the parties would not undertake in advance to accept the decisions of the mediator. While the profile of this "honest broker" form of mediation remains much the same, this is obviously an even weaker form.

At this point we enter into a far less formal process, called conciliation, in which there is little effective decision making by the third party, who offers little more than "good offices," making it possible for the parties to communicate more directly. In practice this is a process that is relevant only in situations in which parties are not in a declared state of war, and where parties are prepared to be known to interact. It can be modelled thus:

Participation   ——————————

Communication   ——————————

Third Party   ————

The next "weaker" form is direct negotiation between parties. This brings us back to our starting point: the profile is the same as the one with which we commenced. It is the profile of conflict. The process and its outcomes reflect the relative power of the parties. There may be a settlement, but it is likely to be short-lived, as it rests on the power relationship remaining static. In modern conditions means of violence are available to even the least powerful of parties, and instability is assured if there is a settlement forced on one party by another:

Participation   ——————————————————
Communication   ——————————————
Third Party   –

SUMMARY VIEW

We could have included many other variations in this sequence, especially so at the "weaker" end of the spectrum. There is, for example, "collaborative problem-solving" where a third party brings together parties to a dispute, such as in a reorganization of a corporation. All present have common goals, but different choices as to how to achieve them. Disputes are over choices rather than any human need issues. The role of the third party is that of a chairperson keeping records and guiding discussion. There are variations which apply to community disputes. There are other forms involving compromises manipulated by a third party, or exploitations where a dominant party is in a position to impose its interests by reason of greater resources thrown into the process, as appears to be the case in many environmental disputes (see Amy, 1987).

We could thus list a variety of processes in the total range from courts to direct confrontations:

Courts
Quasi-judicial settlements
Arbitration
Binding mediation
Non-binding mediation
Shuttle diplomacy or caucusing negotiation
Conciliation
Collaborative problem-solving
Direct power bargaining

Let us note again that as forms become "weaker" the role of the third party weakens, while there is a progressive increase in the participation of the parties and communication between them.

It will be seen that domestic societies and the world society are at a crucial stage in the management of conflict. The failure of power-based unilateral decision making has led to a crisis situation in decision making, reflected in the failure of conflict management procedures that rest on degrees of coercion or manipulation.

The whole range of possible devices from direct power confrontation to legal judgements, and back again to direct confrontations, has been tried. We have, over half a century, been able to do no more than make power bargaining more sophisticated, playing largely into the hands of the more powerful, and of those who are better equipped to take advantage of the more sophisticated processes now available.

AN HISTORICAL PROCESS

The trend toward weaker forms of mediation, that is the step-by-step reductions in the decisive role of third parties, is not just an analytical progression. It is also an experienced historical one. At the international level, for example, the International Court was the intellectually preferred means of conflict settlement after the First World War. In practice it has not been used in any significant way to deal with international conflicts. There are few cases of major conflict that have been handled by any international tribunal. Under the United Nations there have been some instances of non-binding mediation, as for example, in the case of Cyprus (see the Mediator's Report, UN Security Council Document s/6253, 1965). Such mediation has not been effective. In the Cyprus case there was no direct interaction between the parties, and the mediator was working on certain assumptions about the intentions of the parties about their relations with Greece and Turkey which could not be checked in the absence of any direct interaction. These assumptions proved, finally, not to be valid.

At the domestic level, courts have been less and less effective in dealing with intense conflicts that take place within societies. It is possible to make arrests, to punish and to jail; it has not been possible for courts to deal with underlying problems. Courts are confined largely to adjudicate infringements of law, and to disputes between parties over negotiable interests. As courts have become overwhelmed, jurisdiction in some of these latter cases in some countries is being handed over to privatized processes of dispute settlement which share the traditional assumptions about the nature of conflict.

It will have been noted that each of the decision making models we examined in Chapter 12, from stimulus–response reactions to more considered decisions, had its counterpart in conflict management which, as has been seen, progressed from authoritarian settlements to more considered mediation that involved to some degree the parties to the dispute. In decision making, the historical trend showed more and more interaction before final decisions were made, and more and more consideration of the nature of the decision to be taken. In conflict management there was the parallel tendency: more and more participation and communication by those affected, and less and less coercive third-party intervention.

What is clear from this historical series of decision making and conflict management models is that each failed, and led to the next, until there was a return to the original power-oriented bilateral conflict that the models were supposed to avoid. In the historical series we ended up where we began, that is with direct power negotiation, perhaps modified to some degree by very weak forms of third-party intervention.

By failure, we mean first an unwillingness of parties to conflicts to use the means available to them. Having tried forms of mediation they have finally shown a preference for direct negotiation, even violent conflict.

An even more important source of failure has been the results of these processes when they have been used. There are many examples of mediation in one form or another that have led to protracted conflicts. The Cyprus situation has persisted for twenty years. The Israeli–Palestine problem shows no prospect of solution despite many attempts at mediation and shuttle diplomacies. So with many local disputes, such as environmental disputes, zoning battles and gang wars. The inadequacies of the processes employed may be an important part of the total problem.

It is only when we have discovered the precise nature of the behavioral dimensions which have led to the conflict that we can determine what are the politically acceptable and effective processes of conflict resolution. To that we now turn. Then we will return to decision making, and to parallel models of conflict resolution, but this time to decision making and conflict resolution that incorporate a behavioral dimension.

THE BEHAVIORAL COMPONENT

There must be a reason for these common trends in decision making and conflict management. It is not some accident or temporary influence that accounts for them. Whether in the family, in industry, in commerce, in community relations or in international relations, there is some influence at work that explains these persistent trends toward greater participation by the parties involved. Whatever it may be, it has to be taken into account when we explore the forms of decision making and conflict handling that are likely to be acceptable, and to work.

There is a conspicuous behavioral component in these historical trends. First, the trend toward "weaker" forms reflected difficulties in having matters of importance, for example non-negotiable values such as are involved in ethnicity conflicts, or issues involving security and defense, determined by authoritative third parties. Second, the trend reflected the need for total satisfaction of important values, and the avoidance of compromises, if there were to be a resolution of the problem, rather than a temporary settlement of the dispute or conflict.

LESSONS FROM THE PAST

Experience shows that there must be full *participation* by the parties in any process dealing with conflicts that are deep-rooted for the process to be acceptable and effective. (This is one reason why courts and arbitration have limited applicability.)

Experience does not show that full and direct *communication* between parties is always desired, though direct communication is the final result in power political negotiation or direct violence. If, however, we assume that there must be problem-solving and not just settlement for an outcome to be lasting, and since problem-solving must take into account the hidden data of human values and needs, we can assume that some process of direct and complete communication is essential.

Such high quality communication is unlikely without the assistance of a *third party*. However, the third party in this case has a role quite different from the third party to which we referred when discussing conflict management. The role of the third party in judicial settlements, and "weaker" forms, such as mediation, is a decision making or quasi-decision making one. It is this role which has been resisted by disputants. It is clear from empirical evidence that parties to disputes that involve values important to the disputants require decision making to be wholly in their own hands until final and acceptable options have been discovered and agreed. The third-party role in problem-solving is one confined to promoting communication between the protagonists, and helping them in their analysis of their relationships, and the discovery of options.

There are, therefore, these three variables to be taken into account in any profile of the conflict resolution process: participation, communication, and a third-party non-judgemental, non-authoritative facilitating role.

The profile changes from those depicted when we considered conflict management. It will be recalled that the conflict management (mediation) profile was:

Participation   —————————————
Communication   ————————
Judgemental Third Party   ——————————————————————

Now it becomes:

Participation   ——————————————————————————
Communication   ——————————————————————————
Facilitating Third Party   ——————————————————————————

This sets us on a quite different course; we move from settlement toward analytical problem-solving conflict resolution, requiring outcomes that are positive for all concerned.

THE MAIN VARIABLES

The simple diagram in Figure 13.1 depicts the differences between coercive and problem-solving approaches.

Segment *A* is the area in which third parties impose terms of settlement that are designed to be favorable to all the parties in dispute in the absence of their participation – as, for example, when Britain, Greece and Turkey imposed a constitution on Cyprus in 1960. Segment *D* in where the outcome is win–lose, but the rules are accepted, as in a game (for example, changes of government by electoral processes). Segment *C* is the traditional area of thought where it is assumed that outcomes must be win–lose, inviting conflict or requiring authoritative settlements. Segment *B* is the area in which both parties gain as a result of interactions, and require no external coercive decision making: their conflict can be resolved, as distinct from settled.

Segments *C* and *B* are those that are of immediate interest to us. *C* represents power politics, bargaining and coercive settlements,

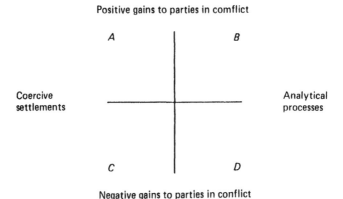

Positive gains to parties in comflict

A   B

Coercive   Analytical
settlements   processes

C   D

Negative gains to parties in conflict

Figure 13.1 Coercive and problem-solving approaches

giving rise to win–lose outcomes. *B* represents such problem-solving that there are positive gains to all parties.

The essential feature of any shift from the lower left to the upper right quadrant in Figure 13.1 is a shift from an emphasis on the preservation of the status quo and its institutions by the use of power, to the satisfaction of the goals of those concerned by some interactive process. This raises some fundamental questions of political philosophy – for example, the issue of the common good and the individual interest – that rest, in turn, on some fundamental questions concerning the human being.

THE QUESTIONING OF ASSUMPTIONS AND PERCEPTIONS

The questioning of assumptions and perceptions is a key to discovery of the nature of a particular conflict and its underlying sources, and also to the nature of acceptable options. It is this which is the resolution process.

Imagine a clock-face. At 9 o'clock there is *A*, representing Application, Action, the Actual steps taken to deal with a particular situation. At 6 o'clock there is *M*, representing the Means that have been decided upon to deal with the situation, the Methods authorities or other parties involved in the dispute have determined. These will reflect their perception of the situation, their role, their philosophy and ideology, and generally any influence which determines policy (see Figure 13.2).

It is usually the case that the policy formation process, whether it be at the level of government, in industry or in the family, is taken almost intuitively, on a hunch, on the basis of observable information,

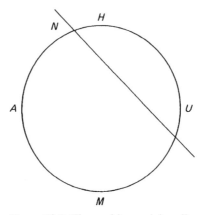

Figure 13.2 The problem-solving diagram

and without a great deal of questioning of perceptions, and within some ideological framework. Typically political considerations, such as electoral support, personal popularity and status enter into the decision making process. It is not typical to conduct a careful analysis in interaction with others who might be affected before decisions are taken. A realistic and longer-term costing of the consequences of actions to be taken is, therefore, not part of the traditional process.

If a policy decision is made in this way, and particularly when it has been justified in public (and again this could be at management or union level, even the family level no less than at official level), then the probability is that any failure of the policy will lead to more of the same medicine. Failure by violence or some form of threat or coercion to quell a riot, to suppress an opposition, to control a work force, or the behavior of children in a family or a classroom, tends to lead to increased coercion.

To move from settlement to resolution it is necessary to move to 3 o'clock, to a point *U* in Figure 13.2, which represents some adequate and *U*nified theory of behavior that would guide policy and ensure that the action taken is not self-defeating, and will accomplish its objectives.

A UNIFIED THEORY

The notion of a *unified* theory arises because reactive policy is greatly influenced by separate disciplines, that is by segments of total knowledge available.

There is available a wealth of knowledge in the social sciences, but it is scattered and in separate segments. We know a great deal about decision making, institutions, legitimacy, and other "islands" of knowledge available to a facilitator in a conflict resolution situation. But we have difficulty in integrating it in a way that makes it available in a particular situation. At a personal intellectual level this is a problem. It is a major problem at the highest levels of government where decision making becomes a conflict in itself between separate agencies each dealing with a small amount of the total information that could be available.

HYPOTHESES

It is not possible to achieve a unified theory unless we have already determined the basic and fundamental hypotheses on which we are to operate. This brings us back to H, representing *H*ypotheses, at 12 o'clock in Figure 13.2.

What are the ultimate goals of society, of civilizations, of people that must be reflected in any decisions taken in respect to a particular situation? Is it the political status of decision makers, and if so at what cost to future goals? Is it pursuit of some belief system that has been inherited, but not necessarily adapted to changed conditions and increased knowledge? Are we able to get down to some fundamental assumptions regarding the nature of the human being, such as those implied in needs theory? The quality of decision making rests on consideration given at point H.

Conflict resolution, on the other hand, rests on an assumption that there are such objective criteria. It is the discovery of these that is implied in the emphasis placed on the examination of hypotheses in the facilitated conflict resolution process. The third party is in an analytical, almost a teaching situation, drawing attention to false assumptions, and opening up possibilities of arriving at potentially realistic ones.

PROCESS

We have, therefore, moved toward a process that is a substitute for the series of stronger and weaker forms of third-party intervention that have proved unacceptable whenever there are important values at stake. In summary form it is one that starts with basic assumptions, works through to explanations of the conflict situation, provides guides to policy and ends up with the acceptable option.

Invariably there will be adjustments to be made to whatever is decided in principle. There may be failure to achieve a lasting solution. Then there must be the feedback of *new* data from A to H. It was for this reason that we inserted a point N between 9 and 12 o'clock in Figure 13.2.

SOME ADDITIONS TO THE MODEL

In practice there is a line drawn (Figure 13.2) from the point N at about 11 o'clock to a point at 5 o'clock. What is on the left is in the field of official negotiation – a policy decision to act in a certain way, and its implementation. What is on the right is the pre-negotiation analysis – examinations of assumptions, development of explanations and theories, and the discovery of viable options. In practice both might be carried out by the same persons, especially in local disputes where the participants are representing themselves. At more complex levels the two processes are likely to be separated, the pre-negotiation stages being conducted by persons who are in a position to recommend to decision makers, who then must negotiate.

Another addition to the model is between 3 and 6 o'clock. At some stage between explanation or theory and means and action it is necessary to consider what steps are to be taken to move from a situation of conflict to one of cooperative relations. Finding an agreed option is a start, but implementing it without destroying it in the process is an important consideration. Some tension reduction measures may destroy any prospect of reaching the desired goal. For example, peace-keeping forces tend to institutionalize and perpetuate conflict. Consideration of these issues is a stage in the implementation of an agreement, a stage between M and A in Figure 13.2. But the details of moving from a conflict situation to the desired outcome must be regarded as part of the pre-negotiation stage.

THE HUMAN DIMENSION

We have been playing a game here in choosing the letters to mark points on the clock face model. They read "HUMAN." This is a game with a purpose. What we have done is to stress the human element in conflict and conflict resolution. This is not, once again, for reasons of idealism: we are concerned with the political realities. Ultimate "power" rests with those whose needs and aspirations are not negotiable and must be met, as we have seen from experiences in Northern Ireland, Cyprus, Sri Lanka, South Africa, the Middle East and elsewhere, and as we are beginning to see in the streets within industrial countries, including the major thermonuclear powers.

The stages of the process must be directed toward revealing and satisfying this human dimension. Part of the process must inevitably be accurate assessments of the consequences of using positions of power to avoid such satisfaction – the costs of making puzzles out of problems. This costing aspect runs through the whole process, and explains why it is possible to maintain even among participants of different bargaining power an analytical approach to the problem at hand.

THE TASK AHEAD

Models are merely abstracts designed to point to some of the key variables in a process. The main task still remains: to examine in detail the theoretical and practical details of a conflict resolution process. Why do we assume that there can be agreed options in cases in which there are non-negotiable issues at stake? Why should we assume that parties that are powerful, and especially leaderships with a short political time-span, will be prepared to cost the consequences of their policies? What are the principles which govern the role of a third party? How can we adjust theories that have been developed within separate disciplines to the realities of the total person? We turn to this and related questions in Chapter 14.

14 Conflict Resolution as Problem-solving

Given the tension between the preservation of institutions in the interests of social stability, and the satisfaction of the needs of individuals within a social setting, at all societal levels political decision making is forced into a problem-solving framework in which conflicting interests and strategies have to be taken into account and costed. Indeed, the decision making models of conflict resolution that we have depicted in Chapter 13 are meaningful only in the context of the notion of problem-solving. It is problem-solving to which their historical trends point.

THE CHARACTERISTICS OF PROBLEM-SOLVING

In the Introduction to this overview we noted that problem-solving in conflict resolution was concerned with identifying causes, and for this reason it must be analytical. In elaboration it has four distinctive characteristics. First, *the solution is not an end-product*. It establishes another set of relationships that contains its own set of problems. A problem-solving process might, for example, achieve economic growth or increased leisure. Once achieved it may present a set of anticipated and unanticipated problems, such as inequalities and class conflict, or the problems of adjustment to increased leisure. It is a continuing process rather than a final determination.

Second, problem-solving frequently requires a new synthesis of knowledge, new techniques and a *change in conceptualization* of a problem. When deviance cannot be contained by coercion, a quite different strategy is called for, based on a quite different analysis and theory of behavior.

Third, problem-solving deals with a situation in its *total environment* – that is, the parts of a problem are subject not merely to interaction among themselves, as is the case with a jigsaw puzzle, but to interaction with a wider environment over which there can be little or no control – as though the parts of the jigsaw were changing their size and shape over time. It is the open nature of behavioral systems, unlike laboratory-controlled systems, that is part of the problem. Employer–employee relationships occur in a wider political, economic and social environment, and are affected by them and affect them.

Fourth, to be effective problem-solving goes back to *sources and origins*. The maladjusted individual who commits a crime has a history that made this a high probability. There are, for example, large numbers of teenagers in affluent societies who are alcoholics and who will have on-going problems; there are persons who have felt from early years that they have been discriminated against; there are nations and communities that feel they have not been accepted as equals; there are persons in societies who feel continuously that they are regarded as lesser persons because they have a particular color, religion or sex. When we witness the eruption of a conflict we are inclined to attribute it to some immediate causal factor, and find difficulty in justifying the response by reference to the apparent stimulus that triggered it. We fail to place the stimulus and the response in the total causal setting. In a personal interaction some trivial remark can trigger an aggressive response that can be understood only in the context of the past relations and experiences of those concerned. The Rushdie affair of 1989 in which Iran threatened death to the author of the novel *Satanic Verses* was beyond the comprehension of those who accepted this as a response of Iran and Muslim leadership to a particular event. It was understandable and explicable only in the context of Western treatment of Muslim societies as colonial and backward territories over many years. Only by redressing this past could there have been a solution to that problem.

Because of the difficulty of dealing with these complexities, there has always been a tendency to cope with social and political problems by more direct and simple reactive processes, that is, by taking some *ad hoc* action as and when this seemed unavoidable, with little attention being given to background and wider implications. Police and military interventions are usually of this character. There is a great deal that is associated with conflict *management* which is of this "first aid" order. It is to this attitude to social problems that problem-solving conflict resolution offers a challenge.

THE PROBLEM-SOLVING PROCESS

These features of problem-solving – its on-going nature, the reconceptualization required, the need to deal with the totality of a problem, and to deal with it at source – determine problem-solving processes.

The traditional approach in social sciences is for the observer or analyst to stand at a point outside the situation or events under study, and to come to some seemingly objective conclusions. Nevertheless, the situation is still perceived by the observer in terms of his or her own normative standards, interpretations of behavior, and knowledge of various pieces of history, sociology, and politics. Conflict resolution seeks, by contrast, to be the study by protagonists of the patterns of their own overt behaviors in an intimate and analytical interaction in which there can be detailed checking. The only reality which is relevant is that of the participants. It is not for the third party, or some "specialist," to define the reality. It may be that the reality as perceived by the protagonists may alter as a result of increased knowledge; but it is their reality that must be accepted in any problem-solving process.

We are led, therefore, to seek conditions in which observations of patterns of behavior are made from within the situation, by the protagonists themselves. These same conditions are those in which knowledge communicated by professionals in human affairs about common patterns of behavior in similar circumstances can be fed back to participants, allowing them to select what is perceived to be relevant, and giving them the opportunity to alter their perceptions as new information seems to require.

These conditions suggest themselves. The parties to a conflict need to be placed in a setting that enables them to check on their perceptions of each other, and on the relevance of their conflictual tactics in terms of possible consequences, and to explore alternatives that are available once reperception and reassessment have taken place.

The third party is an observer in a scientific role. The third party makes no assessments, judgements or value interventions. The third party does, however, play an active and greatly influential role by communicating relevant patterns of behavior drawn from other situations and from theoretical knowledge. It is wholly supportive of all actors, and adopts a no-fault and neutral position. It is not for the third party to be the expert on their situation. For this reason it is well for the third party not to be or to include an area or regional specialist. The third party will, of course, engage in clarifications and interpretations of facts and events.

The particular and detailed outcome of this process is unknown in advance. It is likely to be very different from the expectations of the parties because of likely changes in preferences and cost assessments of pursuit of goals, and whatever relevant knowledge about organizational behavior that is brought to bear.

The role of the third party has, therefore, little relationship to the traditional role of a chairman, a mediator or judge. Rather than work from ascertained "facts," or norms and practices in a particular situation, the task of the third party is to apply general theories about conflict and human behavior to the particular situation being examined, thereby helping the parties to analyze it. It is the detailed analysis by the parties of the particular conflict, not normative observations by a third party, that leads to the resolution of the conflict.

There is a hypothesis that once the relationships have been analyzed satisfactorily, once each side is accurately informed of the perceptions of the other, of alternative means of attaining values and goals, and of costs of pursuing present policies, possible outcomes are revealed that might be acceptable to all parties. The justification of this hypothesis is in the theory of behavior outlined in Part I: deep-rooted conflicts are related to needs that are held universally, needs that are not material goods in short supply. Their acquisition can best be obtained through choosing from many options those satisfiers that are not a threat to others, and which, desirably lead to valued exchange relationships.

THE SPONSORING ROLE OF THE THIRD PARTY

In handling conflicts in which there are more than two parties it is necessary, if the analytical procedures are to be followed, for a third party to make an initial analysis of parties and issues, and to bring together in the first instance those parties that are in conflict over specific issues, commencing with those that are at the center of the conflict, that is those whose relationships have been most damaged by the conflict. In a multi-ethnic conflict that has international implications, for example, it is necessary to commence with the local communities, not with the external powers interested in the dispute.

The third party has, therefore, a sponsoring and structuring role.

Tentative assessments must be made as to which are the parties, and which are the issues relevant to these parties, that are to be discussed. As the process gets under way alterations may have to be made – as, for example, if it turns out that there are some issues to be resolved between factions within the parties selected. Typically, deviant behavior involves many parties in addition to those engaged in the deviant act. Juvenile crime involves parents, schools and peer groups, not just as parties that can assist the deviant in returning to conforming behavior, but as causes of the deviance, and as means by which the environment of the deviant can be altered. In this sense, authorities concerned with living and working conditions may be parties to the conflict. So, too, in wider conflicts. An industrial conflict involves many unions and many different levels of organization within unions, each of which experiences conflict within its organizations, and this applies also to management. Local and regional conflicts typically involve many parties. (These and other aspects of process are dealt with in Book 4 in which, also, procedures are set out in detail.)

CONFLICT RESOLUTION AS AN ANALYTICAL AND LEARNING PROCESS

In Chapter 15, which deals with cultural aspects, we will be arguing that there is a universal or human culture that favors reasoned attempts to contend with problems. The interactive and problem-solving procedures of conflict resolution are not uniquely part of any regional culture. They are essentially the same for peoples of all cultures as any analytical situation would be. There is a problem area to examine, a body of knowledge to be applied, persons whose role it is to convey knowledge and facilitate consideration of it, and those who will integrate new information into their own thinking for their own uses.

Let us note that the subject matter of a conflict resolution interaction is relationships, and the fundamentals of human behavior. It does not dwell on law or history. Parties to a dispute tend initially to argue their cases on legal and historical grounds because these have been their justifications, and this is what is expected of them in a public relations forum. Facilitators in a conflict resolution forum must divert them into an analytical approach. Problem-solving is concerned with analysis of relationships, not with normative rules and past events.

Parties to a conflict in a facilitated resolution setting have certain expectations, in particular the expectation of being better informed. They are already equipped with some basic knowledge of geography, comparative politics, institutions and political thinking. Some will probably already have a conceptual framework in which to place any new information or thinking. It is the role of third-party facilitators to broaden and deepen their understanding of their situation. Attention is lost if there is any attempt by the third party to provide some alternate perspective that does not relate to the participants' values and experiences. Their problem has to be resolved in the context of their perspectives (and that of those whom they represent).

The perceptions of reality of participants, who may come from various cultures and who may have different belief systems, are the starting-point of facilitated analysis. Their individual computers are already programmed: analysis cannot turn off the current and cannot wipe out this programming, though it may be able to alter it, add to it and increase capabilities.

There are, in addition, practical reasons for starting within the frame of reference of the participants: unless participants can identify something relevant to their experience and belief systems, they cannot easily internalize and learn. Experience is that in facilitated interactions between parties to a conflict there is a high level of concentration, interest and learning. This is particularly so when the inputs from the third party build on the interests and experiences of the participants. The question facilitators should be asking and posing to participants is whether existing positions, which have led to conflict, comprise the total of possible positions, whether the conservative–liberal–radical positions are not, in respect of many fundamental conceptual notions, the same position, and whether a paradigm shift is possible that would lead to other positions richer in explanatory and predictive power.

The role of the facilitator is to provide participants with tools of analysis, and how to question and to think. Questioning of existing information and assumptions is a key element in the analysis of any complex human situation.

THE PROBLEM OF SCOPE AND THE QUESTION OF RELEVANCE

It would be expecting too much both of participants and of facilitators to be familiar with all the available behavioral knowledge that is relevant to a particular human situation. Yet there can be no limits on the theoretical knowledge that might be relevant. There can be a focus on a particular topic; but even in respect of this there can be no boundaries. A cultural or ethnic conflict can be examined from several perspectives. There will be a perspective based on traditional power political, legal and authoritative assumptions, defining the conflict as a problem of law and order within the existing political system, perhaps a majority government system. There is the perspective of the minority participants who are eager to grasp at any input that seems appropriate, but unable to judge with any degree of certainty what to accept and what to reject. Should the minority accept a minority situation within the wider majority law and order framework, or are there some reasons why this cannot be expected?

Then there will be the perspective of the third-party facilitator who endeavors to synthesize traditional and specialized perspectives and make them relevant to the situation or area of interest. As part of the synthesis there will be an attempt to filter out classical and traditional notions and assumptions that seem not to be relevant to the contemporary situation and conditions.

On what basis can fundamental questions be answered, or must such questions always remain open as subjective judgements? What should be accepted and rejected among the many ideas that come from classical literature, separate disciplines, and the attempted synthesis of the facilitator?

THE FILTER

What is required in a problem-solving forum is a "filter" to screen out false assumptions and implications from existing knowledge, cultural and ideological orientations and personal prejudices. Probably the main task of the third party is to provide this filter. If the participants can use this filter, then they will be able to perceive realities accurately, to assess available theoretical and empirical knowledge, and arrive at reliable conclusions.

In Chapter 13 we modelled the analytical problem-solving process by using a clock face diagram (Figure 13.2), the focus being on 12 o'clock, the point at which basic assumptions were questioned. Only when assumptions had been examined could there be a move to theory at 3 o'clock, and approach at 6 o'clock, and application at 9.

Failure to resolve the problem would be fed back to 12 o'clock and assumptions would be re-examined. This is a filtering process: false assumptions are eliminated. The intellectual activity at the 12 o'clock mark is the foundation of problem-solving.

This filter becomes an important tool of analysis. In filtering out false assumptions, the vacuum left invites the introduction of alternative theories. For example, if in an ethnic conflict the idea is filtered out that the majority has the right to expect obedience while the minority has the obligation to obey, then an alternative notion of authority relationships and democratic constitutions is invited.

In a conflict resolution interaction the filtering out of perceptions and prejudices is an important part of the proceedings. Ultimately it has to be accomplished by protagonists – it is only they, by their own reasoning and testing, who can arrive at revised conclusions. But the third party has to be the agent inspiring the necessary questioning.

Education generally includes the three Rs. The option we have in discussing a particular situation in depth is to provide some knowledge of the processes of reasoning, the fourth R: how thought occurs, how change in thought takes place, the means that can be employed to challenge existing thinking and to arrive at alternative hypotheses. This effectively builds on the knowledge and capacities of the participant, no matter what the cultural or ideological background.

This is what we mean by providing a "filter." It is this filter that is the main requirement of a process that deals with deeply-rooted conflict.

CONCEPTS AND MODELS

It can now be seen why we have argued that a great deal of attention must be given to language and the precise meaning of words, to concepts and their underlying assumptions, to models that are implicit in thinking, and to the assumptions that underlie judgements as to what are the salient variables to be included in models. Complex situations can be analyzed effectively by doing little more than entering into discussion about the meaning of conceptual words, many of which are in everyday use and which are taken for granted – authority, legitimacy, legality, norms, obligations, power, relationships, democracy, coercion, deterrence, development, elites, participation, and ethnicity, among others. The value is not only in learning the content of concepts, and how each requires almost a general theory of behavior for its understanding, but in the habit acquired to analyze words, concepts and their underlying assumptions. Parties to conflicts become greatly involved in this, and it enables them to delve into their problem in ways that make it an almost intellectual discussion rather than a confrontational one.

The nature of the "filter" thus begins to emerge. It is the process of questioning assumptions, the clarification of concepts, the consideration of the salient features of relationships, and the political systems and their processes, all within the context of a study of the problems of induction, the limitations of deduction, and the processes of reasoning. The filtering process is to assist in checking preconceptions and in observing the participants' own "realities" – whether it be a particular class reality, a foreign cultural reality, or an ideological reality. The filter is to provide means of adjustment at a pace and in a way that is acceptable and relevant to each participant. Supplying this filter is the main contribution of the facilitator in a conflict resolution interactive situation.

SUMMARY

This approach to the conflict resolution forum helps to make clear its nature. The third party – usually a panel of facilitators – is professionally trained in a wide spread of behavioral studies, in addition to the philosophy of science and the supportive processes of facilitating communication between the parties. It is not unlike the role that the teacher enacts when inviting members of a class to question and to analyze.

It also draws attention to the supportive nature of the third party. Participants arrive with all manner of ideological and value orientations, all kinds of culturally-based perceptions of others. The facilitation role is to help the protagonists work through preconceived notions and find their own "truth."

15 Culture

We cannot complete an analysis of decision making and conflict resolution without making special reference to culture.

Amongst those interested in conflict resolution there is a widespread interest in culture and cultural differences, perhaps because cultures have been brushed aside as evidence of some inferior status throughout periods of greater power domination. There appears to be a reaction against colonial impositions of Western norms in the handling of conflicts in other cultures, that is imposing Western legal norms and processes that are alien, even in the handling of conflicts amongst peoples of the indigenous culture. Whether this is the reason or not, there is a tendency in dealing with conflicts to give culture some special status, and to introduce it into both analysis and process in ways that are not relevant and probably dysfunctional.

Culture is obviously a value to be protected: empirical evidence is that the protection of culture is something for which peoples will make personal sacrifices. The active preservation of cultures is a driving force in all ethnic conflicts in multi-ethnic societies. Culture has this vital importance because it is a satisfier – that is, a means by which to achieve and to preserve human needs of identity and recognition. For this reason culture and human needs must be differentiated, the latter being universal and the goal, and the former being specific to some identity groups and the means of attaining goals that are universal. There could be social conditions in which culture becomes less of a value because identity and related needs are satisfied by job opportunities, social status and other conditions that promote autonomy.

Different cultures typically have different means of dealing with conflicts. In some there is resort to violence, in some there is leadership arbitration, and in some there is resort to traditional or legal norms. Where there are disputes within societies, especially disputes that have origins in clashes of cultures, it is important to recognize such differences as substantive issues in the conflict to be management or resolved. But it needs to be understood that cultural differences are part of the problem to be resolved. They are not, especially in a multi-cultural conflict, an inherent part of the management or resolution *process*. Culture, either as a satisfier or as a means of dealing with conflicts, should not influence the problem-solving process, a process that must be capable of cutting across cultures.

THE CONCEPT OF CULTURE

In considering these issues we immediately run into a problem of meaning. By "culture" is meant "the act or process of tilling and preparing the earth for crops; cultivation of the soil" (Webster's). The meaning is extended to other forms of growth and development, until finally the term refers to concepts, habits, skills, and manners of a given people at a given period of development. Culture is, by definition, acquired.

If culture refers to behaviors that can be acquired by societies or communities it becomes difficult to know where to draw the line between on the one hand, different ethnic or major community behaviors, which are continuing behaviors and, on the other hand, behaviors associated with particular groups at particular points of time. Part of the New York diplomatic United Nations Mission "culture" seems to be to arrive late for meetings, part of Middle East "culture" is to sleep after lunch. There are members of groups within societies who follow an unconventional way of life. Do they form a "culture" within a culture?

If different ethnic "cultural" groups are found to handle conflicts differently, may it not be that groups within cultures also have different ways of handling conflicts? We could get down to the level of individuals and their different habits.

CULTURE AND THE HUMAN DIMENSION

Whatever the definition of "cultural," it is separate from that which we have termed the human dimension. It is for this reason that we have employed different terms to represent the goals of each. When we have referred to "values" we have been referring to those behaviors that are acquired and specific to a particular society or group. They could change over time, and according to different circumstances. When we have referred to "needs" we have been referring to those goals that are ontological or universal in the human species, and which are probably genetic, and which, therefore are not subject to change even in changed conditions.

The link between the two is an intimate one. For example, cultural differences are associated with ethnic differences in cases in which religion, language, food and other cultural phenomena are associated with ethnicity. At the same time ethnic identity probably has its roots in the human need for security. It becomes difficult in practice, therefore, to make a clear distinction between the two, even though a distinction exists analytically.

Cultural values are important to most members of a community, even though the consensus values themselves are subject to change over time, and even though members of communities are able to adopt the values of other communities to which they may migrate. In some cases it may appear that they are so important that they are fought over just as are human needs.

It is far from clear, however, that this is the case in practice. The so-called "religious" conflict in Northern Ireland may not be primarily a religious conflict. It has far more the features of a class conflict consequent upon discriminations. So it may be with some of the conflicts in the Middle East, where it is assumed that religious fundamentalism is a major source of communal and inter-state conflict. It is likely that religion is frequently made the vehicle of protest against discriminations, and against the treatment of some nations by greater powers as if they were colonial territories.

The reality is that human needs, cultural values, and economic interests are tied together in ways that sometimes defy analysis in a particular situation. Their separation conceptually, however, is important in any analytical attempt to define a situation. For example, it is evident that cultural issues become most important when there are unfavorable economic and political conditions. The defense of cultural values can readily become a means to security, just as identity groups are a means of protecting and promoting human needs. In this way cultural values can be confused with human needs, and such confusion could lead to a confused analysis and inappropriate outcomes.

THE PROCESS ISSUE

It is in respect to process, however, that the cultural dimension promotes most confusion. Social scientists can point to different means of dealing with conflicts in different cultures (Horowitz, 1985). These comparative studies are valuable because they point to possible options, and stimulate thought about processes and procedures.

It should not be concluded, however, that cultural norms in dealing with conflicts should necessarily be encouraged even within a particular culture. Execution is one means of eliminating a conflict, duelling is another. The "eye for an eye" or revenge philosophy is an "instinctive" reaction that is a part of the "culture" of many peoples. The Western traditional culture is dominated by feudal traditions of coercion by authorities. The study of processes of conflict resolution is necessary just because cultural traditions in the handling of conflicts are so frequently dysfunctional.

Even should it be found that there are some distinctive means of handling disputes in different cultures, however they be defined, there is a good reason for trying to find processes that cut across cultures. Many if not most deep-rooted conflicts have an inter-cultural – or an inter-class – dimension, and these require processes that are culturally neutral. When we are dealing with deep-rooted conflict, that is conflict that involves human needs, it is necessary to have a process that is capable of delving into human needs, despite different religions, languages concepts, habits, time-frames and other cultural or class differences.

The justification for the study of analytical conflict resolution is that conflict has been handled in most cultures, if not all, by coercive and authoritative means, or by violence. Conflict resolution does not favor the processes of one culture above another, but is critical of most if not all, especially those that have emerged within societies that are elite dominated, and where legal norms reflect elite interests.

Problem-solving conflict resolution processes, by contrast, are nothing other than the exploitation of abilities of analysis and thought common to the human species, thus favoring and prejudicing none. All varieties of the human species have abilities to think, and with or without help can follow a logical and analytical thought process. All have abilities to solve problems, though in most cases some assistance may be required. Analytical problem-solving, especially when facilitated by a third party of the type that we have described is, therefore, an ability that is generic, cutting across cultures, even cutting across levels of education and experience. Perhaps it is part of a universal human culture.

This is not to argue that cultural characteristics are irrelevant to the process. For example, it is said that Chinese are more long-term-oriented than peoples from Western cultures. This could be a political system consequence, or it could be something more fundamental such as tradition. In either case, such differences will emerge in any interactive process, and the participants will become aware of them, and make their assessments accordingly.

CULTURE AND ATTITUDES

Attitudes, like culture, are acquired. They are sometimes confused with culture in relationships. For example, it could be argued that there is evidence of a great power "culture," a symptom of which is arrogance in the treatment of less powerful nations: the latter are expected to adopt the values of the former. Similarly there appears to be a small power "culture," the symptom of which is a struggle for independence and recognition as an independent entity. There are class cultures. These attitudes come between parties to disputes in subtle ways.

Accommodating to the cultural habits of others is important in social relationships, and is a matter of etiquette. In a conflict situation, however, etiquette is not likely to be a preoccupation. It is far more likely that cultural differences will be treated as measures of incompatibility. In this sense culture may enter into the conflict resolution process, and is one component of which a third party should be aware, along with all the other personality and procedural influences that are part of the dynamics of any interaction process.

Culture as such, however, we must conclude, is not an important consideration in a facilitated analytical problem-solving conflict resolution process. It would be condescending, and seen to be condescending, if processes were designed to accommodate to one culture and not to another – which would make actual procedures very difficult.

In recent years analytical approaches may have come primarily from scholars in the Western world. If this is so it could be because it is the Western world that has suffered the most from major conflicts, and because it is in the developed world that certain types of domestic violence are most prevalent. It cannot be deduced that analytical problem-solving is part of Western culture, being imposed on other cultures. On the contrary, Western culture leads strongly to the coercive management of conflict. Problem-solving is not the product of a culture: it is a product that relates to the abilities of the human species, and is designed to reveal and to promote in a particular circumstance the needs of members of that species. Certainly experience to date suggests strongly that participants in a conflict resolution forum feel more comfortable in it than they do in what appears to be more traditional in most cultures, that is power bargaining and negotiation.

Empirical evidence such as that gathered by anthropologists and regional specialists tends to emphasize differences, for this is what is being researched. The differences recorded tend to be differences in means, not goals. Given an assumption of generic needs it could be that the same anthropologists and regional specialists might discover that earlier and smaller societies were more inclined toward rituals that led to cooperative problem-solving than to the type of confrontations and power bargaining strategies that are now typically Western.

16 Acceptability of Conflict Resolution

Should there be a political consensus that the social costs of repressed conflict are unacceptable, and that appropriate problem-solving conflict resolution processes should be institutionalized (something we discuss in Part V), would such processes be perceived as acceptable and practical in the particular case?

THE COMPLEXITIES OF CONFLICT RESOLUTION

The power political procedures are clear cut and direct. The conflict resolution procedures, by contrast, are complex. They must be deeply analytical, and for this reason facilitated and exploratory, and finally result in outcomes that are seen by the disputants to be a fair resolution:

1. *Analytical*, so that needs may be revealed and defined accurately, thus leading to an agreed definition of the problem, and to an opportunity for all parties accurately to assess and cost the consequences of allowing frustration of needs to continue.
2. *Facilitated*, so that interactions between the disputants are indeed analytical and lead to consideration of acceptable options, while avoiding power bargaining in any form.
3. *Exploratory*, so that there are no formal commitments or even expectations of agreements, as would be the case were there formal and public knowledge of interactions before there were agreement.
4. *Resolution*, because an outcome in which the conditions are acceptable to the parties, and also socially acceptable in the sense that the disputants are not seen to resolve their conflict at the expense of the rest of society (which would in the longer term be dysfunctional to them), is the only kind that is likely to be stable.

At present authorities and publics understand and operate in an environment in which there is an acceptance of the simple and direct means of power and coercion as a means of dealing with conflicts. Is it realistic to expect them to pursue the seemingly complex processes of problem-solving conflict resolution?

RESOLUTION PROCESSES

Should the resolution of conflict be preferred to the costs of conflict and its containment, the answer to the question whether it will be acceptable and pursued will finally be based on two main considerations, one dealing with goal achievement, and the other dealing with process.

First, can there be an agreement that meets the non-negotiable needs of those involved in conflict, including the non-negotiable needs and cultural values of those presently in authority in the case of an internal conflict?

Second, are conflict resolution processes such that they will lead reliably to early outcomes which in fact preserve non-negotiable needs and values, and the goals of social and political stability?

The first precondition is taken care of, at least theoretically, by the processes of conflict resolution. Conflict resolution processes leave final decisions with the parties involved. With this veto, there is no question of relative power or weakness entering in the exploratory interaction. A coercive third-party decision making role was the reason for failure of judicial and compulsory mediation processes, and is why, as we saw in Chapter 13, "weaker" forms of intervention – that is those that are not judicial or in other ways determinative – have been the only acceptable ones. There has to be total satisfaction of basic needs without the compromises required in bargaining and negotiation.

It is the second precondition that is the crucial one: a credible assurance that the process will, in fact, lead to a resolution in these terms and, furthermore, not be a protracted or conflictual process, possibly leading to a worsened situation that would have to be subjected to coercive controls.

It is only in this context that a value decision can be made as to whether it is more cost effective to control conflict by repressive means or not. On the one hand, there are the on-going costs and economic consequences of the conflict; on the other, there are the uncertainties of the resolution process and outcome.

There is empirical evidence that no bargaining, negotiation, mediation or any other such process is acceptable to authorities when they believe they have the coercive power at least to contain a situation. Wars such as that between Iran and Iraq in the 1980s go on for years despite many attempts by the United Nations and other interventions, until the costs become unacceptable. In the case of an internal conflict, such as an ethnic conflict, authorities who believe that they are legal, and that there is an obligation on the part of the minority to obey, will permit the destruction of the economy rather than admit the need for dialogue. This is the case at all social levels, in industry, in community relations, and internationally.

There are many complex psychological–political reasons for this traditional reluctance of an authority, government, industrial or other, to admit that coercive power does not succeed, and to insist that, in any event, there cannot be dialogue with the opposition. Mostly they arise out of the power political conceptions that are so deeply ingrained in consensus thinking. The hint of a willingness to negotiate can be perceived as an admission of defeat or at the very least, as a sign of weakness, and this would prejudice future bargaining positions. Negotiation is, after all, part of the power process. A willingness to negotiate is a surrender. In addition there are personal role positions being defended.

On the other hand, there have been many cases in which authorities have sought after, and have been prepared to enter into problem-solving processes in relation to high level conflicts once they were aware of the nature of the conflict resolution process (Burton, 1969; Kelman, 1972; Azar and Burton, 1986). In each case this was possible because the facilitated conflict resolution process was perceived as an opportunity to confirm strength, not weakness. When a party is prepared, prior to any negotiation, to argue its case, define the causes and nature of the conflict, within an analytical framework before a third party, this can be interpreted only as a sign of confidence in its position, and the justice of its cause. There is no evidence of weakness, there being no precondition of ending conflict prior to interaction. Indeed, the usual response of parties when approached is that they would be willing to enter into such a dialogue, but the other side, having in their view a poor case, would not.

In such a setting, protagonists are not perceived to be negotiating with the opposition, because interactions are informal, exploratory and usually hidden from public attention at least until there is an acceptable basis for negotiation. At this stage of public thinking, still very much influenced by power political norms, such secrecy can be justified as falling within ethical bounds.

The situations referred to, however, have been situations that had become costly and intractable. There had been the "ripening" referred to by the power theorists. There is no evidence as yet that there is the understanding of the nature and sources of conflict that would lead authorities to predict conflict, to preassess the inevitable costs, and to accept conflict resolution processes to prevent those costs, or themselves take the necessary steps to prevent further escalations of conflict.

The answer to the question whether resolution processes will be preferred to the costs of conflict seems to be, therefore, that a precondition of acceptance of conflict resolution is a far better understanding of both the nature of deep-rooted conflict and the non-negotiable issues that are at stake, and the nature of the analytical process. This points to the need in a particular case for sponsors of third-party intervention to communicate clearly to the protagonists the nature of the approach, remembering that they are communicating with persons whose culture and thinking is within a power political framework.

THE POWER OF IDEAS

We have traced thought and practice from *settlement*, where an outcome results from authoritative decisions or from superior bargaining or military power, through normative and related negotiating and mediation processes, to *resolution* in which the parties interact and explore acceptable options. There is one other "process" still to be noted which underlies both the effectiveness and the acceptability of conflict resolution. This is the generation and promotion of ideas that could resolve problems even without parties interacting.

While some disputes may be settled by interactive processes, and within the constraints of the prevailing system, the handling of deep-rooted conflicts requires something more than process. It requires an input of knowledge and innovation not usually associated with negotiation, mediation or other forms of conflict management.

It is in practice not possible to persuade parties to a deep-rooted conflict to interact, or to "come to the table" as it is sometimes put (Laue, 1988), unless the table that is to provide the interaction, first, is appropriately constructed and, second, has on it an inviting menu.

The construction of the table is the process – bargaining, negotiating, problem-solving or some other. Parties to a dispute or conflict will not voluntarily come to a "table" that could prejudice their position in relation to a matter of vital concern. As observed, judicial settlements, arbitration and compulsory mediation take away from responsible leaderships their decision making control. The US withdrawal from the jurisdiction of the International Court of Justice in 1985 over Nicaraguan action against the US was dramatic evidence of this. Authorities will not accept such limitations on their sovereignty until there is an agreement which meets their needs. Furthermore, any forum that suggests bias or lack of neutrality, or which by implication attaches blame to one side, or seeks to apply social norms in any arbitrary way, will be avoided.

The table construction must be problem-solving. Discussion of details, that is those arrangements that do not involve political decision making, can take place only after an agreed framework has been discovered. Our concern when considering acceptability is, however, primarily with the menu provided at the table. The menu, the satisfiers, clearly must be one that is attractive to all parties involved.

When the Greek and Turkish Cypriots were in conflict in the 1960s, the United Nations negotiator could not persuade them to meet together. Each had the precondition that its own draft constitution would be the basis for discussion. In their traditional bargaining framework neither side could afford to prejudice its position by accepting the draft of the other as a basis of discussion. This is generally the case: parties believe they cannot afford to negotiate from any position other than the bargaining strength advantage given by taking their position as the starting point. But the negotiator then had no menu which enabled the parties to select, and finally to negotiate over, alternative satisfiers.

A United Nations mediator was appointed to visit one party, then another, trying to find out what the problem was, and making suggestions. The whole process was a failure. The mediator found some circumstantial reasons for the failure, but there were process reasons far more damaging. The suggestions made were not well-founded for a basis for discussion. He concluded that no purpose would be served in continuing separate consultations (see United Nations Security Council document s/6253 of 26 March 1965).

This mediation approach has been a common one. It arises out of a false assumption about the nature of conflict: the assumption that given goodwill and adequate communication, preferably direct communication, there can be agreements based on reasonable compromises. After the failure of mediation as a process in the early days of the United Nations there was, especially in the US, a strong tendency for scholars and persons who regarded themselves as professionals in the area of conflict negotiation to descend on parties to a dispute or conflict and expect them to "come to the table," the table being, let us remind ourselves, only a process. The belief, shared by the mediators, was that if only parties would interact with some degree of good faith and mutual confidence, there could be agreement. The third party would create that good faith and confidence by assisting communication. The third-party role was the conduct of the meeting, recording observations, and attempting to provide clarity in communication.

This approach assumed that options, mainly involving compromises, would be generated by the parties, implying that a possible solution was within their conceptual frameworks, and that all that was necessary was for them to interact in good faith. This approach ignores the main characteristics of a deep-rooted conflict. First, there are issues on which there cannot be compromise, and second, with all the goodwill in the world there may not be within the conceptual framework of anyone involved in such a conflict any options outside those that have been within their experience or knowledge. They might desperately desire and seek an agreement, but there is nothing within their conceptual frameworks that meets their needs.

Take, for example, the many ethnic conflicts throughout the world society. In every case the assumption is that there can be some kind of "democracy" characterized by some kind of "power sharing." Negotiations on this basis do not get very far, for power sharing can never be translated into equal power. Power sharing can be symbolic of some desire to cater to minority needs, just as an opposition political party represents minority needs; but ethnic power sharing places the minority in the role of a permanent and ineffective minority. Its political identity remains that of a minority, as is its social identity.

There is, therefore, a role for a professional who is outside the system, who can provide a menu which suits the cultural and other requirements of all. It will be an innovative and comprehensive menu that includes the seemingly incompatible needs of all parties – as incompatible as one-man-one-vote and apartheid seem to be in the South African conflict. It has to be a menu that signals no prejudice, no fault, no value judgements, no preconditions, no selected ingredients, but an endeavor to make available whatever ingredients are required to satisfy the cultural values and human needs of all concerned.

The menu has to be one that does not prejudice any of the parties in any way. It has to have ingredients that are generally attractive as means of satisfaction of needs: it must be a menu that is perceived as an opportunity to satisfy personal tastes, separate cultural preferences, and national choices, prepared in ways that make possible total compatibility. If there are not opportunities for complete satisfaction it can be assumed that there are ingredients missing, or that the combination of ingredients are found not to mix.

It is in the suggestion of satisfiers, not the provision merely of the table, that a facilitating third party has most to contribute. It is in this field that there must be knowledge of the dietary requirements that are universal, and an ability to innovate to fit the requirements of the diverse consumers. It is not until there is a non-threatening, and positively acceptable menu on the discussion table that parties can be expected to come to it and interact with each other at it. This means that there have to be discovered, and made known in advance, dishes and combinations of dishes that are likely to be a departure from traditional social and political satisfiers, promoting a paradigm shift in thinking about satisfiers.

THE NEED FOR A PARADIGM SHIFT

Throughout this study we have emphasized the need to question assumptions, and to be clear on concepts. It is this creativity which is at the heart of the facilitation process – the provision of an acceptable menu. We have discussed the widely used term "democracy." According to the way in which they see that their interests would best be satisfied, it can mean different systems to different parties. It could mean for those who feel excluded from the political process a form of compulsory voting to ensure total participation (which some countries, for example, Australia have). It could mean majority government which could alienate large sections of the total population. Parties in conflict are not likely willingly to interact until there is some clarity on meanings of such terms because what is implied by them, like the different constitutions of the two Cypriot parties in the 1960s, would predetermine the interaction.

There are many models, concepts and definitions of terms which get in the way of meaningful analysis and communication. "Integration," "equality," "freedoms," like democracy, can be perceived as threatening, not merely to interests, but to deeply felt needs also. There is an ontological need for autonomy, but also for identification with an identity group. There is seemingly an incompatibility between these two, especially in a multi-ethnic situation. The need for identity and its associated autonomy reflects something important in the development of the person and group. The need for identification reflects a need for security. "Integration" of different identity groups can be perceived by them as threatening both to their autonomy and their security. Cooperation between different groups within a framework that preserves autonomy and security can, at the same time, be valued greatly. Conflict between groups is the consequence of institutionalized means of cooperation that prove to be threatening of identity and security. It is an important part of the role of the third-party facilitator to give terms like "democracy" and "integration" a meaning that accords with needs theory, and to be creative in finding appropriate institutional frameworks that meet the requirements of the redefined concepts.

As we saw in Chapter 9, ethnicity seems to be a special case. But we have already rephrased it in a way that applies it to relationships between the person and society: in all relationships there is a tension between the needs of separate autonomy and valued relationships. Problems of relations that must cater for personal autonomy and also identification with an identity group, can readily be extended to group autonomy and identification with the wider society. But because ethnicity is a clear example of this tension, let us stay with it for this analysis. In any event, ethnicity conflicts are important in the global picture, in addition to providing a clear example of related class and identity problems generally.

In the Cyprus case, a group of research scholars in London in 1966 arranged a meeting between nominees of the leaders of the two rival factions. The assumption that had guided the United Nations mediator was that the Greek Cypriots sought "Enosis" or union with Greece, and the Turkish Cypriots, in self-defense, sought "Double Enosis" or union with Turkey. What was revealed very clearly at these analytical discussions was that *both parties* valued more their relations with each other than with their neighbors Greece and Turkey. Yet they, and especially the Turkish minority, sought their own separate identity within Cyprus (Burton, 1984).

Another group of scholars in 1984 brought together in Washington nominees of the main leaders in Lebanon. After some days of intensive interaction in which neither side could believe what they were hearing, it became clear that both Christian and Muslim factions valued their special relationship, and even a separate kind of culture, that had emerged over the centuries, over their relationships with external national groups of the same religion. Yet, once again, they were seeking a separate identity (Azar and Burton, eds. 1986).

The menu to be offered before there could be any formal negotiation had, therefore, to include means of satisfying the separate identity needs of both Christian and Muslim groups, and factions within each, and the needs for valued relationships with those same groups from whom a separate identity was sought. Clearly, conventional political integration, majority government and related devices could not be acceptable. They did not provide a basis for negotiation. Another menu had to be provided. It had to be provided by the third party adopting an exploratory and inventive review of alternatives.

CREATIVE THINKING

Frequently there are models within experience that have not been thought of as relevant because they are in different spheres. There is, for example, a prime example of a smoothly working system that includes many minorities, small and large, but which has the image of being conflictual. This is the model of the world society to which reference was made in Chapter 8. In practice it is a very cooperative model. Considering the number of parties (160 or so), their cultural, linguistic, ideological and other diversities, they work together on a functional basis very effectively. Planes and ships obey international rules, communications of all kinds flow, even in some cases where there are no diplomatic relations, trade flourishes and every unit is equal in the sense that it can exercise a veto. Cooperation is based on a value attached to the rules, and the functional relationships they establish.

Parties engaged in a conflict, however, stick rigidly to their frames, and it would be beyond their imagination to perceive an international model – conventially regarded as conflictual – as providing one useful to them. Such a model, however, could help in dealing with major ethnicity national problems, as in states such as South Africa and the Soviet Union amongst others, and could, with imagination, be adapted to the needs of both the minorities concerned and the states in which they are to interact.

This is but one example of a model, and it helps to make the point that there is always required something more than process in dealing with a current or future problem. There is a need for a theoretical framework that takes into account the human dimensions of the problem, and the structures that might be appropriate. This can be formulated in ways that make for an agreeable dish on the table.

Such ideas, because they are based on a theoretical framework, have a general application. Only the negotiable details are unique to the particular case. This means that the major contribution to the resolution of the particular case will come from analysis and discussion outside the boundaries of the particular case. A group of relevantly trained persons sitting around a table in another country, a potential facilitation panel, can construct both the table and what is to be served without involving the parties until there is an acceptable framework in which there can be an analysis that includes all concerns and, later, negotiation.

South Africa could be regarded as such a case at this time of writing. The future could be open civil war, as took place in Northern Ireland and Cyprus, leading to massive population movements and separate entities – a logical extension of apartheid – before any positive steps might be taken to resolve the conflict. Both sides are bound to their own definitions of the future, and no compromise seems possible.

It could be that the goal of blacks to create a single nation by one-man-one-vote with no discriminations as exist in other multi-ethnic nations could be viable. The blacks, having been a minority, could be willing to see that whites were not so treated in a unified nation. This was the approach of Rhodesia, subsequently renamed Zimbabwe. The small minority of whites were not required to accept the average living standards of blacks, and were able to maintain their separate status to a large degree, even though political power was curbed. Perhaps it is easier for a majority, previously an underprivileged minority, to accord respect to a minority, than it is for majorities, not knowing what it is to be a minority, to accord respect to minorities under their control. We do not have many examples of underprivileged majorities assuming political power. But the white minority in South Africa would have to be convinced of this. They would want some guarantees.

If there were an "idea," some conceptual framework that included what seem to be wholly incompatible satisfiers, as are integration and separation, this could provide an agreed basis for the interactions necessary to arrive at an agreed outcome. The global model combines the possibilities of both separate identity and interaction. The world order model of functional relationships could be applied to any ethnically divided country. It might provide for the establishment of separate community boards or legislatures, each with a veto, relying on values attached to the benefits of functional cooperation as the force that keeps the groups together. It could be argued that this could lead to security, stability and, therefore, to increased cooperation generally far quicker and more reliably than some coerced settlement on the basis of some traditional form of majority government. Some such model could be formulated without any prior consultation with the parties, being based primarily on a theoretical analysis of multi-ethnic relations generally. It would be up to the parties in a facilitated interaction to apply the model, if they were to find it a basis of discussion, to their particular situation. All manner of constitutional and functional details would have to be worked out by an interactive process, but there would be established, if the "idea" were accepted in principle, an alternative to the two opposing preconditions that had led to stalemate and the danger of civil war. This is very different from trying to promote an interest in negotiation without a known "table," and without any inviting dish on the table, and nothing to attract the parties, even though it could well be that the protagonists were most anxious to avoid what they saw to be ahead.

CREATIVITY AND MANIPULATION

It is important in conflict resolution that there should not be interventions that might be or be interpreted as manipulative. For this reason, there are those who take the view that intervention roles should be confined to recording the observations of the participants, hoping thereby to facilitate communication between them (see Book 4, *Conflict: Practices in Management and Resolution*). But this does not allow for the need for ideas, models, innovations and the challenging of meanings and assumptions, as a means of establishing a framework and menu for interaction.

In the South African case the US applied sanctions against South Africa. For what purpose? What was the US wanting the South African Government to do? What was the "solution" the US Government had in mind? Did it expect the South African Government to adopt one-man-one-vote or some such "solution" to the problem? Observers with some knowledge of ethnicity knew full well that this was a recipe for future civil wars between different factions. Threats and coercive techniques such as sanctions may have some domestic political value to those employing them, but they do not solve problems to which solutions are not known.

This stress on the role of creative ideas and models for discussion makes the study of conflict, its resolution and provention, into a profession in much the same way that medicine and engineering are professions. Clients seek advice, and it is professional advice that is usually adopted. This does not eliminate interactive problem-solving processes, but is preparation for them where there are cases of intractable conflicts. Given an adequate theory of conflict, given an adequate analysis of the particular conflict, options can be advanced that would provide the basis of interaction with some perceived prospect of meeting the requirements of all concerned.

Like any product, its acceptability is determined by its relevance and usefulness. There has been a clear movement away from authoritative and judgemental processes toward problem-solving ones, and the acceptability of the latter depends no less on the way in which non-negotiable needs are seen to be preserved and advanced by the process. If parties do not come to the table, whether the table be a court, arbitration or conflict resolution processes, it will be because it is not seen to be beneficial, making the risks and costs of conflict the only option.

There is another factor to be taken into account in assessing acceptability, and that is awareness and knowledge of the process. Facilitated conflict resolution is a novelty. This places an even greater obligation on professionals to make both the table and the menu attractive and understandable.

IV
Provention

Chapter 17   From Resolution to Provention   233
Chapter 18   Second-order Change   239
Chapter 19   The Intellectual Challenge   252

Introduction to Part IV

In Part I, *The Problem Area*, we argued that conflicts arising out of any frustration of human needs cannot be suppressed or *settled* for long, and that authorities had no option ultimately but to seek to *resolve* them.

In our exposition we consistently referred to conflict resolution and provention together, the one being the short-term and case-by-case approach to conflict, and the other being the longer-term policy approach to eliminating the sources of conflict. We argued that the insights from conflict *resolution* would help to provide the policy direction for *provention*.

The link between these two became all the more obvious when we stressed the exponential increase in conflict that results from containment policies, and the consequent inadequacies of resolution processes in coping with the resultant conditions.

In Part II, *The Political Context*, we referred to the philosophical implications of needs theory, such as the nature of legitimization, and the principles of intervention. Once again we treated resolution and provention as being closely linked: it was this philosophical background within the framework of needs theory from which would be deduced both faciliated conflict resolution processes and provention policies.

In Part III, *Conflict Resolution*, however, we were concerned more specifically with the actual processes of facilitated conflict resolution, showing how they are an extension of decision making.

Now, in Part IV, *Provention*, we return to conflict provention, and examine it also as a separate phenomenon. While facilitated conflict resolution could be described in detail as a process, conflict provention, being concerned with longer-term policy rather than with procedures, cannot be treated in the same way. There is the same costing of options to be assessed, but in different time-frames. There is the same problem of parties and issues, but in this case the parties are not specific ones, but total societies, and the issues are the far broader issues of the common good, and of political interests and ideologies.

Furthermore, while conflict resolution processes have been tried and tested, while they relate in one form or another directly to decision making experience and are, therefore, conceptually within our grasp, with provention we are approaching the unknown and virtually untried.

Indeed, provention is even more elusive in that in practice it must be either a documented failure or, if successful, seen as an attempt to deal with a problem that arguably may never have developed! A conflict, by comparison, is tangible and observable. In other words, we are dealing with policy making that could mean changes in institutions, probably affecting many interests adversely in the short term, without being able to demonstrate with certainty that the costs were required.

From a theoretical point of view there is the simple proposition that if certain human needs are not satisfied, there will be conflict. The conflict will be of such a character that no suppressive means will contain it. Attempts to suppress it will lead, on the contrary, to exponential increases in conflict. One could go on to predict a total catastrophe. But this is a prediction deduced from a largely theoretical argument. The empirical data do not exist outside the theoretical argument. There is little chance that the argument will persuade existing interests to make the required proventive changes. Such provention has not been possible in the field of ecology, which directly affects everyone, and where there are on-going empirical data to support theoretical projections.

We are, however, not engaged here in some abstract intellectual exercise. We are dealing with phenomena that are far more threatening to civilizations than even long-term ecological and environmental damage. We are dealing with QOL issues that are probably more threatening to civilized survival than are the possibility of nuclear wars. Furthermore, they are issues that can trigger nuclear wars. Conflict provention as a policy is a requirement of survival in a nuclear or any other age (see Burton, *Dear Survivors*, 1982).

In Part IV *Provention*, therefore, we examine this problem by looking first at the concept of provention more closely than we have so far (Chapter 17). We then deal with problems of change and try to find why it is that realistic costing does not take place, and the circumstances in which it might (Chapter 18).

We then move on in Chapter 19 to consider some of the intellectual challenges that this broad problem poses. The underlying thesis is that these practical problems to which we have referred will be overcome only when scholarship provides the necessary analytical framework, the discoveries, that practitioners require. It is also our contention that needs theory, in so far as it is an adequate theory of

Provention

behavior, potentially provides the basis of a synthesis of strands of thought that up to date have been in separate and contending belief systems.

This is not as seemingly abstract or remote as may seem to readers interested in conflict resolution. The link between resolution and provention is a reciprocal one: not only does experience with cases point to provention policies, but knowledge of the framework of provention and some of the practical problems to be experienced provides a necessary background for facilitated conflict resolution. Options discovered in that setting have to stand the test of time, and not be merely temporary expediencies that suit the convenience of the parties at the table.

17 From Resolution to Provention

As noted at the very beginning, we had to invent the word "provention." The absence of a suitable word reflects the fact that prevention of an undesired event by removing its causes, and by creating conditions in which it cannot occur, has not been a focus of attention of societies or of scholars. The reluctance or failure to give provention a high priority goes to the root of the increasingly disturbing problems societies and civilizations now face. Societies usually react to adverse conditions only after it is too late to do much about them. They have been and are oriented toward remedial measures. Conflict *resolution* is an advance on *settlement*, but it cannot cope with the increasing incidence of conflict and violence. We have noted the exponential nature of the increase in violence and conflict. Resolving one case of domestic violence, gang warfare, ethnic conflict, or confrontation with another nation, does nothing to prevent the next incident. The source of and reasons for problems must be tackled if such conflicts are not to occur.

PROBLEMS OF PREDICTION: PROBABILISTIC PREDICTION

It is not being overly dramatic to state that unless civilizations can make this step from remedial measures to provention, exponential factors will, within a time framework of immediate concern to living generations, lead to environmental and social conditions that are unacceptable in human terms.

Provention, doing something about problems before they cause conflict, presupposes prediction. It could be that our inability to predict is our main problem in conflict *provention*. Prediction is a general problem of decision making. In practice prediction tends to be based on expectations of behaviors consistent with the requirements of the system in which they occur, not on any adequate theories of behavior. Employees are expected to be "rational" and not to strike if a strike is likely to threaten the company and, therefore, their futures. We term "irrational" behaviors of some Heads of State if

233

these behaviors do not accord with our expectations. The label becomes the explanation of behavior. False predictions lead to self-defeating policies, ranging from the collapse of major companies, to false interpretations of data by intelligence agencies, and to involvement in wars that cannot be won. What kind of prediction do we require for the *provention* of conflict?

There is a kind of statistical prediction on the basis of past experiences – for example, experiences of ethnic conflicts – that could predict future conflicts in similar circumstances. Experiences of past car accidents are a means of predicting the likelihood of future ones. Authorities make such predictions constantly. For instance, prior to some political protest meetings or political anniversaries they make the necessary police and military preparations to prevent trouble.

This prediction of probability based on experience leads merely to avoidance of anticipated events. It is the basis for containment policies, and remedial measures generally. It does not require any explanation of conflict. It does not depend on or provide any insights that could lead to *provention*.

During the 1960s and 1970s there were in the social sciences many attempts to be quantitative. This led to criticisms that phenomena of greatest interest, such as values, might not be subject to operational definitions and quantification. The quantification that took place seemed to be without a theoretical framework that would enable results to relate to any theory of human behaviors. An even more severe criticism is that, in the absence of such a theoretical framework, prediction on the basis of quantification of past happenings is likely to direct attention away from happenings that may be crucial, but to which attention has not been directed because they have yet to be experienced.

GAMES WITHOUT END

There is another type of prediction that takes place within what, as we have already noted, Osgood (1962) describes as "games without end." Games without end are thought systems and the policies they promote which are based on self-fulfilling assumptions and prophecies.

There is the strategic game in which deterrent strategies of peace through strength lead to constant increases in arms levels until resource scarcity or political pressures lead to arms control negotiations. Arms control negotiations require, it is argued, increased arms as bargaining tools in negotiation. In the event of an arms control agreement the reduced arms are then compensated for by modernization within the limits set by the new agreement. The basic predictive assumptions of the game – that is, that there is constant threat of aggression by others, and that such threats can be deterred by threat – are not questioned. The extent of the threat and the success of deterrence are evaluated by those within the game, thus ensuring its continuation. It becomes a game without end, at least until it becomes apparent that the costs and failures of deterrence have led to conditions that render domestic conditions a more serious threat to the nation than does any external threat. A game without end is a self-determining, and therefore a misleading basis for prediction.

ANALYTICAL PREDICTION

When we look to prediction as a step toward the *provention*, rather than merely the avoidance or *prevention* of conflict, we are involved in discovering the causal factors that must be dealt with. The knowledge of what to look for, the discovery of what conditions provoke the behaviors to be prevented, requires an adequate theory of human and societal behaviors, including a reliable theory of conflict and conflictual behaviors.

Needs theory suggests that, despite the obvious difficulties, reliable prediction of conditions that provoke conflict may now be possible. We are catching the first whispers of a theory of human behavior that argues that the human being, whether or not by nature evil or anti-social, or requiring socialization by parents and society, has certain needs that are human, that are not malleable, that must be satisfied if there is to be development and conforming behavior.

To the extent that needs theory provides us with an explanation of behaviors, it provides us with a basis for prediction. Any set of circumstances, any institutions, any social relationships, that deny identity, recognition, autonomy or the preconditions for a human drive toward development, creates an environment of conflict, and puts societies at risk. In such an environment there are no containment, coercive or deterrent strategies that can for long avoid conflict, and probably violent conflict in one form or another.

For many years we have had what are termed "future studies," and these have an important role to play in promoting thought. Their concern has been primarily with steps toward desired futures, but, having reviewed their approaches, what is missing is some detailed, codified way of deciding which futures are better than others. These studies have acted more as a warning than as a means of dealing with the undesired and promoting the desired.

While needs theory may have the potential of providing a framework, it is as yet at an early stage of development. There can be generalized predictions based on observing levels of needs satisfactions. It can be predicted that ethnicity conflicts will escalate, that nations will be broken up into less integrated units and perhaps separate units, that societies will become more divided between those who have opportunities for development and those who have not, that identity groups will become smaller as conditions become more threatening, that such defensive identity groups will become more violent and self-seeking, and that authorities will have less and less success in exercising coercive powers. As yet, however, these predictions must be subject to reservations until more is known about levels of apathy and opportunities for protest, and the lengths authorities are prepared to go in the defense of their roles and institutions. In short, we are at a very early stage in prediction, having in the past not attached importance to it.

PROVENTION IMPLIES CHANGE

Civilizations have dodged *pro*vention to date partly, no doubt, because of these problems of prediction. But there has been a more pressing reason. Explanations of behavior that direct attention to the need to adjust systems to people, rather than the other way around, provide a predictive base that usually points to the necessity to alter environments and conditions as the means of provention. For this reason, prediction and provention of conflicts in most policy areas are unwelcome. While remedial treatments of specific cases can be made within the existing structures and institutions of a society, provention could require far-reaching changes in them. Say, for example, research were to discover that a major societal problem such as drugs, teenage pregnancies, or domestic violence, could be provented only by a redistribution of available resources to the extent necessary to provide conditions for all members of society to attain both individual development and social bonding. This would mean the provision of rewarding jobs, suitable accommodation, and – perhaps most important of all – the stimulus of education and opportunities for establishing valued relationships. A program with these ends in view would be costly, and would be seen to threaten the immediate interests of most of those who determine economic and social priorities. It is far easier politically to concentrate on punitive tactics like incarceration, or remedial conflict management measures, case-by-case as and when circumstances require, even though the longer-term costs prove to be far greater than would be the costs of *provention*.

VESTED INTERESTS VERSUS UNCERTAINTIES

There are, however, understandable and valid reasons why societies and leaderships have been reluctant to abandon traditional remedial means of dealing with future threats. There are, obviously, serious practical problems associated with predictions and proventions. If there were convincing predictions, and if there were a high degree of certainty that relevant policies would achieve their goals, the costs of provention might be acceptable even to those who would have to foot the bill. For example, if it could be demonstrated that health care reduced health and industrial costs in the future, some resource reallocations, even reallocations away from defense budgets, might receive political support. If it could be shown that business would profit from trade far more if educational systems were expanded, then authorities could receive support for activities which competitive businesses could not promote separately. If it could be demonstrated that adequate housing, community organization and education could with certainty reduce the number of single-parent families and associated problems of development among alienated persons, there could be more support than there has been for such provention activities. In short, it is understandable that there will be resistance to provention unless and until prediction is surer and provention more than a vague ideal.

CONFLICT RESOLUTION AS A MEANS OF CHANGE

Even if there were support for *provention* policies that are likely to be reliable in achieving their goals, we would still need processes of change that are not socially disruptive, for only such processes are acceptable and beneficial.

We have not yet discovered means of change that are continuous, non-threatening, and generally beneficial. The scholarly literature on change is sparse, except that which is devoted to discontinuous change. Structural and institutional change by improved decision making processes, by means that preserve and lead to the satisfaction of the legitimate interests and needs of all concerned, has not attracted scholarly attention.

Interactive, analytical problem-solving processes of conflict resolution may be the key to solving this problem of social evolution. Problem-solving in the specific situation can suggest processes and norms acceptable in that situation, and which can have a general application. The resolution of a particular street gang conflict, or an ethnicity conflict, for instance, points to the specific conditions needed to eliminate and provent the problem of street gang warfare and ethnic conflict in general. Success in the specific context can pave the way for acceptance of similar measures applied more widely. This fearful dilemma of change is one to which analytical problem-solving can make a special contribution.

It is to this change problem that we now turn. It is this on which the concept of provention rests.

18 Second-order Change

REFRAMING

In resolving a social problem, either by resolution processes or by provention policies we are, in effect, dealing with changes within systems, and in some cases changes of systems. It is the growing realization that certain types of conflict cannot be contained, and that changes in institutions and policies are required if societies are to be reasonably conflict-free, that has led to the study of problem-solving as a supplement to, or substitute for, system maintenance as an approach to the problem of conflict.

In Chapter 10 we made reference to "primary" and "secondary" change, primary change being that which is environmental and beyond human control, and secondary change being the policy or institutional adjustments that are required as a consequence. Paul Watziawick, John Weakland and Richard Fisch made a similar distinction in a book devoted to *Change: Principles of Problem Formation and Problem Resolution* (1974). To facilitate exposition they referred to "first and second order change," the former being the problem as it emerges within a system, and the latter being the solution brought about by system change. In their view there is a need for "reframing" the situation, and redefining the problem before there can be a positive step taken in dealing with it.

As a means of explaining the need to reframe, these authors referred to Osgood's observations (1962) on deterrence theory, to which we referred in Chapter 17. Osgood argued that "the policy of mutual deterrence includes no promise for its resolution." It is, therefore, "a game without end" and finally the attempted solutions become the problem. For example, in arms control negotiations the negotiation process becomes the problem. Placing members of street gangs in prison is such a game without end. A high proportion leave prison even more socially maladjusted, leading to a need for more prison accommodation, and to a shortage of police and detention facilities as the next problem. A first step in "reframing" is to recognize the existence of the game and its rules so that policy makers can break out of it and find a solution to the problem.

IS PROVENTION BY CHANGE WHAT IS SOUGHT?

These writers of 1974 were aware of the opposition there would be to any attempt at problem-solving by getting to the roots of problems, and initiating change to deal with them. Mindful that there is a strong political preference for direct, coercive means of containing a conflict situation, rather than going through the far more complex process of resolution and provention, they observed that "Second-order change appears unpredictable, abrupt, illogical, etc., only in terms of first-order change, that is, from within the system."

The question which we wish to pose in this assessment is whether problem-solving conflict resolution, involving second-order change, is the practical way forward, or whether the more traditional approach of authoritative controls is more practical politically. With improved and collaborative techniques, maybe it is more likely to give stability without system change, and this may be more in the interests of societies and their members.

There is a costing factor that must be considered. Is it better, for example, to experience the value costs of political repression, (including the political reactions of others outside the system), rather than to suffer the costs and uncertainties of institutional and social change? Perhaps this is the most important and prevalent question asked today in world society: there are few countries free of internal social problems, conflicts and violence, few that do not have to make these value and procedural choices. As we would expect, the consensus among authorities seems to be strongly in favor of system, and role preservation.

To assess the longer-term costs of conflict, especially economic costs and the effects on freedoms and quality of life generally, it is necessary to determine with some degree of credibility:

First, in what conditions second-order change is likely to be required.

Second, the nature of the changes that are inherent in the idea of resolution or provention by second-order change.

Third, what reliance there can be on problem-solving conflict resolution processes and provention policies achieving their objectives.

We will deal with the first two of these in this chapter, and the third separately in Chapter 19.

THE SITUATIONS REQUIRING SECOND-ORDER CHANGE

We have made a distinction between *disputes* over material resources that can be the subject of bargaining and negotiation, and *conflicts* over human needs issues that are not for trading. This distinction, however, while analytically convenient, may be a distinction without a difference: are there such separate categories, and if so, how are cases within each to be determined?

The distinction between conflicts that can or cannot be managed within a system is not one made within the traditional power framework. This is itself one reason why resolution is not yet within the conceptual thinking of many authorities and societies – including many scholars. The power political position is that all disputes and conflicts, domestic and international, have to be, and furthermore can be, dealt with by coercive means.

To recapitulate our earlier discussion, the traditional view, a power political view, is that:

1. Human beings in their social relationships, leaders and nations, are aggressive by nature, and, therefore, conflicts are inevitable and will have outcomes determined by relative power (Morgenthau, 1948).
2. This aggressiveness, if not innate, is due largely to evolutionary competition for control of scarce material resources, and for leadership and power roles which help in securing these resources, and, therefore, persons and nations are obliged to be aggressive in acquiring and protecting their possessions and territories.
3. Economic development is the promotion of consumption as a means to increased production, and this drive to consume takes precedence over such non-material satisfactions as valued relationships, thus making acquiring behaviors, and even some anti-social behaviors, part of the norms of society.
4. While competition and aggressiveness are natural and even desirable attributes of systems and persons, extremes must, in the interests of system preservation, be contained by deterrence, threats and other such measures exercised by authorities.

As we have seen the conflict resolution position, by contrast, is based on a different set of assumptions regarding the nature of conflict. Both agree that human aggression is not biologically mandated, and to the extent that it is promoted by problems of scarcity and the need for material acquisition, it is probably a product of behavior required by competitive economic and distributive systems. Where the two schools depart is over the "political realist" assumption that these causal competitive conditions are inevitable and even desirable.

The assumptions of conflict resolution are:

1. Conflict that is protracted and frequently violent is typically a direct consequence of frustration of non-material human needs, especially individual and group recognition and identity.
2. Human needs, being ontological, cannot, by definition, be traded or satisfied by power bargaining and negotiation, and cannot be contained by deterrence and threat.
3. Unlike material goods and interests, non-material human needs are not necessarily in short supply. Satisfaction of human needs promotes their satisfaction in others: the more security and recognition one party to a relationship experiences, the more others are likely to experience.
4. Conflict arises, therefore, not because of scarcity of resources or goal opportunities, but because of the selection of satisfiers or means chosen to achieve goals. Material resource control and acquisition, and status seeking, are possible choices of satisfiers, not goals.
5. A change of focus from resource competition to goals, from means and tactics to ultimate objectives, opens up possibilities of discovering cooperative and non-scarce material options as means of satisfying human needs.
6. Because there is no scarcity factor in human needs goals, there are opportunities for agreed organizational changes and for conflict resolution.

These two theories of conflict are clearly in opposition: the one attributes conflict to human aggressiveness that must be controlled by authorities, and the other to human needs for which institutions must cater. The one assumes that deep-rooted conflict can be contained, the other that real power finally resides in persons and identity groups. These opposing assessments of the power of human needs lead to wholly different assessments of the conditions in which conflict can be managed or resolved within a system, and in which second-order change is required.

The two theories give substance to the distinction we are making between situations that may be contained, and those that require second-order change. Situations such as those that emerged in

Northern Ireland, Cyprus, Sri Lanka, the Basque country, Tibet, and many others fall into the category of deep-rooted conflict that cannot be contained by "authoritative within system" measures. Empirically they seem to have demonstrated the power of human needs in a way that justifies the distinction. Nonetheless, each of these cases has been treated by the authorities concerned as within their power to control. Failure by authorities to control one situation has not led authorities in similar situations to apply the lessons experienced. Each case is perceived as being unique.

THE PRACTITIONER'S PERSPECTIVE

There has been in the distant past a measure of success in the repression of symptoms of problems. Feudal and other authoritarian or totalitarian systems have been maintained over long periods of time. Many contemporary systems that are repressive, including some that fall within the category of "democracies," but which contain dissident ethnic or religious minorities, have been maintained by these means.

In some other cases there have been attempts to accommodate minority demands with unfavorable results. Demands for lands made by indigenous populations so as to establish their identity (for example, in New Zealand, Australia and the United States), have led to further demands, followed in due course by hostile reactions from the majority populations. Such cases might seem to provide empirical evidence that favors strong controls rather than resolution processes. These may, however, be examples of responses based on a false definition of the problem. Demands for land rights are merely a symptom of underlying human needs for identity and recognition that can be satisfied ultimately only by distributive justice, non-discrimination and valued relationships within the wider society. Making available the satisfier, land, does not of itself make possible the goal, identity and autonomy.

In other cases societies have managed both problems and the disputes and conflicts that are their symptoms by learning to live with them. Societies tend to put off solving a problem. Environmental pollution is one example. There are problems of family violence, poverty, education, rusted bridges, old planes, and others that are managed by ignoring them, at least until there is a crisis, such as accidents, deaths, protests or system breakdowns. Even then the remedy is often some politically acceptable minimum intervention. International conflicts have also been managed, or contained, in this way. Great powers have deterrent strategies, and the United Nations has employed peace-keeping forces over long periods of time as means of containment.

These means of containment may make even more difficult a final resolution in the particular instance, and they certainly do not contribute to the solution or provention of other conflicts of the same kind. But they do help to prevent violence in the short term. From a practitioner's perspective, containment may be the expedient means by which conflicts can be controlled and tensions reduced, without disturbing the existing system.

So much have societies accepted *management* as a solution, that it has come to be regarded as problem-solving. Indeed, the two terms are frequently employed interchangeably. It is certainly tempting, especially for those who are in control, to seek means of management and containment, rather than to deal with the total situation in all its complexities.

Can we justify, in these circumstances, this distinction we have made between *disputes* that are part of the system, and which can be taken care of by existing institutionalized means, and *conflicts* that have sources in human needs and require second-order change? Even if these are two fundamentally different types of relationships, may not the same straightforward coercive techniques be appropriate in both cases?

WITHIN-SYSTEM DISPUTES AND CONFLICTS

In all societies there are confrontations that relate to non-material resources, which we have termed conflicts involving, in particular, cultural values and human needs of recognition, identity and development.

Because needs – and, to a lesser extent, values – are not negotiable, conflicts in these cases tend to be protracted or intractable if dealt with by within-system judicial or any non-analytical processes. They, far more than major interest disputes, are potentially violent and destructive of human development, relationships, property and life.

Interest disputes, unless quickly and equitably settled are likely to generate defensive role behaviors, and perceived threats to values, thus becoming value conflicts. For this reason it is expedient in many cases of interest confrontations to have speedy settlements by traditional court or authoritative processes on the basis of recognized social norms.

At the same time, it cannot be assumed that what appears to be an interest dispute is in fact only that, or can be dealt with as such. Courts sometimes deliver verdicts that are felt to be unjust, with unforeseen consequences. (There are on record cases of murders of solicitors and judges involved in child custody cases.) Those administering judicial and alternative processes require a training that alerts them to the possibility of the presence of underlying issues.

Adding to complications in defining disputes and conflicts, it is sometimes difficult to identity values and needs, and to separate them clearly from the means employed to pursue or to satisfy them. Goals can easily be confused with tactics, which are negotiable. In its conflict with Iraq in 1987 Iran insisted that its major goal was to get rid of the leadership of Iraq. This was a tactic, the goal being, perhaps, to avoid any further aggression, or to satisfy some personal leadership or religious values. The underlying goal was not as clearly stated or understood as was the tactic, and this is usual in conflict situations. Until goals and satisfiers in a particular conflict are clearly separated and defined, the distinction between disputes and conflicts is not clear, and any positive outcome to conflict management processes is unlikely.

The question arises whether there is a continuum from normal or healthy conflict, through interest conflict, through tactic or satisfier conflict, to value and needs conflict. Are all these the same type of dispute escalating from one level of intensity to another, or do they have separate origins and explanations, requiring quite different treatments? How can the practitioner assess and come to a decision as to whether to employ coercion or resolution?

Disputes, whether normal or not, have at least the following six primary characteristics:

1. there are degrees of complexity, by which is meant the number and nature of protagonists
2. there are structural elements, by which is meant that disputes may have, directly or indirectly, institutional and structural origins
3. there are role components, by which is meant the degree to which role preservation and role seeking are means by which to pursue or defend interests, values and needs

4. there are personality aspects, by which is meant that disputes involve personality problems, different knowledge levels and different levels of communication and perception
5. there are elements of depth, by which is meant that there are different levels of negotiable interests, and non-negotiable values and needs
6. there are manifest and hidden conflicts, the latter frequently being the more complex and difficult to resolve.

An empirical analysis along these lines helps in differentiating those conflicts that are normal or systemic, and those that cannot be so regarded. For example, a dispute between two persons of shared knowledge and perception, over an issue of choice that does not involve a high level of material interests, or any level of value or need, would be normal, that is a within-system dispute. There is no problem to be resolved that would call for second-order change. Or again, a dispute over material resources that takes place within the system in which resources are allocated, and which does not involve values or needs, presents a case for within-systems management. It would be desirable, of course, if in the management process there were an awareness of any human dimensions that could not be dealt with by judicial or power-bargaining processes.

A conflict, on the other hand, that involves many parties and issues, values and needs, or is structurally or institutionally based, in which there is little possibility of communication or shared perceptions, is bound to be potentially destructive of persons and society. It is such conflicts that would require either imposed constraints as an expedient, or the application of problem-solving conflict resolution processes if a long-term solution were to be sought.

The range of normal disputes varies with the type of social structure in which persons and groups interact. In a traditional society, for example a small tribal society, each member has a role and an identity, there is face-to-face interaction, there are non-competitive means of survival, and there are accepted norms governing behavior. Normal disputes would be limited to some social and personal interactions, such as disputes within a family or in relation to working relationships. Any more serious conflict would be dealt with by accepted traditional means.

In a command society, such as a feudal society or a centrally planned society, normal disputes would similarly be confined to immediate relationships. In such societies, roles are clear and relationships are largely determined by the imposed structure. It could be stable over long periods of time, at least until knowledge and awareness of opportunities for increased individual development threatened its legitimacy.

In more developed and complex societies the extent of normal disputes is much greater. The typical industrial society is highly competitive. Normal and interest disputes are promoted within a competitive environment. Competition is a form of dispute. However, competition within a system that is based on competition must be defined as normal. It is promoted and governed by market mechanisms and by dispute settlement processes, such as bargaining and negotiation, which are an inherent part of the system. There is, in fact, a merging of normal and interest elements as economic and social institutions merge. The work place, the source of income, is as much a social setting as is the family. Both forms of dispute, normal social disputes and interest disputes, are within-system disputes and, while they are analytically different for dispute management purposes, they can be treated as one, or one as the extension of the other in a continuum.

CONFLICT AND SYSTEM FAULT

Every system has its problems, such as lack of incentive, an absence of political participation, corruption, unemployment, discriminations, inequalities of opportunity and others, leading usually to more complex and intractable social problems. Within-system responses are made by whatever processes are appropriate to the system. In practice such system problems are usually not solved, but merely contained. As a result, if they lead to conflicts rather than disputes – that is, if they involve human needs and not just interests – there will be a continuing problem. The reality is that it is unlikely that within-system processes can be effective in dealing with conflicts that arise out of system fault. Within-system processes are designed to support existing institutions. They are likely to be effective within legitimized systems in dealing with negotiable interests. But conflicts which have sources in human needs, as is the case with ethnic conflicts, and major discriminations involving denial of opportunities, may be contained by within-system processes, such as police constraints, but are unlikely to be so resolved. There will be protracted conflict until there is second-order change.

In the consideration of the conditions in which second-order change may be required we could conclude, at this stage of knowledge and experience, that "normal" and "system" disputes are different analytically and in practice from "value" and "needs" conflicts. The one may be contained, while the other requires system change. The evidence seems to be, also, that they require different treatments because of their differences in kind.

This generalization having been made, it becomes clear that whether a situation is a dispute or a conflict, whether second-order change is or is not required, may not be determined finally until the treatment processes are under way. The failure of containment of a dispute would obviously suggest that the situation had underlying sources. If the nature of a dispute or conflict cannot be known for sure until a problem-solving process is under way, it suggests that even situations that seem clearly to be within-system, normal disputes, like a demand for increased wages, should be dealt with by persons trained at least to be able to detect the symptoms of a conflict if they should emerge.

THE TYPE OF CHANGE REQUIRED

This brings us to the second question we posed above: if system change is necessary, what will be the nature of the changes that are likely to be the outcome of resolution and provention by second-order change? Clearly, the nature of changes that may be required is a major factor in determining the acceptability of conflict resolution. An authority in deciding whether to opt for an authoritative settlement or a problem-solving approach to conflict must assess the type and extent of second-order change that might be required.

In the South African case second-order change would include major constitutional changes and reallocations of power, and this would be seen to be threatening to the white minority unless they were aware in advance of the possibility of some acceptable option. In the gang violence case, the changes required could include major additions to, or reallocations of, educational resources, job training provisions, housing, and such measures that could fit into the system, but which would probably require changes in social norms, and probably income redistribution through taxation, on a scale that could be politically unacceptable.

Politically unacceptable change, even though consistent with system operations, has to be regarded as second-order change. This places authorities in a dilemma: calculations could lead to a conclusion that without change there will be costly disruption of society, while the changes required cannot be made within the existing political environment. In practice, the short time-span of political decision making is sufficient to guarantee that the dilemma will be resolved in favor of traditional coercive treatments. Only when there is a consensus understanding and when acceptable policies are seen to have social pay-offs in the longer term, even though politically unpalatable in the short term, can there be constructive policies and within-system remedies.

ACCUMULATED ADJUSTMENTS

So far we have been assessing the relevance of problem-solving processes as a means of discovering options that would resolve problems in social organization, thereby proventing situations of conflict. Implicit has been that we are assessing a process that is a continuous one: there would be constructive responses by authorities to changed conditions as required.

For the kinds of reasons we have examined – for example, ideological commitment and interest pressures, and the exercise of power to contain rather than to solve problems – the challenge authorities face in all societies is not how to cope with the flow of change, but how to respond to accumulations of need for change to which no adjustments have been made in the past.

The early demands for change that were made in South Africa, Cyprus, Sri Lanka, Northern Ireland, Chile, the Philippines and many other countries were resisted and suppressed, until overt and violent conflict was unavoidable. Adjustments made earlier could possibly have avoided the intensity of conflict that emerged, thus requiring less fundamental change. Similarly in national life, there have been accumulations of race discriminations, leading to educational and skill discrepancies that result in even more disadvantage to those who have been discriminated against. There are income, property and other monopolistic accumulations which are difficult to deal with in the absence of major challenges and disruptions to existing institutions and interests.

A large component of what is called "progress" has been this accumulated inheritance of social and political problems which have not been faced. Second-order change will occur, despite constraints, and probably by means of violence, if there are no decision making processes that would enable adjustment where such accumulations have occurred.

THE NEED FOR VIABLE OPTIONS

One precondition of successful change is that there are clear and viable options. For change to be possible, there must be clear opportunities for the pursuit of human needs by those who may have to give up their dominant role positions. For example, the governments of countries with ethnicity problems cannot promote alterations in constitutions that do not preserve the identity needs of existing power elites. They have their needs to pursue no less than those demanding the opportunity to pursue theirs. In most cases of accumulated adjustment the options are not clear: those that would be relevant usually involve constitutional and functional systems that still have to be discovered and explored.

These considerations take us back to the first question – in what circumstances are second-order changes necessary and inevitable? They suggest that our search is not for new systems or even altered systems, but rather for decision making processes that both continuously, and in special circumstances, can deal with the dynamics of any system in such a way as to adjust to change at an early stage, and thereby preserve and promote institutions that cater for human needs. The problem is not necessarily with systems, but with processes within systems that can ensure that they do not run into problems that render them vulnerable to second-order change. Second-order change may not be required if the situation is one that has recently emerged, but will be required if there has been an accumulated resistance to required change.

In practice, we have little option but to observe, once again, that the amount and nature of second-order change that might be required is a calculation that cannot be made outside the context of a problem-solving interaction between the parties involved, or outside the investigations and research necessary for policies of provention. Sometimes declared values are not more than tactics by which to promote or to preserve the interests of particular groups. Take, for example, the issue of prayer in schools. Prayer in schools may be promoted by many who believe in and practice prayer out of conviction. It is also promoted by others who have no inclination to pray, but who see this institution as a symbol of the legal and other social norms they seek to promote. There are other ways of preserving the norms of society, for example, having adequate teaching facilities so that the values attached to relationships with the teacher and the institution are sufficient to ensure the desired social behaviors.

It is not until the nature of a situation in all its aspects are revealed that there can be a true assessment of the kind of changes that might be required: confrontational demands and negotiating positions do not reveal the nature of disputes and conflicts, or their possible outcomes.

THE RELIABILITY OF PROCESSES

Our third question relating to the acceptability of conflict resolution and provention, and of second-order change that is implied, was the reliability or credibility of resolution and provention processes.

There are empirical means of assessing the value of facilitated conflict resolution processes, and previous references have been made to case studies. In any event, these processes are facilitated interactions between parties to a conflict, and outcomes are the consequence of costing by the parties.

Provention raises different issues. Reliability and credibility finally rest on an understanding by those concerned, that is authorities and electorates that choose authorities, of the issues at stake, of the framework in which predictions are made, of the variables that affect the particular prediction and its time-span, and other factors that have to be taken into account when costing provention against containment of conflict.

This means that the processes of provention must be even more exacting and analytical than conflict resolution processes. This leads us into realms that in the practical world of democratic politics are challenging, nebulous, perhaps far beyond consensus understanding. Yet, as we pointed out in the Introduction to Part IV, the future of civilizations probably depends on decision making that is based on such an analysis. So for an assessment of this third issue in provention and second-order change, we turn to Chapter 19, *The Intellectual Challenge*.

19 The Intellectual Challenge

What lies behind a seemingly universal failure of decision making processes to achieve stated goals and to protect the future? Why do modern industrial societies, renowned for their scientific achievements, seek to deal with their social and political problems by means of containment that prove costly and frequently dysfunctional? Why is there so little provention?

Interest pressures are a major factor, especially where pressure groups dominate the decision making process. But interest groups, like the community as a whole and its members, have a stake in the future. Must there be reliance on treatment of symptoms, leading to increasing levels of containment and coercion, until some major catastrophe occurs? Must there be a "ripening" effect, as is thought by some to be the case, in making conflict resolution possible before interests and authorities will face the realities of the future? Must there be unmanageable situations before there is planning to provent them?

RELIABILITY AND CREDIBILITY

In Chapter 18 we dealt with two influences that determine the extent to which prediction and provention will be acceptable in decision making. These were, first, the conditions in which second-order change is likely to be required; and second, the nature of the changes that are required for provention of conflict. The third influence, which we then noted and which we wish now to discuss, is the perceived reliability of provention processes in achieving their goals.

We have chosen to treat this separately because it seems to be the main determinant: only if authorities and interests find prediction and provention credible and reliable will they shift from their more traditional and tried containment and management policies.

This consideration puts the ball of the future back into the court of scholarship. There is a major intellectual challenge here. Until research findings make possible the development of a consensus in favor of problem-solving approaches, the defensive practices of

252

deterrence and coercion will prevail. The future of civilizations probably depends on a consensus shift in thinking from power to problem-solving. At the conceptualization and articulation stages this is not the responsibility of political leaders and administrators: it is an intellectual challenge and responsibility.

THE RECENT NATURE OF THINKING ABOUT PROVENTION

This study of conflict and its provention is not one of philosophy or learning as such, but such a study draws attention to the recent nature – and by implication, the inadequacy – of thinking, and of what has been termed "scientific method," as applied to this field.

Provention, as distinct from prevention, itself is an unfamiliar notion, and conflict provention policies anticipating the future are novel. The concept develops directly out of a focus on opportunities for human development rather than on institutional constraints. But provention is but one of many concepts that emerge from such a shift in thinking. There are many others with which we are familiar that have a changed meaning once a human dimension enters into thinking and policies. In Chapter 5 we dealt with terms and concepts. We delayed such definitions until we had explained the conceptual framework, for it is this which gives meaning to terms. Now that we have explored the field in greater depth we can give others meaning.

ALTERED CONCEPTS

In Part II we dealt at some length with the concept of *legitimization* and its origins, making a clear distinction between authorities that are legal, and those that are legitimized. We used this distinction to explain the way political institutions sometimes aggravate and promote, for example, ethnic conflicts. There is no need to repeat those observations. It cannot be stressed too much, however, the way in which this quite fundamental distinction between what is legal and what is legitimized arises directly out of an analytical framework which includes a human dimension.

Closely related is the concept of *democracy*. The proper meaning of democracy is government by the people – that is, a government that passes the tests of legitimization. In practice, however, democracy has come to mean at best majority government, and usually not even this test is passed. In the major contemporary "democracies" leaders and representatives are elected by 25 or so per cent of the total population. Sometimes as many as half of the potential electorate do not vote due to apathy or to problems with registration procedures. Those who do participate tend to be those with a stake in government – that is, they have acquired interests to protect. In any event, once elected, leaders and representatives are subject to pressures from organized interest groups, thus pushing aside even more the concerns of the underprivileged. In the longer term their neglect, through low priorities given to housing, education, health, and the stimulus of useful jobs, affect the economy and social relations of the total society, and in due course even the relatively privileged suffer.

Where there are ethnically mixed societies there is not only the problem of unrepresented classes, but also unrepresented ethnic groups. Threats to cultural values, including language, reinforced by discriminations in jobs, housing and role, lead to conflicts in multi-ethnic societies. Misconstruing these problems, greater powers try to insist that smaller nations copy their "democratic" institutions, and wonder why they meet resistance.

There are further implications when there is a focus on a human dimension rather than on institutional norms. There are many within Western systems who attach importance to *integration* as a goal for others. They have a strong preference for integration of multi-ethnic societies rather than autonomies. There are those who have been advocating integration as the ideal among the states of West Africa. From a behavioral perspective, however, separation may be a more acceptable option in many situations, and possibly the means by which to achieve integration in the longer term. The separation of Greeks and Turks in Cyprus gave a degree of security from which members of the two communities could move toward cooperative activities. Associated with this kind of thinking is the idea of *federations* as a compromise. But federations are a disguised form of integration. The minority becomes an institutionalized sub-group within the federation. The numbers game is still played.

There are other means of cooperation that avoid voting, and depend on an informed consensus. As has been pointed out, the international functional system works smoothly, sometimes even during wars, and without any central legislative organization: there are agreed international regulations that govern many activities – health, trade, air and sea navigation, and others. These are all based on agreements negotiated on the premise that each participant has a veto, but at the same time has a strong interest in arriving at agreements and in observing agreed rules. This is also a model for cooperation between nations within states.

THOUGHT PROCESSES

Earlier we referred to the way in which we seem to be able to think only when we have symbolic *models* (Deutsch, 1963). Historically, certain models provided the only explanations possible. Unmanageable conditions were due to the wheel of fortune or the swing of the pendulum (see Boulding, 1956). These models provided not just analogies. They were total explanations. Further enquiry was not called for; there were uncontrollable forces, perhaps supernatural or divine, that were responsible. Such explanations were evidence of, and contributed to, the total fatalism that prevailed.

We have seen how the same superficial attitudes are shown to public policy generally. Juvenile crime is a problem: there are many variables to be explored. But this complex problem can readily be treated in the short term by ignoring the complexities, that is by sending the delinquents into detention. Power bargaining in industrial relations avoids any need for recognition of underlying relationship problems. In international relations we avoid analysis of complexities and opt for deterrent strategies.

When there is an inadequate explanation of a situation – when, that is, there is not a full analysis and understanding of it – there is no option but to treat it in this manner. In finding one's way through the bush, in dealing with mechanical faults that are not immediately understood, and sometimes in working out relationships, *trial-and-error* dominates. Failure requires another new start, and another, until by chance there is achievement.

In Kuhn's terms (1962), there is a paradigm or accepted belief system to which we hold tenaciously until situations occur that clearly cannot be explained within it. Then a new one begins to emerge. Add sets of interests to outmoded and inadequate explanations and there is a basis for *ideologies*, or summaries of ideas, focusing on only some aspects of the total problem, and from particular perspectives. Ideologies are statements of belief that emerge when there is inadequate information on which to base a common consensus. Ideologies have decision making or policy implications, but they cannot, by their nature, provide a basis for resolving problems.

The need for educational processes that encourage problem-solving orientations and approaches is clear. It would be expedient to have teaching courses on how to think and how to solve problems for all entrants into higher education, and perhaps earlier. This could be a most profitable investment for the future in all societies.

Being analytical, questioning assumptions, seeking clarity of concepts and language, implies the possibility of breaking away from existing patterns of thought. For many this is uncomfortable and even dangerous in political affairs. Yet the crucial task of preserving and promoting human values and appropriate institutions cannot be achieved by thought systems and policies that do not take into account all the variables that are relevant. A simplistic or reductionist approach to politics is necessarily destructive of the basic goals of persons and societies.

It was for these reasons that in the late 1960s interest in the posthumous works of an American, C. S. Peirce, who died in 1914, exploded. Writing at the turn of the century, he had advocated "abduction" which means, essentially, to make sure the original hypothesis reflects all knowledge and experience available. He called it "critical common-sensism." This contradicted prevailing beliefs that the original hypothesis was a matter merely of personal choice, and that the testing or falsifying process was the essence of science (see Rescher, 1978).

It is a critical common-sensism that people do not normally seek to destroy each other and themselves, and would welcome viable alternatives. If they do not use existing institutions in helping them to deal with their conflicts, there is something unacceptable about the institutions.

The essence of conflict resolution and the problem-solving process generally is the questioning of assumptions and alleged facts, careful analysis of the total situation and clarity on concepts and language. In short, it is a facilitated exercise in how to think. So, also, conflict provention is a step toward bringing knowledge back into a whole, and developing processes that make available to public policy and social relations the totality of knowledge.

There is nothing new here for successful businessmen, lawyers, diplomats, managers and administrators. People who are successful in their calling know, by definition, how to handle problems. They start with a carefully thought out definition of a problem in all its fundamental aspects and the goals to be achieved. They take all variables into account, variables ranging from facts to feelings, needs and values. They then construct a theory relevant to the situation. This theory guides them to an approach, a policy, a method. Then there is application with the results fed back into the original hypothesis and changes made when necessary. It is a kind of informed common-sense, as Peirce observed.

REMEDIAL AND PROVENTION APPROACHES: TWO DIFFERENT FIELDS

Remedial and proventive approaches to any problem area are very different, requiring different curricula for two quite different professional callings. In the conflict area remedial measures are for those interested in a profession of facilitated conflict management, and focus largely on process. Any limited background study of the phenomenon of conflict is thus attuned to that particular purpose. *Proventive* measures, on the other hand, are relevant to those who are concerned with policy making at local, regional, corporate, administrative and parliamentary levels, and in international organizations, and require a far deeper background knowledge of the sources of conflict, and of the environmental changes that would be required to *pro*vent it.

Is there a call for professionalism in the area of conflict *pro*vention in addition to conflict management and resolution? May it not be that societies, rather than undertake the necessary and far-reaching changes, will choose to continue the use of traditional means of containment, coercion and deterrence, with whatever help can be given by courts and alternative dispute resolution processes, and case-by-case conflict management procedures?

This is certainly tempting from a practical and political perspective. The aim of prediction and *pro*vention is to be proved wrong! Only by failing to *pro*vent that which is to be *pre*vented can the prediction of the event be fulfilled. It is a no–win game. But it is a game that scholarship, if not politics, should be prepared to play.

In fact it is not possible to train professionals to be adequate facilitators in the particular case of deep-rooted conflict unless they have an understanding of what makes an environment of conflict, and of the changes that are required to eliminate it. In scholarship we must move forward into the area of *pro*vention. Only when scholarship manages to articulate the basis of reliable prediction, and the means of provention, can we expect any shift in understanding from a containment or remedial approach to conflict toward a proventive approach.

V
Conclusion

Chapter 20   Conflict Resolution as a Political System   261
Chapter 21   A Summary Assessment   269

Introduction to Part V

Protest against the present, which is a virtually universal and continuing phenomenon, does not necessarily include a recipe for the future. All systems, authoritarian and democratic, are facing insurmountable problems and are, as a consequence, being challenged. Is the problem one of systems, or one of process? Does the study of conflict resolution and provention contribute in any way to the great debate (Chapter 20)?

We have traced the theory of decision making from coercive settlements, through management process, to resolution and to provention. Judicial, arbitration and management processes are well established and institutionalized. We have argued that there is a wider political significance in conflict resolution, but we have yet to deal with the institutionalization of resolution and provention as an applied process. Ultimately, however, the problem of conflict, its resolution and provention, comes down to the need for a paradigm shift from a power to a problem-solving framework, and this means that it is a problem of education, first the education of facilitators and policy makers at all social levels, but finally education leading to a popular consensus (Chapter 21).

20 Conflict Resolution as a Political System

POLITICAL MOVEMENTS IN PERSPECTIVE

This study has been written in, and indeed was provoked by, what would seem to be an unprecedentedly widespread condition of unrest and conflict in the global society and within each of its members. In particular, towards the end of the 1980s there was a persistent and effective challenge to political authorities in most countries. National politics were separated, not just by law, but in protest movements, between those who claim a right to govern, and those whom they assume have an obligation to obey. The challenge, always there but latent, appears to have been brought to the surface to an unusual degree in the 1980s by overt evidence that those who claim the right to govern are not usually adequately representative and responsive to the needs of those whom they seek to control and, furthermore, tend to act in their own interests, in many cases corruptly.

Amongst these challenges in the 1980s were remarkable developments in the Soviet Union, China, Poland and other communist countries as a result of domestic protest that could not be attributed to any foreign covert interventions or to a phase in the "cold war." In addition there were forty or so countries in which ethnic minorities, comprising more than a quarter of total national populations, were experiencing threats to their cultural security and human needs generally. There were minorities comprising lesser proportions in almost all other countries whose rights were similarly at risk (Gurr and Scarritt, 1989). There were, also, reactions against military dictatorships, especially in Latin America.

From a Western perspective the challenges in communist countries were seen as a validation of Western-type economic and political systems, especially those, like the US and Britain, that had rejected economic and social controls by central authorities. They justified deregulation and privatization processes, which had become the formal policies of these and many other governments, and which were stimulated by reactions against past failed policies of economic and social intervention. Resistances to authoritative and bureaucratic interventions that were taking place in the communist world in the cause of freedom and democracy were understood in the Western free-enterprise world as validating the movement that favored non-interventions by central authorities in their economies and in social life generally.

This euphoria in free-enterprise systems, and the widespread global situations of tension and overt conflict elsewhere which stimulated it, diverted attention away from no less serious problems arising within such systems. Deregulation and privatization policies were proving not to be the answer to emerging class and ethnicity problems in free-enterprise systems. They are not likely to be the answer in communist countries either, for there are in these countries major problems of underdevelopment, and also ethnicity problems, that will not be resolved by the introduction of Western-type democracy or by altered economic systems. In fact these acute problems are further accentuated by such processes in both systems. In both, it should be noted, it was the relatively privileged who, in the name of "freedom," were reacting against interventions. In the free-enterprise systems, while the wealthy became wealthier, the poor (usually minorities) became poorer, worse educated and more alienated. The "trickle-down" economic theory was falsified. In the communist countries the relatively underprivileged and minorities were not likely to benefit from more consultative systems dominated by majorities.

In both cases the problems were wrongly defined. The public demand in communist states was for democracy and freedoms as the means by which to end corrupt practices and to improve economic development. But given such democracy and freedoms there would not be a resolution of such pressing social problems. They existed in the West where there was such democracy and freedoms. The issue for both was not democracy and freedoms, or regulation and deregulation, or intervention and non-intervention. It was what kinds of democracy, freedoms and intervention were appropriate to the circumstances, what kind of within-system change was required, and when and what kinds of second order change might be required to resolve problems and to provent them occurring – the problems we introduced in Chapter 11 in relation to conflict *resolution*, and in Chapter 18 in relation to conflict *provention*.

The answer to these questions is not found in structures of economies and governments. All types are vulnerable, obviously some more than others, in the absence of an adequate predictive knowledge on which to base policies, and in the absence of processes by which policies can evolve on such a basis. Such processes would include feedback or self-monitoring mechanisms to ensure that policies define and target goals accurately.

Trends away from authoritative control were self-reinforcing. Social problems created by deregulation and non-intervention soon grew out of control in developed Western systems, promoting further withdrawal and denial by authorities of their responsibilities. High levels of urban violence, drug addictions and other consequences of lack of educational, occupational and communal opportunities were widespread. Associated with these overt signs of system breakdown, problems of non-representation, corruption and ethical violations became major political issues. What students in China complained about, an absence of democracy, and associated with this, corruption in administration, were not confined to that system and clearly would not be cured merely by moving toward more representation and more market freedoms.

These separate situations of protest and system breakdown in different countries, taking their own distinctive forms, were apparently symptoms of something that was being experienced in common, and perhaps universally. It could not have been accidental that changes forced on an administration in the Soviet Union were followed by changes in many countries not under Soviet control, and accompanied by tensions and conflicts within non-communist systems thought to be fundamentally different.

What appears to have happened is that changes in Soviet policies, initially instigated by the urgent need to deal with domestic problems, led in the West to altered perceptions of threat, which in turn made possible increased attention to domestic problems of deprivation and violence, including an expanding drug problem. In short, the reduction in great power tensions led to far more concentration in the US and elsewhere, including China, on domestic problems.

This interpretation of events follows from our previous analysis. We have from the outset rejected the more conventional approach to conflict that treats it as a different phenomenon at different societal levels. We have been trying to find an explanation of this universal relationship problem, one that helps to explain conflict at all societal levels. We are as much concerned with relationship conflict at the family, industrial and community levels as at the international.

A UNIVERSAL PHENOMENON

There are many reasons why this 1980s phenomenon of protest at all levels and in all communities could be unusual, if not unprecedented. There are reasons to believe, also, that they could all, though separate situations, relate to a common behavioral phenomenon.

The environmental circumstances were unprecedented. First television provided a means of world coverage, resulting in a sense of support and of achievement for those involved, placing authorities on the defensive. Second, there were sophisticated means of protest, both violent and non-violent, at the disposal of those who otherwise lacked political and military power. Third, there was an unprecedented spread of populations, through migrations, student exchanges and business contacts, that ensured external support for protest movements that otherwise might have received none. These were recent developments, perhaps changing the nature of protest, changing the balance of power between elites and others.

More fundamentally, however, there was a common cause, a common phenomenon. In all these cases of protest we have noted the goal was not change in the political system, the industrial system, the family system. On the contrary, existing systems seem to have been acceptable and even valued, regardless of what they were. The Chinese students were not opposing communism, and those involved in conflicts with authorities in the West were not opposed to the free-enterprise system. We have noted that ethnic minorities have favored their relationships with majorities comprising another ethnicity over relationships with neighboring communities of the same ethnicity. Deviant children who are in conflict with parents are not protesting about the family as a unit. Protest movements in all types of authoritative systems, at all levels, are deeper than that. In all cases the struggle is to find that form of authority, from the family to the national, and to the global society, that is legitimized, that establishes the necessary balance between the person and the social good, and that resolves and provents conflicts in ways that establish an environment of harmony and stability in which there can be individual development – which in itself contributes to social harmony and development. Polish trade unionists, Chinese students, ethnic minorities and alienated young people who formed street gangs, were seeking the same goals, the same kinds of alterations, not in systems, but in the ways in which they operated, including the ways in which systems could be adjusted to altering circumstances and altering demands made on them.

SYSTEM AND PROCESS

In these events a quite fundamental phenomenon is revealed. Traditionally there have been struggles over types of systems. The world has been threatened by conflict between capitalism and communism. A world war was fought between capitalism and fascism. What is now revealed is that system differences may not be a problem. Seemingly malign and irrational behaviors of authorities, even seemingly dictatorial authorities, may not be the major problem. There could be the same situations of conflict in conditions in which all nations were democratic, in which all leaders were well intentioned, in which industry sought to be profitable, and in which the family sought to pursue social values. The problem that gives rise to conflict is not a system problem. It is a problem that arises out of the processes within systems by which decisions are made, by which goals are determined, and by which they are pursued.

We would come to this observation even without the empirical evidence with which we commenced. We have been concerned in this analysis with the underlying trend that has given rise to protest. We have asserted that it is a shift from an emphasis on the obligation on the part of the person to adjust to institutions, to a growing demand that institutions cater for the ontological needs of people. The balance between individual and identity group needs, on the one hand, and the common good, on the other, must be determined in this framework. Whatever the system, deep-rooted conflict must be endemic unless this balance meets the ontological needs of persons and the groups with which they identify.

RIGHTS AND NEEDS

To the Western observer this could sound like a justification of the Western emphasis on human rights. But why are Western systems also in trouble? The shift we have been discussing can be redefined in terms of rights and needs. Within the institutional framework in which the emphasis is on the preservation of systems, rights within that system are upheld. These are, in practice, the norms that preserve the system, the norms that finally ensure conformity and the suppression of needs. Take, for example the "right" of free speech. Those who exercise this right are those who control the media and means of ensuring conformity. The right of political participation is one that results in not more than 50 per cent of a population in many Western "democracies" voting at elections. Others feel alienated, and in many cases are excluded because they are not able to cope with the registration processes required. Freedoms include the right to employ expensive lobbying tactics in the interests of small interest groups, both in getting persons elected and controlling their behaviors while they are in office. Within the same system there is no "right" for a stimulating job, or a job of any kind. Rights as such are no more than a means of preserving a particular type of system, and do not go to the root of the problems societies face.

It is needs, not rights, that have to be satisfied if there is to be stability in relationships. Provided a system satisfies human needs, it can avoid conflict. There are examples of benevolent dictatorships and very traditional societies that are legitimized. These are frequently smaller face-to-face societies. The system structure is not the problem, it is system operation that determines whether human needs are met. This emphasis shift to the role of institutions in catering for the needs of people could fundamentally change relationships between different political systems worldwide.

THE FUTURE

Like all transitions, especially those that are unplanned and *ad hoc* responses to conditions, the present has potentials that are both positive and negative. The assumption by private enterprise of responsibilities to resolve economic and social problems could be regarded as a positive trend, a positive form of anarchy, that had tremendous long-term benefits for political systems, if it were to observe decision making processes that were analytical and interactive by those concerned. But the same privatization could also take a special interest orientation, and be dysfunctional and conflictual. The latter is the probability, bearing in mind consensus thinking that favors interest-dominated and power-political solutions rather than problem-solving ones. These are problems of process, not of systems (see Rubenstein, *Group Violence in America*, 1988, and Burton,

Conflict Resolution as a Political System, 1988).

What was disturbing about movements of protest in the 1980s is that no options or alternatives emerged. Demands for democratization do not provide models for democratic systems. Demands for freedoms do not provide recipes for economic systems. Demands for ethical probity do not prescribe forms of administration that do not lead to corruption. These were reactive situations – in none did there emerge any contributions to political thought. The social good was, in fact, submerged by the claims for further privilege for the already privileged. The result would be an even greater gulf between those who expect to have a right to rule, and those who can have no such expectations, and the emergence in even starker form of class and class warfare, perhaps now more usually called ethnic conflict.

PROBLEM-SOLVING PROCESSES WITHIN SYSTEMS

The task which is defined by a consideration of conflict, its resolution and provention, is not to create some ideal political system, but to discover the processes that are required within any type of system by which relationships can be handled to resolve or provent conflict, in other words to satisfy basic needs. Clearly, the norms that would evolve over time in dealing with conflict situations would alter structures, and maybe in time different systems would move toward some as yet undiscovered form of polity; but this is not the goal. The goal is to resolve or provent conflict, that is to promote a harmonious society, by processes that ensure human needs are promoted. Systems are treated as satisfiers, means to ends. The goal is, therefore, a process goal, a means by which systems and institutions within them alter and evolve in response to demands that reflect human needs. It is in this sense that the study and practice of conflict resolution and provention is removed from debates over systems, and in this sense, also, a departure from the contending framework of classical political philosophy.

The question posed in this chapter is, therefore, whether there is a role for institutionalized conflict resolution and provention to supplement or even, in the future, to move political systems in the direction of greater legitimization and the democracy and freedom that legitimization implies. In Part II we dealt with the political context of conflict resolution and provention, questions of legitimization, and the individual in society. We concluded Part II by introducing the idea of constructive intervention. It was in this context that we examined decision making and conflict resolution in Part III. When we turned to provention in Part IV we were once again concerned with problems of change and adjustment to change, and the intellectual challenges they presented.

The question we need to address at this stage is whether conflict and its provention, within this altered framework, can be institutionalized, and in ways that do not create dominant interest groups that seek only to preserve institutions.

21 A Summary Assessment

RESIGNATION

Today, almost in the third millenium, AD, there is still an emphasis on *settlement*, usually coercive settlement, and the treatment of symptoms of problems, rather than on their *resolution*. There is still no consensus conceptual framework for conflict provention. Yet the danger signs are clear: QOL that includes the satisfactions of human needs is on the decrease, conflict and violence are destroying economies as well as people, and the environment of conflict is increasing at an exponential rate. Why is there no action to get at the roots of such problems?

The reason lies not just in vested interests. Conflict has seemed to be inevitable, a cost to be born, even glorified by memorials and anticipated in symbols of nationalism. There continues to be a kind of resigned acceptance of the inevitability of conflict, and wars, as a means of "resolving" conflict at all social levels. It is seen as a normal part of human existence, along with disease, famine and natural catastrophe, and beyond human control perhaps even more than these natural disasters.

It could be argued that ordinary social disputes, the kind of disputes we earlier defined as normal and constructive conflict, even though physically damaging in some instances, are nonetheless inevitable and an ontological part of human relationships. These are conflicts that have sources in misperceptions, intellectual disagreements, negotiable disputes, and personality differences. With better understanding of relationships, facilities for dispute resolution, and more conducive environments, their incidence could probably be reduced. But they cannot be eliminated, nor would be it desirable to eliminate all such disputes.

This resigned acceptance, however, has no rational justification when we are dealing with conflicts brought about by frustrated deep-rooted human needs. The only possible intellectual justification is that within the limits of existing knowledge nothing can be done about such conflicts. This implies that human evolution is still at a stage at which there is not the capability of conscious control of the social environment, or that nothing can be done because the causal social–political structures are too entrenched to be altered signifi-

269

cantly, even though intellectually the changes required might be conceptualized.

RESOLUTION AND PROVENTION AS A CHALLENGE TO RESIGNATION

Conflict resolution challenges these beliefs, arguing that an inability to effect change and to resolve conflicts is more likely to be due to an absence of thought given to problems of change, and the relevant and effective problem-solving processes. With problem-solving conflict resolution resignation gives place to a search for the appropriate processes. The study of conflict, its resolution and provention provides a framework for thought that is abductive – that is, challenging of assumptions. It is analytical, non-judgemental, problem-solving, a-disciplinary, and at the same time highly empirical in the sense that it is dealing with situations and human responses at the micro-level. Within such a framework the assumptions of separate disciplines and traditional consensus beliefs are given a different perspective, leading to different kinds of questions and answers.

Thinking on matters of polity has dealt primarily with questions about who should govern, and revolutions have taken place over the issue. Conflict, its resolution and provention direct attention to how authorities, whoever they may happen to be, in whatever system they operate, and at whatever social level, must behave if they are to be legitimized and to achieve their goals; what relationships are required between authorities and those over whom they exercise control; what constitutes valued reciprocal relationships; and, most importantly, what is the nature of ultimate human goals.

In this sense the study of conflict, its resolution and provention, brings back into focus issues of political alienation, and lack of individual development and recognition that provoked many past thinkers to seek solutions to polity problems. But the tendency in the past was to seek institutional solutions, and being institutional, they did not get to the roots of the problems they were seeking to solve.

Conflict resolution and provention seek the processes by which relationships can be harmonious by getting at the roots of problems in relationships, thus subjecting to scrutiny any institutions (class or other) that are a source of conflictual relationships. Conflict resolution and provention seek to incorporate a continuing analytical problem-solving process within whatever political structure happens to exist: it is a process relevant to all systems.

THE CREATIVE ROLE OF PROFESSIONALS

Conflict resolution does not impose solutions, or designate alternative systems, or advocate in a particular case. It contributes a process, a process of analytical and interactive problem-solving and costing, that enables participants to determine for themselves, in the light of the analysis made, whether they wish to meet the costs of policies that might be conflictual and dysfunctional in the longer term. This is a process that is open to persons within communities concerned with their own disputes, and also to community representatives who have a mandate to take a longer-term view of the interests of those whom they represent.

The emphasis on process, the focus and concentration on process, a process that leaves decision making within the purview of those concerned, is the feature that separates conflict resolution from any past means of handling conflicts. It is a process that, even in the interests of the powerful, makes relative power irrelevant, for it is resolution that is sought, not a negotiated or power settlement that could be costly in the longer term.

It implies, however, something that is demanding of those engaged in conflict: the obligation to be analytical, and to get to the roots of the problems that cause the conflict, and to cost out the consequences of policies and options. Because this is demanding on parties engaged in conflict, parties who inevitably will be involved ideologically and emotionally, conflict resolution processes usually include some form of facilitation by professional persons to ensure a deep analysis of the problems being confronted.

The study of conflict resolution, the study that such a facilitator must make, is a wide study of human nature and the total environment. In a typical conflict resolution forum dealing with a major conflict, such as an international or ethnic conflict, a professional third party will be a panel of professionals, for four or five persons are required to fulfil the challenging requirements of such a role (see Book 4, *Conflict: Practices in Management, Settlement and Resolution*).

We have emphasized the need for interaction between protagonists, and for them to arrive at options that meet their needs, the facilitator acting as a catalyst. We stressed in Part III, however, the creative role, the way in which a facilitator can place a particular situation within a theoretical framework in which viable options can be considered. A panel of facilitators will ususally spend as much time interacting with each other as they do with their clients. It is their function to bring to bear in a continuing way whatever professional knowledge there is to their particular case. The professionalism involved is the same professionalism required by those concerned with provention. It is a professionalism that is outside process, and places the facilitator in the same role as any other professional who gives advice. There is a distinction to be made between the macro-conditions required as a precondition of resolution or provention, an area of concern to the professional adviser, and the micro-conditions that apply in the particular case and which will be determined by the protagonists.

This is a professionalism that has yet to develop. It challenges those within the wider field of dispute and conflict management who focus almost exclusively on process and micro-analysis, implying that there is no role for professional advice to protagonists other than a facilitation role in an interactive situation. This process role will in due course be a secondary one, the major one being an advisory role to parties in conflict, both in how to resolve a current conflict and in how to avoid conflict in the first place.

THE AVAILABILITY OF CONFLICT RESOLUTION

A question still to be addressed is, how do conflict resolution and provention processes become available to those who require them? Societies have courts and other means of arbitration, and these have evolved over generations. Where does conflict resolution fit into existing institutions? How can it be made available to those who need it?

The availability of conflict resolution is a matter of institutionaliz-ation. Conflict provention, by contrast, is a far more complex problem of paradigm shift, education and consensus formation.

The institutionalization of conflict *management*, in many forms, has evolved in recent decades, largely as a result of crowded and expensive judicial processes, and the demand for processes less mandatory than arbitration. Up to the present they have been sponsored primarily by private organizations. While governments have their own agencies, (for example, the Administrative Conference of the US's promotion of *"Agencies' Use of Alternative Means of Dispute Resolution"* adopted in 1986), most of the work in this area is performed by small professional groups, standards being set more and more by professional organizations such as the Society for Professionals in Dispute Resolution (SPIDR) in the US. It is safe to say that any parties to disputes that seek such assistance can usually find persons or organizations that can help them to communicate.

Resolution processes, as distinct from *management* processes, have been confined largely to university centers because of their greater concern with deep-rooted conflict, largely international and intercommunal so far, and in-depth analysis of situations within a theoretical framework (see Burton, 1969: Azar and Burton, eds. 1986; Kelman, 1972; Mitchell, 1981b).

As yet conflict resolution processes have not been adopted officially in diplomacy. While the Foreign Service Institute of the US Department of State has reported on them (see McDonald and Bendahmane, 1987), they are processes little known because of the confidential nature of the interactions promoted. Furthermore, unlike most management processes, they require some special knowledge of analysis and behaviors because of the more active role played by the third party in promoting an in-depth analysis in exploring possible options.

Availability depends, therefore, on some institutionalized means yet to be found. Possibilities are in the training of diplomats so they can enact a facilitating role in the normal course of their work. This, however, runs into trouble because governments tend to take sides in disputes between other parties, and this prejudices the role of their diplomatic representatives. It might be relevant only to diplomats from countries that are seen to be neutral in their relationships.

Another possibility is an agency of the United Nations, such as the United Nations University, or the Secretariat itself which becomes involved in mediation and usually seeks the assistance of a diplomatic representative to the United Nations from a small and neutral country. Neutrality of itself, however, does not provide the knowledge of theory and process required.

The probability is that a form of institutionalization will evolve only when processes are more widely known, and when more cases can be documented. Theory and processes deduced from theory can be set out in detail (see Book 4 of this Conflict Series), and are there to be applied as parties to conflict become aware of them, and as institutions evolve that can handle them.

While there are opportunities to promote the resolution of conflicts in particular cases, and while, therefore, there is a need for more professionals who can do this, and for some institutions within the nation and in the global society to make services available, it would be grossly misleading to suggest that the availability of conflict resolution processes will relieve civilizations of their present crisis situation. There is a large number of major ethnic conflicts globally, and there will be many more. They are protracted conflicts requiring major structural changes. Deep-rooted conflict is widespread in every society, especially in ethnically divided societies. Interventions in particular cases can make a contribution, but each one would need follow-up to a degree that would be beyond the resources of large professional offices.

The value of such specific interventions is primarily in the learning and knowledge that can be gained from the experience, both by the parties concerned, and by the third party, and the demonstration to a wider public of an alternative to resignation and despair.

PROVENTION AS THE MAJOR POLICY FOCUS

Provention is a far more challenging problem than the availability of facilitated resolution. It raises the fundamental questions of political philosophy with which scholars and practitioners have struggled for generations.

We have been concerned with problem-solving processes, on the one hand, and resistances to any challenging analysis on the other. The link between the two is costing, and costing has an important time dimension. What are the costs now and in the future of refusal to deal with the roots of problems? Because individuals survive in the present, the future is usually beyond their immediate concern, and this means that the thinking required may have to be promoted by a defender of the future. Since authorities also live in the present, it is difficult to imagine who or what can be the guardian of the future. Who is to take care of entropy, which is important for the future of the human race, of the forms institutions take, and social policies generally? Apart from costing, which is long term and may not influence current policies and decisions, what is there to promote the institutionalization of problem-solving and provention?

Indeed, this is the problem of modern civilizations: there appear to be few significant political institutions that have the role of looking to the future, even the short-term future that affects persons now living. Responsibility for control of unnecessary resource exploitation and environmental contamination is not accepted by any authority, national or international. The reason is that there are no credits for such control, and there are many political debits. There are future costs to society of children born to drug addicted parents, there are future costs of alienation, inadequate educational and health facilities, but the political institutions of most countries cannot cope with such future costing. There are inadequate means of planning for the future.

Conflict resolution and provention, analytical problem-solving, seeks to add this longer time dimension to decision making. It becomes generally available, however, only to the extent that it becomes part of the thinking of peoples in facing up to the realities of relationships that affect them. The corporate manager with a responsibility for the longer-term success of the corporation, the public administrator who must look ahead in developmental projects, the educator who has to plan the environment in which children will function, all have to cost the present by reference to the future. Conflict resolution is an extension of this process to those who are caught up in situations in which they have difficulty in costing the consequences of their behaviors.

There is, clearly, a call for professionalization along these lines within the legal profession and in diplomacy. It would seem an obvious requirement for foreign policy advisers so that, for example, governments could avoid taking sides with one faction or another in some conflict between other parties. But nowhere is it more necessary than in public administration and in politics.

Availability of provention processes has finally to be the same kind of availability that we observed has taken place since the early 1960s, with developments in decision making. It is an experience-based consensus form of availability that touches on every aspect of decision making affecting conflict and its resolution and provention: this means almost all decision making, both in the private sector and in the public. In other words, formal availability of conflict resolution should not be necessary if conflict and its resolution were understood and part of everyday life, as are bargaining and negotiation today. A major paradigm shift in thinking is required.

A PROBLEM OF EDUCATION

The problem of availability of conflict resolution and provention processes is therefore, a problem of education. The thrust of scholarship in most behavioral disciplines is toward the preservation of existing institutions, the treatment of symptoms, and the socialization of the individual accordingly. One result is that even many of those who claim to be in the conflict area are well within the traditional framework of preserving that which exists, and *settling* disputes within this framework by manipulative or coercive tactics. Their educational and cultural backgrounds in one discipline or another have oriented them in this direction.

The availability of conflict resolution and provention, therefore, is first and foremost the inclusion of problem solving in the classroom at all educational levels, (see Beyer, 1987), and where possible, the inclusion of problem-solving approaches in existing professions, especially those professions that are concerned with human interactions. The student of conflict, its resolution and provention, is not only a potential third-party facilitator in a conflict situation. The student of conflict, its resolution and provention, is the potential high-quality corporate manager, politician or political adviser, administrator, social worker, teacher, policeman, strategic planner, diplomat, lawyer, and most importantly of all, the ordinary citizen. It is the educational system, a system that is a-disciplinary and oriented towards problem-solving, that can promote the availability of conflict resolution and provention.

THE NEED FOR THINKING SKILLS

It will be an unsatisfactory conclusion to policy makers at all social levels and to people generally that the problem of conflict, its resolution and provention, depends on thinking skills. In her *Thought and Knowledge: An Introduction to Critical Thinking* (1984), Diane Halpern observes "Although the ability to think critically has always been important, it is imperative for the citizens of the 20th and 21st century. For the first time in the history of the human race, we have the ability to destroy all life on earth. The decisions that we make as individuals and as a society regarding defense, the economy, conservation of natural resources, and the development of nuclear weapons will affect future generations of all peoples around the world." This is a valid emphasis. The dangers of conflict, not resolved or provented, are even more fundamental, and require even more critical thinking.

One could conclude that "the slow and weak progress of conflict resolution is due mainly to the obstruction of the status quo ideology. That ideology has produced a theory that explains policies 'scientifically' and justifies them empirically. We call for a paradigm shift. The difficulty is that while the forces of the status quo *do* have a paradigm, and it must be removed before we can progress, we do not have what appears to them to be a satisfactory alternative. I suspect that the new paradigm will not be seen until *after* the old one has gone, or at least has been discredited. That could be too late! The challenge is to produce an acceptable alternative even while the status quo ideology still exists" (Banks, 1989).

A Short Bibliography

Below there is a short bibliography, a selection of eight books, with a brief commentary on each, that at the time of publication of this Volume were readily available. They could further introduce the reader to this subject of Conflict, its Resolution and Provention. A longer annotated bibliography is included in Volume 3 of this Conflict Series.

Box, Steven (1971) *Deviance, Reality and Society*, Holt, Rinehart & Winston.

Steven Box, working at the University of Kent at Canterbury, England, was a creative rebel. His assertion that deviant behavior must be treated as being one and the same as ordinary behavior was a major challenge at the time. For him deviance was merely behavior that did not happen to fit in with the rules of society, which tolerated as part of its economic and political system gross anti-social behaviors. It was legally possible for persons already wealthy to "rob" on a large scale through many institutional devices, but a minor theft by someone in need was punished. Such an oversimplification does not do justice to a major work that alerts the reader to some political–philosophical problems that have yet to be tackled.

Burton, John W. (1972) *World Society*, Cambridge University Press (University Press of America, 1987).

Included in this short list is a book by the author of this Volume on *Resolution and Provention*. It has been included mostly for historical reasons: this was among the first teaching texts that went into some detail on conflict resolution and its processes. It reflected experience with several international situations. The emphasis was *not* on human needs – in 1972 the conception had not become part of thinking. The assumption was that perceptions were the main problem, only implying that there were hidden motivations that a facilitated process could help to unveil. Little thought was given at the time to their nature.

Coate, Roger A. and Rosati, Jerel A. (1988) *The Power of Human Needs in World Society*, Lynne Reinner Publishers.

This collection of essays brought together the major contributions available at the time to this new mode of thinking. The title was an apt one, reflecting the concerns of the 1980s that authorities no longer had a monopoly of power. The book was written before upheavals in China and the Soviet Union and the failure of the United States to control the drug traffic and the violence of the cities.

Haworth, Lawrence (1986) *Autonomy: An Essay in Philosophical Psychology and Ethics*, Yale University Press.

What is of interest and significance in the history of thinking about human needs, and to which we sought to draw attention in Chapter 6 of this Volume, is the way in which thinkers have come to an emphasis on identity and related human needs from many different perspectives and disciplines. Indeed, there is evidence that this has happened on an individual basis, with very little interaction among scholars from different disciplines, or even within them. Hence the use of different terms. "Autonomy" is used by Haworth to mean more than its dictionary meaning of self-government, and far more in the sense of Sites's term "control," implying the need for the individual or the identity group to be in control of those conditions that affect the pursuit of needs.

Lederer, Katrin (ed.) (1980) *Human Needs: A Contribution to the Current Debate*, Oelgeschlager, Gunn & Hain (Cambridge, Mass.).

The fact that a conference was held to discuss the notion of human needs, and that there were papers produced is probably more important historically than the content of the papers. Many of the participants of that conference were subsequently participants at a conference convened to apply needs theory to conflict resolution, and it is their contributions that are the content of Volume 2 in this Conflict Series. It is interesting to compare the two contributions of many of the same people, in the one case concerned with human needs in relation to a theory of development, and in the other, to a theory of conflict resolution.

Mitchell, C. R. (1981) *Peacemaking and the Consultant's Role*, Gower.

Here we come to the applied side, but with a firm base in theory. This is a short book, and very readable. It serves as an introduction to conflict resolution, not just at the international level, which is the major interest of the author, but generally because of its theoretical foundations.

Sandole, Dennis J. D. and Sandole, Ingrid S. (eds) (1978) *Conflict Management and Problem Solving: Interpersonal to International Applications*, Frances Pinter (London).

This is yet another collection of essays. Some of these were the result of a conference, and others have been selected and edited carefully by the two editors. The field covered is much wider and perhaps fits more into international relations studies than conflict studies, but the interests of the authors have made their selection most relevant to conflict resolution.

Sites, Paul (1973) *Control: the Basis of Social Order*, Dunellen Publishers.

Many references have been made to this book in this Volume. Perhaps no sociologist has contributed more to the shift in thinking that has taken place from a focus on the socialization of the person toward a recognition of the human need for control. This is one of the foundation works in this emerging field of conflict resolution, and especially conflict provention.

References

AMY, DOUGLAS J. (1987) *The Politics of Environmental Mediation*, Columbia University Press.

ANDREWS, FRANK M. (1986) *Research on the Quality of Life*, University of Michigan.

ARDNEY, ROBERT (1966) *The Territorial Imperative*, Dell.

ARGYRIS, CHRIS (1983) *Reasoning and Learning, and Action: Individual and Organization*, Jossey-Bass.

AZAR, EDWARD E. (1986) "Protracted International Conflicts," in AZAR and BURTON (1986).

AZAR, EDWARD E. and BURTON, J. W. (eds) (1986) *International Conflict Resolution: Theory and Practice*, Wheatsheaf (UK).

BANKS, MICHAEL (ed. and contributor) (1984) *Conflict in World Society. A New Perspective on International Relations*, Wheatsheaf (UK).

BANKS, MICHAEL (1986) "The International Relations Discipline: Asset or Liability for Conflict Resolution?", in Azar and Burton (1986).

BANKS, MICHAEL (1989) Personal communication to the author.

BARASH, D. P. (1977) *Sociobiology and Behavior*, Elsevier.

BAY, CHRISTIAN (1958) *The Structure of Freedom*, Stanford.

BECKER, ERNEST (1968) *The Structure of Evil: An Essay on the Unification of the Science of Man*, Braziller.

BECKERMAN, WILFRED (1987) "National Income," in *The New Palgrave Dictionary of Economics*, vol. 3, Macmillan.

BEYER, BARRY K. (1987) *Practical Strategies for the Teaching of Thinking*, Allyn & Bacon.

BLAKE, ROBERT R., SHEPARD, HERBERT A. and MOUTON, JANE S. (1964) *Managing Intergroup Conflict in Industry*, Gulf Publishing Co.

BLAU, PETER M. (1964) *Exchange and Power in Social Life*, Wiley.

BOEHM, W. W. (1958) "The Nature of Social Work," *Social Work*, vol 3. no. 2.

BOULDING, KENNETH E. (1956) "General Systems Theory – the skeleton of science," *Management Science*, no. 2.

BOULDING, KENNETH E. (1962) *Conflict and Defense: A General Theory*, Harper & Row.

BOULDING, KENNETH E. (1966) "Conflict Management as a Learning Process," in DE REUCK and KNIGHT (eds) (1966).

BOX, STEVEN (1971) *Deviance, Reality and Society*, Holt, Rinehart & Winston.

BRECHT, ARNOLD (1967) *Political Theory*, Princeton.

BUCHANAN, JAMES M., TOLLISON, R. and TULLOCK, G. (1980) *Toward a Theory of Rent-Seeking Society*, College Station, Texas A and M University Press.

BURNS, JAMES MACGREGOR (1977) "Wellsprings of Political Leadership," in *The American Political Science Review*, LXXI (March).

BURTON, JOHN W. (1941) *Restrictive and Constructive Intervention*, University of London.

BURTON, JOHN W. (1962) *Peace Theory: Pre-conditions of Disarmament*, Knopf.

BURTON, JOHN W. (1965) *International Relations: A General Theory*, Cambridge University Press.

BURTON, JOHN W. (1969) *Conflict and Communication: The Use of controlled communication in International Relations*, The Free Press (NY).

BURTON, JOHN W. (1972) *World Society*, Cambridge University Press (University Press of America, 1987).

BURTON, JOHN W. (1979) *Deviance, Terrorism and War*, Martin Robertson; St Martin's Press (NY).

BURTON, JOHN W. (1982) *Dear Survivors*, Frances Pinter (London).

BURTON, JOHN W. (1984) *Global Conflict*, Wheatsheaf (UK); The Center for Conflict Management, University of Maryland.

BURTON, JOHN W. (1987a) *Resolving Deep-Rooted Conflict: A Handbook*, University Press of America.

BURTON, JOHN W. (1987b) "Three Qualities of a Secure Nation," in Macy, Mark (ed.), *Solutions for a Troubled World*, Earthview Press.

BURTON, JOHN W. (1988) *Conflict Resolution as a Political System*, Working Paper 1, Center for Conflict Analysis and Resolution, George Mason University.

BURTON, JOHN W. and MITCHELL, CHRISTOPHER R. (1987) "Middle Powers Report," Center for Conflict Analysis and Resolution, George Mason University.

BURTON, JOHN W. and SANDOLE, DENNIS (1986) "Generic Theory: The Basis of Conflict Resolution," in *Negotiation Journal* (October).

CARPENTER, SUSAN L. and KENNEDY, W. J. D. (1988) *Managing Public Disputes*, Jossey-Bass.

CIBA (1966), *see* DE REUCK and KNIGHT (eds) (1966).

CLARK, G. and SOHN, L. (1960) *World Peace Through World Law*, Harvard University Press.

CLAUDE, INNIS (1959) *Swords into Plowshares: The Problems and Progress in International Organization*, Random House.

COATE, ROGER A. and ROSATI, JEREL A. (eds) (1988) *The Power of Human Needs in World Society*, Lynne Reinner Publishers.

COMMISSION ON CRITICAL CHOICES FOR AMERICANS (1976) *Qualities of Life*, Lexington Books.

DATOR, J. and ROULSTONE, M. G. (eds) (1988) *Who Cares? And How? Futures for Caring Societies*, World Futures Studies Federation.

DAVID DAVIS MEMORIAL INSTITUTE (1966) *Report of a Study Group on the Peaceful Settlement of International Disputes*.

DAVIES, J. C. (ed.) (1971) *When Men Revolt and Why: A Reader in Political Violence and Revolution*, The Free Press (NY).

DE REUCK, ANTONY and KNIGHT, JULIE (eds) (1966) *Conflict in Society*, a CIBA Foundation Volume, J. and A. Churchill Ltd.

DEDRING, JUERGAN (1976) *Recent Advances in Peace and Conflict Research*, Sage Publications.

DEUTSCH, KARL (1963) *The Nerves of Government*, The Free Press (NY).

EASTON, DAVID (1953, 1981) *The Political System*, Knopf.

ENCYCLOPEDIA OF PHILOSOPHY (1967), vol. Six, Paul Edwards (ed.), Macmillan; The Free Press (NY).

ENVIRONMENTAL PROTECTION AGENCY (1973) *The Quality of Life: A Potential New Tool for Decision-Makers.*

ETZIONI, AMITAI (1988) *The Moral Dimension Toward a New Economics*, The Free Press (NY).

FISHER, A. G. B. (1935) *The Clash of Progress and Security*, Macmillan.

FISHER, A. G. B. (1945) *Economic Progress and Social Security*, Macmillan.

FISHER, ROGER, and URY, WILLIAM (1978) *International Mediation: A Working Guide*, International Peace Academy.

FOX, WILLIAM M. (1987) *Effective Group Problem Solving: How to Broaden Participation, Improve Decision Making, and Increase Commitment to Action*, Jossey-Bass.

FRASER, NIALL M. and HIPEL, KEITH W. (1984) *Conflict Analysis: Models and Resolutions*, North-Holland.

FROMM, ERIC (1961) *May Man Prevail?*, Doubleday.

GALTUNG, JOHAN (1969) "Violence, Peace and Peace Research," *Journal of Peace Research*, no. 3.

GOLDBERG, S. B., GREEN, E. D. and SANDER, F. E. A. (1985) *Dispute Resolution*, Little Brown and Co.

GOULET, DENIS (1973) *The Cruel Choice*, Atheneum.

GURR, TED R. (1970) *Why Men Rebel*, Princeton.

GURR, TED R. and SCARRITT, JAMES R. (1989) "Minority Rights at Risk: A Global Survey," *Human Rights Quarterly* (August).

HALPERN, DIANE F. (1984) *Thought and Knowledge: An Introduction to Critical Thinking*, Lawrence Erlbaum Associates.

HAWORTH, LAWRENCE (1986) *Autonomy: An Essay in Philosophical Psychology and Ethics*, Yale University Press.

HEILBRONER, ROBERT L. and THUROW, LESTER C. (1975) *The Economic Problem*, Prentice-Hall.

HIBBERT, J. (1963) *The Roots of Evil*, Greenwood Press.

HOROWITZ, DONALD L. (1985) *Ethnic Groups in Conflict*, University of California Press.

JANIS, IRVING L. and MANN, LEON (1977) *Decision Making: A Psychological Analysis of Conflict, Choice, and Commitment*, Free Press (NY).

KELMAN, HERBERT C. (ed.) (1965) *International Behavior: A Social Psychological Analysis*, Holt, Rinehart & Winston.

KELMAN, HERBERT C. (1972) "The Problem-Solving Workshop in Conflict Resolution," in Merritt, Richard L. (ed.), *Communication in International Politics*, University of Illinois Press (1972).

KELMAN, HERBERT C. and COHEN, STEPHEN P. (1976) "The Problem-Solving Workshop: A Social Psychological Contribution to the Resolution of Conflict," *Journal of Peace Research*, vol. 2. no. 3.

KLINEBERG, OTTO (1964) *The Human Dimension in International Relations*, Holt, Rinehart & Winston.

KUHN, THOMAS S. (1962) *The Structure of Scientific Revolutions*, Chicago University Press.

LASSWELL, HAROLD (1966) "Conflict and Leadership: The Process of Decision and the Nature of Authority," in DE REUCK and KNIGHT (eds) (1966).

LAUE, JAMES H. (1988) "Getting to the Table in Policy Conflicts," *Mediation Quarterly*, no. 20 (Summer) Jossey-Bass.

LEDERER, KATRIN (ed.) (1980) *Human Needs: A Contribution to the Current Debate*, Oelgeschlager, Gunn & Hain (Cambridge, Mass.).

LENSKI, GERHARD, E. (1966) *Power and Privilege: A Theory of Social Stratification*, McGraw-Hill.

LEWIS, ANTHONY (1985) *New York Times*, 28 April.

LLOYD, DENNIS (1964) *The Idea of Law*, Pelican Original.

MANDEL, ROBERT (1987) *Irrationality in International Confrontation*, Greenwood.

MASLOW, ABRAHAM H. (1954) *Motivation and Personality*, Harper Bros.

MASLOW, ABRAHAM H. (1972) *Self-Actualization*, San Fernando (California).

MASLOW, ABRAHAM H. (1976) *The Farther Reaches of Human Nature*, Penguin Books.

McDONALD, JOHN W. and BENDAHMANE, DIANE B. (1987) *Conflict Resolution: Two Track Diplomacy*, Foreign Service Institute, US Department of State.

McVICAR, JOHN (1974) *John McVicar*, Hutchinson.

MILES, IAN (1985) *Social Indicators for Human Development*, Frances Pinter (London).

MITCHELL, C. R. (1981a) *The Structure of International Conflict*, Macmillan.

MITCHELL, C. R. (1981b) *Peacemaking and the Consultant's Role*, Gower.

MITCHELL, C. R. and WEBB, K. (eds) (1988) *New Approaches to International Relations*, Greenwood Press.

MITRANY, D. (1944) *A Working Peace System*, Oxford University Press.

MODELSKI, GEORGE (1962) *A Theory of Foreign Policy*, Pall Mall Press.

MONTVILLE, J. and DAVIDSON, W. (1981–2) "Foreign Policy According to Freud," *Foreign Policy*, no. 45.

MONTVILLE, J. (1987) "The Arrow and the Olive Branch: A Case for Second Track Diplomacy," in McDONALD and BENDAHMANE (1987).

MOORE, BARRINGTON (1978) *Injustice: The Social Bases of Obedience and Revolt*, Pantheon Books.

MORGENTHAU, HANS (1948) *Politics Among Nations: The Struggle for Power and Peace*, Knopf.

NATIONAL ASSOCIATION OF AMERICAN SOCIAL WORKERS (1958) *Social Work*, vol 3, no 2.

OLSON, M. (1965) *The Logic of Collective Action*, Harvard University Press.

OSGOOD, CHARLES (1962) *An Alternative to War or Surrender*, University of Illinois.

PATCHEN, MARTIN (1988) *Resolving Disputes between Nations: Coercion or Conciliation*, Duke University Press.

PEIRCE, C. S. (1978), *see* RESCHER (1978).

PERETZ, P. (1978) "Universal Wants: A Deductive Framework for Comparative Analysis," in Ashford, D. E. (ed.), *Comparing Public Policies: New Concepts and Methods*, Sage (1978).

PIRAGES, D. (1976) *Managing Political Conflict*, Praeger.

POPPER, KARL (1957) *The Poverty of Historicism*, Routledge & Kegan Paul.

PRINGLE, MIA (1974) *The Needs of Children*, Hutchinson.

PRUITT, DEAN and RUBIN, JEFFREY (1986) *Social Conflict: Escalation, Stalemate, and Settlement*, Random House.

RAJARATNAM, K. (ed.) (1983) *Quality of Life: A Collection of Seminar Papers and Group Reports*, Center for Research on New International Economic Order (Madras).

RAPAPORT, ANATOL (1966) "Models of Conflict: Cataclysmic and Strategic", in DE REUCK and KNIGHT (eds) (1966).

RESCHER, NICHOLAS (1978) *Peirce's Philosophy of Science: Critical Studies in His Theory of Induction and Scientific Method*, Notre Dame Press.

RESTON, JAMES (1984) *New York Times*, 21 November.

RESTON, JAMES (1985) *New York Times*, 28 June.

RIFKIN, JEREMY (1986) *Entropy: A New World Vision*, Viking.

ROBBINS, LIONEL (1934) *The Great Depression*, Macmillan.

ROBBINS, LIONEL (1936) *An Essay on the Nature and Significance of Economic Science*, Macmillan.

ROTHSTEIN, ROBERT L. (1981) *The Third World and US Foreign Policy: Cooperation and Conflict*, Westview Press.

RUBENSTEIN, RICHARD E. (1987) *Alchemists of Revolution: Terrorism in the Modern World*, Basic Books.

RUBENSTEIN, RICHARD E. (1988) *Group Violence in America*, Working Paper 2, Center for Conflict Analysis and Resolution, George Mason University.

RUMMEL, R. T. (1970) *Applied Factor Analysis*, North Western University Press.

RUMMEL, R. T. (1972) *The Dimensions of Nations*, Sage.

SANDOLE, DENNIS J. D. and SANDOLE, INGRID S. (eds) (1987) *Conflict Management and Problem Solving: Interpersonal to International Applications*, Frances Pinter (London).

SANDOLE, DENNIS J. D. (1988), *see* MITCHELL, C. R. and WEBB, K.

SANDOLE, DENNIS J. D. (1988), *see* BURTON, J. W. and SANDOLE, J. D.

SCARMAN, L. (1977) "Human Rights," *University of London Bulletin*, no. 39.

SCHWARZENBERGER, GEORG (1941) *Power Politics: A Study of World Society*, Stevens.

SCHWARZENBERGER, GEORG (1964) *Power Politics: A Study of World Society*, Stevens (3rd edn).

SCIMECCA, JOSEPH (1981) *Society and Freedom: An Introduction to Humanistic Sociology*, St Martin's Press (NY).

SCRUTON, ROGER (1980) *The Meaning of Conservatism*, Barnes & Noble.

SECURITY COUNCIL, *Cyprus Mediator Report*, (1965) s/6253.

SITES, PAUL (1973) *Control: the Basis of Social Order*, Dunellen Publishers.

SIVARD, RUTH L. (1988) *World Military and Social Expenditures: 1978–88*, World Priorities.

SKINNER, QUENTIN (1983) *The Return of Grand Theory in the Human Sciences*, Cambridge University Press.

SNYDER R. C., BRUCK H. W. and SAPIN B. (1962) *Foreign Policy Making: An Approach to the Study of International Politics*, Free Press (NY).

TOWLE, CHARLOTTE (1973) *Common Human Needs*, United States Bureau of Public Assistance.

WALTZ, KENNETH N. (1954) *Man, The State and War: A Theoretical Analysis*, Columbia University Press.

WATZIAWICK, PAUL, WEAKLAND, J. H. and FISCH, R. (1974) *Change: Principles of Problem Formation and Problem Resolution*, Norton.

WEDGE, BRYANT (1971) "A Psychiatric Model of Intercession in Intergroup Conflict," *The Journal of Applied Behavioral Science*, vol. 6. no. 7.

WEINER, B. (1979) *Human Motivation*, Holt, Rinehart & Winston.

WILL, GEORGE (1989) *Washington Post*, 30 April.

WILSON, E. (1977) Preface in Barash (1977).

WINFREY, OPRAH (1988) *Gangs*, WLS-TV, Transcript W4322 (May).

WOLFERS, ARNOLD (1962) *Discord and Collaboration*, Johns Hopkins University Press.

YOUNGHUSBAND, E. (ed.) (1964) *New Developments in Casework*, Macmillan.

ZARTMAN, WILLIAM (1986) "Ripe Moments and Mediation", in BEN-DAHMANE, D. B. and McDONALD, J. W. (eds) *Perspectives on Negotiation: Four Case Studies and Interpretations*, Foreign Service Institute US Department of State, US Government Printing Office (1986).

ZAWODNY, J. K. (1966) *Man and International Relations*, Chandler Publishing Co.

Index

abduction 19, 256
abnormalities 29–30
  see also deviance
accumulated adjustments 249–50
Afghanistan 165
Afro-Americans 163
aggression 31, 32, 34, 73, 241–2
AIDS 16
alienation 91, 93–4
Amy, D. J. 192
analysis
  prediction and 235–6
  problem-solving and 206–7
Andrews, F. M. 59
arbitration 57, 190–1, 192, 195
  see also mediation; negotiation
Aristotle 68
arms control negotiations 234–5
arms reductions 164
assumptions, questioning of 197–8
attachment 92
  see also valued relationships
attitudes 215–16
Australia 140, 144, 223, 243
authoritative decision making
  189–90
authority
  challenges to 79–80, 261–3
  erosion of 126, 129–30, 154
  legitimization of *see* legitimization
  power of 112–14; limits 115–17
  relationships with 67–9, 72–3
  repression and 69–70
  role 158
autonomy
  local 140–1, 142–3
  personal 60–1, 93, 153, 223–4
availability
  conflict resolution 272–4
  provention 275
Azar, E. E. 22, 40, 219, 273
  Lebanon 42, 142, 225

balance-of-power 85–6
Banks, M. 101, 116, 277

Barash, D. P. 93
bargaining *see* negotiation
Basque country 119, 243
Beccaria, C. 30
Becker, E. 31, 33
Beckerman, W. 58
behavior 2
  coercion and 4, 14, 27, 79–80
  conflict management/resolution
    194–5; problem-solving
    204–5
  control theory 81–2
  culture and 212
  needs theory and 34–5, 36–7, 235
  power theory and 46, 73, 80–1
  reflexes and instincts 81
  totality of 20–1
  unified theory 198–9
  see also deviance; needs
behavioral revolution 77–8
Bendahmane, D. B 273
Beyer, B. K. 276
billiard ball model 74, 88
Blake, R. R. 85, 176
Boehm, W. W. 84
Boethius, A. M. S. 74
Boulding, K. E. 100, 255
Box, S. 92, 97
Britain 144, 162, 196, 261
  balance-of-power 85–6
  Northern Ireland 125
  protectionism and Japan 87
Bruck, H. W. 176
Buchanan, J. M. 167
Burns, J. MacGregor 92, 95
Burton, J. W. 40, 118, 219
  change 128
  cobweb model 74, 88
  Cyprus 42, 142, 224
  decision making 182
  development 76
  Lebanon 42, 225
  Peace Theory 100
  privatization of problem-solving
    266–7

Burton, J. W. – *continued*
  problems of perception 92, 101,
    178
  provention in a nuclear age 231
  resolution processes 273
  values 22

capitalism 38–9, 42
Carpenter, S. L. 173
Centre for the Analysis of Conflict,
  London University 100
Center for Research on Conflict
  Resolution, Michigan
  University 100
change
  conflict resolution as means of
    238
  exponential 52–4, 233
  legitimization and 127–9
  problems of institutional 66,
    69–70, 71
  provention's implication of
    236–7
  resistance to 55–6, 130
  system 54–5, 130–1, 167, 239–51
chemical weapons 68
Chile 249
China 130, 214, 261, 263, 264
CIBA Foundation 100
city violence 54
Clark, G. 86
class relations 145
Claude, I. 86
Clausewitz, K. von 100, 101
Coate, R. A. 34, 103
cobweb model 74–5, 88
coercion 4–5, 6, 13, 14, 131
  adding to environment of conflict
    52
  compared with problem-solving
    196–7
  costs of 17; negotiation and
    218–19
  by great powers 17, 40
  lack of alternatives to 23–4,
    69–70
  see also containment
Cohen, S. P. 182
Cold War 101

collaborative problem-solving 192
colonialism 80–1, 126, 141
command societies 246–7
Commission on Critical Choices for
  Americans 58
common good 23–4, 46–7, 157
communication 45–6, 78–80
  conflict management/resolution
    189–92, 195, 196
communism 38–9, 42
  challenged 261–2
competition 241, 247
complexities 20–1
concepts 75–6, 209–10
  altered 253–5
  sets of 98–9
  see also language
conciliation 191, 192
  see also mediation; negotiation
conflict
  definition 2
  determinants of 49–50
  escalation 16, 50–2
  institutions as source 147–8
  as non-legitimized relationships
    125–7
  profile of 189, 191–2
  system fault and 247–8
  theory and practice 27–9
  see also deep-rooted conflict;
    disputes; high-level conflict
conflict management *see*
  management
Conflict Research Society, UK 100
conflict resolution *see* resolution of
  conflict
constructive intervention 160
containment 17, 243–4
  see also coercion
control
  challenge to effective 126,
    129–30, 154
  freedom and 66
  interests and 38–9
  legality and 125
  political systems and 133–4
control theory 81–2, 92–4, 97–8
  human needs and 94–7
controversy, political 110–11, 117–18

costing 22, 27, 167, 240, 274–5
costs of treating symptoms 17
courts *see* judicial settlement
creativity
  and manipulation 227–8
  in promoting interactions 220–3,
    225–7, 271–2
credibility 251, 252–3
crime 1, 28–9, 29–30, 206
critical common-sensism
  (abduction) 19, 256
culture 1, 37–8, 211–16
cumulative need for change 128
cybernetic models 176–7, 183, 186
Cyprus 34, 110, 190, 194, 201, 243
  communal chamber 144
  demands for change suppressed
    249
  Government and control 125, 141
  imposed constitution 196
  mediation 193
  negotiation failure 221, 223, 226
  peace-keeping forces 121, 138
  power of identity groups 114
  power sharing 141
  separation and integration 142,
    143, 144, 254
  shared goals 42
  valued relations 142, 224

data, misinterpretation of 77–8
Davies, J. C. 60
De Reuck, A. 100
decision making 47–8, 173–87,
  193–4, 195
  see also policy making
Dedring, J. 102
deep-rooted conflict 15–16, 242–3,
  274
  culture and 214
  human needs and 32–3
  power of ideas 220–3
  resignation 269–70
definition 27
  see also redefinition
democracy 40, 75–6, 223, 253–4,
  261–2
dependency relationships 55–7
deregulation 161, 162, 261–2, 263

determinants of conflict 49–50
deterrence 33–4, 50, 100, 101
  game without end 234–5, 239
Deutsch, K. 100, 177, 255
developed countries 62
development
  economic 61
  human 21–2
  meanings 76
  needs and 51
  policy dilemma 150–1
  relationships and 156
deviance 17, 31, 149, 152–3, 206
  control theory and 96–7
disputes
  definition 2, 241
  private resolution 57, 193
  within-system 244–7, 269
Dollard, J. 81
domestic conflicts 52, 261–3
drug problems 16, 17, 111

Easton, D. 176
economics 63–4
  criticized 62
education 132, 133, 276
Eisenhower, D. D. 101
El Salvador 165
energy consumption 54, 59–60, 62
entropy 59–61, 62
environment of conflict 14, 49–65,
  152–3
  problem-solving and 202–3
  provention and 18–19
  quality of life and entropy 58–65
Environmental Protection Agency
  58
erosion of authoity 126, 129–30, 154
escalation of conflict 16, 50–2
estrangement 91
ethnic conflict 54
  culture and 211, 213
  majority rule 40, 222
  valued relations 224–5
  see also multi-ethnic societies
ethnicity 137–8
evil 30, 31
experts 25–6
exponential change 52–4, 233

facilitation *see* third party
'family control' 134
fascism 44
fault
  issue of 30–2
  system 247–8
federations 254
Fiji 114, 137
filter 208–9, 210
Fisch, R. 239
Fisher, A. G. B. 76
Fisher, R. 16
Fox, W. M. 173
Fraser, N. M. 173
free enterprise 63, 64, 262
freedom 77, 261–2
future studies 235–6
  see also prediction

games without end 234–5, 239
gaming models 86
gang violence 17, 34, 248
Gentleman's Magazine 29–30
Germany 86, 87, 112–13
Ghadafi, Col. M. 34
goals 41–3
  confusion with tactics 43–4, 245
  quality intervention and 163–4
Golan Heights 44
Goldberg, S. B. 16
Goulet, D. 76
great power relations 17, 51–2,
  164–5
Greece 196, 224
Green, E. D. 16
Gross National Product (GNP) 58,
  62
Gurr, T. R. 52, 94, 261

Halpern, D. F. 276–7
Haworth, L. 61, 93, 153, 173
health 132, 133
Heilbroner, R. L. 63–4
Hibbert, J. 29
high-level conflict 85–6
Hipel, K. W. 173
Hitler, A. 87
Horowitz, D. L. 213
Hull, C. 87

human being, concepts of 30–3,
  73–4, 80, 147
human development 21–2
human dimension 4–5, 201
  recent literature 92–4
  trends in thinking 90–2
  see also needs
human law 70
human needs *see* needs, human
human rights 76–7, 99, 265–6
hypotheses, use of 19–20, 199

identity needs 81, 137–9
  facilitation and 223–5
  power and 134, 135
ideologies 255–6
  decision making and 180–1
  goals, tactics and 41–3
  response to circumstances 44–5
  systems and 43
income distribution 56
independence 79
individual, society and 23–4, 31–2,
  38–9, 147–57
industrial relations 71, 85, 206
infant mortality 132–3
input–output model 175–8
institutionalization of conflict
  resolution 272–4
institutions 133
integration 140–1, 254
interactive decision making 174–5
  models 182–7
interest disputes 150, 244–5, 247
interest groups 120, 164, 252
interest policies 109–10
interests 38–9, 40–1, 42
  negotiability 15–16, 39, 78
  vested and uncertainties 237
International Court of Justice 193,
  221
intervention 57, 133
  constructive 158–70
  forms of 189–92
  international 164–6
Iran 34, 203, 218, 245
Iraq 68, 218, 245
Israel 44, 194
Italy 44, 113, 150

Janis, I. L. 173
Japan 26, 87, 160
Jeffreys, Judge 29
judicial settlement 189–90, 192,
  193, 195, 245
  international 193, 220–1
justice 77
juvenile crime 206

Kelman, H. C. 100, 182, 219, 273
Kennedy, W. J. D. 173
Klineberg, O. 81
Knight, J. 100
Korea 25, 151
Kuhn, T. S. 78, 255

labeling 80
labor relations 55
land rights 243
language 74, 75–7, 209–10
  see also concepts
Lasswell, H. 100
Laue, J. H. 220
law
  human 70
  natural 70, 83, 91–2
  political thought and 67–8
  positive 70, 83, 90, 91–2, 98
leadership 154
  dilemmas of 130–1
League of Nations 85, 87
learning 207
Lebanon 37, 42, 140, 141, 142,
  224–5
Lederer, K. 33
legitimization of authorities 98,
  123–36, 176
  ethnic conflict and 145–6
  intervention and 168
  legality and 123–4, 124–5, 127,
    180, 253
  measures of 132–3
  multi-ethnic societies 139–40
  repressive regimes 113
liberalism 139–40
Libya 34
living standards 49–50
  see also quality of life

Lloyd, D. 31, 67–8, 69
local autonomy 140–1, 142–3

majority rule 40, 222, 253–4
Man, the State and War (Waltz) 73
management of conflict 129, 203
  institutionalization 272–3
  problem-solving and 243–4
  trends in 188–96
manipulation 227–8
Mann, L. 173
Marcos, F. 131
Marx, K. 91
Marxism 139
Maslow, A. H. 36, 102
McDonald, J. W. 273
McVicar, J. 152
mediation 57, 180–1, 191, 192,
  221–2
  see also arbitration; conciliation;
    negotiation
mediation panels 170
mental problems 30
Middle East 137, 142, 201, 212, 213
Miles, I. 58–9, 59
military regimes 14
minority groups 34–5, 137, 144, 145,
  179
  see also multi-ethnic societies
Mitchell, C. R. 102–3, 273
Mitrany, D. 100
mixed societies 144–5, 254
  see also multi-ethnic societies
models
  balance-of-power 85–6
  concepts and 209–10
  conflict resolution 197–201,
    208–9
  decision making 175–8, 183–7
  language and 74–5
  world society 134, 225, 226–7
Modelski, G. 175–6
Moore, B. 92–3
Morgenthau, H. 73, 85, 113, 241
Mouton, J. S. 176
multi-ethnic societies 137–46, 254
  see also ethnic conflict
Muslims 203

Nasser, G. A. 68
National Association of American
  Social Workers 84
national interest 76
natural law 70, 83, 91–2
needs, human 36–48, 92–4, 118, 267
  autonomy and 60–1
  conflict resolution and 6, 242
  control theory and 94–7
  culture and 211, 212–13
  deep-rooted 4, 32–3
  interests, values and 37–41,
    78–80
  intervention and 162–3, 168
  prediction and 235–6
  rights and 76–7, 99, 265–6
  significance of approach 33–5
  social problems and 21
  valued relationships 153–4, 205
negotiation 16, 39, 191–2, 192, 194
  arms control 181, 234–5
  winning and 23
  see also arbitration; conciliation;
    mediation
New Zealand 26, 144, 243
Nicaragua 221
North Korea 25
Northern Ireland 121, 190, 201,
    243, 249
  conflicts between factions 19
  identity groups 142
  labeling 80
  minority challenge to authority
    34, 114, 115, 125
  population movements 144, 226
  separation 226
  unemployment 163
  values 37, 213
nuclear age 231

obedience 67–8, 72
Olson, M. 91
options, need for viable 250–1
origins, problem-solving and 203
Osgood, C. 100, 234, 239

Palestine 80, 194
Palestine Liberation Organization
  (PLO) 142

participation in conflict management/
  resolution 189–92, 195, 196
Patchen, M. 173
Peace Research Institute, Oslo 100
peace studies 101–2
Peirce, C. S. 19–20, 256, 257
perception(s)
  problems of 92, 178
  questioning of 197–8
Peretz, P. 93
person, concepts of 30–3, 73–4, 80,
  147
Philippines 131, 249
Pirages, D. 94–5
planned economies 162–3
Poland 131, 261, 264
policies/policy
  dilemma 150–2
  interest 109–10
policy making 23, 198
  entropy implications 62–3
  guidelines for 17–22
  problem-solving conflict
    resolution and 167–70
  problems of 166–7
  provention as focus 274–5
  system change 248–9
  see also decision making
political parties, intervention cycles
  and 161
political realism 71, 114
politics
  controversy and 110–14, 117–18
  movements for change 261–3
  subjectivity and 110–13, 117
pollution 59, 60
population growth 53–4
positive law 70, 83, 90, 91–2, 98
poverty 109–10
power
  authority relationships 72–3
  individuals and identity groups 114
  political theory of 74, 85–90, 173,
    241; decision making
    113–14, 175–9, 183–7
power sharing 40, 141, 222, 253–4
prayer in schools 250–1
prediction 16, 233–6, 237, 257–8
primary change 128

Pringle, M. 84
private enterprise 161, 162–3, 266
privatized dispute resolution 57, 193
privatization policies 261–2
probabilistic prediction 233–4
problem-solving 5
  coercive approach and 196–7
  collaborative 192
  conflict resolution as 202–10
  decision making 186, 187
  individual and society 149–50
  symptom treatment and 121
  see also resolution of conflict
professionalization of conflict resolution/provention 271–5
prostitution, teenage 28
protest 261–5, 267
provention 2, 3, 230–2, 233
  challenge to resignation 270–1
  as major policy focus 274–5
  recent thinking 253–7
  remedial approach and 257–8
  social problems 18–19
  system change 54–5, 169–70, 236–7, 251
Pruitt, D. 38
public choice economics 166–7
public policy *see* policy making
punishment 28–9, 29–30

quality of intervention 159–61, 163–4
quality of life (QOL) 49–50, 58–65

Rajaratnam, K. 59
Rapaport, A. 100, 101
rationality 233–4
reactive decision making 174
  models 176–8, 183–7
Reagan, R. 162
reciprocity 126–8
redefinition 28
reflex responses 174
reframing 239
regional experts 25–6
relationships, valued *see* valued relationships
relevance 207–8

reliability 251, 252–3
religion 213
remedial approach 257–8
repression 28–9, 69–70, 243
  see also coercion
Rescher, N. 19, 256
resignation 269–71
resistance to change 55–6, 130
resolution of conflict 1–2, 2–3, 196–210
  acceptability 217–28
  assumptions of 241–2
  challenge to resignation 270–1
  change and 54–5, 238
  comprehensive approach 20–1
  control and 79
  culture 214, 215
  decision making and 173, 181–2
  international literature 100–3
  policy making 167–70
  as a political philosophy 5–6
  problem-solving 202–10
  processes 218–20, 251; within systems 267–8
  professionalization 271–4
  provention and 18–19, 90, 232, 233
  recent interest 83
resources 59–60, 60–1, 62, 63–4
restrictive intervention 160
retroduction 19–20
Rhodesia 226
Rifkin, J. 60–3 *passim*
rights, human 76–7, 99, 265–6
'ripening' thesis 88–90
Robbins, L. 162
Rockefeller, N. A. 58
Romilly, Sir S. 29
Rosati, J. A. 34, 103
Rothstein, R. L. 88
Rubenstein, R. E. 134, 266
Rubin, J. 38
rules, legitimacy of 68–9
Rummel, R. T. 86
Rushdie, S. 203

Sander, F. E. A. 16
Sandole, D. J. D. 103, 118
Sandole, I. S. 103

Index

Sapin, B. 176
Scarman, L. 92
Scarritt, J. R. 52, 261
school prayers 250–1
Schwarzenberger, G. 85
scope 207–8
Scruton, R. 93–4
secondary change 128–9, 239
second-order change 239–51
  see also system change
separation 140–1, 142–3
settlement 3, 220, 269
  see also judicial settlement;
    management
Shepard, H. A. 176
Sites, P. 92, 95–7
Sivard, R. L. 62, 133
Smith, A. 64
Snyder, R. C. 176
social disputes 269
social organization 55–6, 70–2
social problems 13–14, 18–19, 26,
  56–7, 263
social workers 84
socialization 31–2, 33, 70, 81
Society for Professionals in Dispute
  Resolution (SPIDR) 273
Sohn, L. 86
sources, problem-solving and 203
South Africa 110, 201, 222, 249
  authorities challenged 114, 131
  conflicts within factions 19
  minority control 137, 226
  one-man, one-vote 34, 169, 226
  second-order change 248
  separation 142
  US sanctions 227
  violence preferred to dialogue
    119
Soviet Union 34
  balance-of-power 86
  domestic conflict 52, 115, 261,
    263
  relations with US 43, 79;
    Afghanistan 165
Spain (Basque country) 119, 243
specialists 25–6
spiritual needs 60–1
Sri Lanka 34, 110, 141, 201, 243

authorities challenged
  114, 125
demands for change suppressed
  249
integration and separation 142,
  145
labeling 80
strategic studies 101
street gangs 17, 34, 248
subjectivity in politics 110–13, 117
Suez canal 68
symptom treatment
  costs 17
  problem-solving and 121
system change 54–5, 130–1, 167,
  239–51
system fault 247–8
systems
  conflicts and disputes within
    244–7
  control by 155
  legitimization 132
  preservation of 43, 56–7
  problem-solving processes within
    267–8
  processes and 265

tactics 41–3
  confusion with goals 43–4, 245
teenage prostitution 28
thinking 255–7
  creative 225–7
  need for skills 276–7
third party
  communication 45–6
  decision making 183, 186, 187
  public policies and 22–3
  role 6–7, 169, 195–6, 204–5, 207,
    210; creativity 221–3, 224,
    271–2; filter 208–9;
    sponsoring 205–6
  trends in conflict
    management/resolution
    188–92
Thurow, L. C. 63–4
Tibet 243
Tollison, R. 167
Towle, C. 84
traditional societies 246

transactions (cobweb) model 74–5, 88
Tullock, G. 167
Turkey 196, 224

underdevelopment 62–3, 139
unemployment 148
unified theory of behavior 198–9
unions 145
United Kingdom *see* Britain
United Nations (UN) 124, 125, 218, 273
  mediation 190, 193, 221
  peace-keeping forces 121, 143, 244
United Nations University 58, 273
United States of America (US) 243, 261
  control: cities after dark 125; 'family' 134
  domestic problems 26, 263
  drug problem 111
  economic intervention 162
  energy consumption 62
  independence 79
  Lebanon 141
  military intervention 25, 151; El Salvador 165; Nicaragua 220–1; Vietnam 25, 74, 88, 151
  mixed societies 144
  relations with Soviet Union 43, 79, 165
  South Africa 227
  violent foreign policy 119
Ury, W. 16
US Justice Department Report 14

valued relationships 46–7, 82, 224–5
  demise 154–6
  social good and 153–4
values 21–2, 37–8, 42, 150, 212–13
  interests, needs and 39–41, 78–80
vested interests 237
viable options, need for 250–1
Vietnam 14, 25, 74, 75, 88, 151
  strength from commitment 86
violence 15, 50–2, 54, 66, 119

Waltz, K. N. 73
wants 95
  see also needs
Watziawick, P. 239
Weakland, J. H. 239
Webb, K. 103
Wedge, B. 182
Weiner, B. 93, 94
Will, G. 30
Wilson, E. 93
Winfrey, O. 21
within-system disputes/conflicts 244–7
Wolfers, A. 74, 88
women 35
world government 86
world society model 134, 225, 226–7

Zawodny, J. K. 69
Zimbabwe 226
zonal systems 141–4